Buddhism and World Civilization

Buddhism and World Civilization

Dr. I.N. Singh

PRASHANT PUBLISHING HOUSE
DELHI-110094

Published by :
Prashant Publishing House
C-34, 28 Foota Road, Gali-3,
West Karwal Nagar, Delhi-110094
Phone : 011-22963970, Mob. : 9810396373
e-mail.: prashantpublishinghouse@gmail.com

Buddhism and World Civilization
Reserved
First Published 2018

ISBN 978-81-937193-0-5

PRINTED IN INDIA
Published by Mr. R.K. Jha M/s Prashant Publishing House and Published at H.S. Offset House Press, Delhi.

Contents

Preface (*vii*)

1. Buddhist Philosophy 1
2. Teaching of Theravada 22
3. Buddhist Monasteries 45
4. Disciples of the Buddha 79
5. Buddhist Temples in Japan 127
6. East Asian Buddhism 173
7. The Four Noble Truths 234

Bibliography 267

Index 270

Preface

Buddhism arose between 500-300 BCE, when Siddhartha Gautama, a young man from an aristocratic family, left behind his worldly comforts to seek spiritual enlightenment. He became a teacher commonly known as the Buddha, meaning "the awakened one," and Buddhism spread to become a non-theistic religion that encompasses a variety of traditions, beliefs, and practices largely based on his teachings.

Buddhism is based on an ancient Indian religious philosophy called Sramana, which began as an offshoot of the Vedic religion. Several Sramana movements are known to have existed in India before the 6th century BCE. Sramana existed in parallel to, but separate from, Vedic Hinduism, which followed the teachings and rituals found in the Vedas, the most ancient texts of the Vedic religion. Sramana, meaning "seeker," was a tradition that began when new philosophical groups who believed in a more austere path to spiritual freedom rejected the authority of the Vedas and the Brahmins, the priests of Vedic Hinduism, around 800-600 BCE.

Buddhist teachings explain that Siddhartha was a young man from a respected family, who renounced his family and left his father's palace at age 29 in search of truth and enlightenment through Sramana. Siddhartha began this quest through a period of starvation and, according to legend, grew so thin he could feel his hands if he placed one on his back and the other on his stomach. This explains statues that depict Buddha as thin and withered, rather than the better known depiction of him seated with a large belly.

Buddhism entered China during the Han dynasty (206 BCE-220 CE): The first Buddhist missionaries accompanied merchant caravans that travelled using the Silk Road, probably during the 1st century BCE. The majority of these missionaries belonged to the Mahayana school.

The initial stage of Buddhism is China was not very promising. Chinese culture had a long-established intellectual and religious tradition and a strong sense of cultural superiority that did not help the reception of Buddhist ideas. Many of the Buddhist ways were considered alien by the Chinese and even contrary to the Confucian ideals that dominated the ruling aristocracy. The monastic order received a serious set of critiques: It was considered unproductive and therefore was seen as placing an unnecessary economic burden on the population, and the independence from secular authority emphasized by the monks was seen as an attempt to undermine the traditional authority of the emperor.

Today, Buddhism is practiced by an estimated 488 million people. China is the nation with the largest number of Buddhists, approximately 244 million followers, or more than 18% of its total population. Other countries that have a large number of Buddhists among their populations include Myanmar with 48.4 million, Japan with 45.8 million, Sri Lanka with 14.2 million, Cambodia with 13.7 million, South Korea with 11 million, Thailand, Laos, Singapore, Taiwan, and Nepal. The United States is home to an estimated 1.2 million Buddhists, or 1.2% of the American population.

This is a reference book. All the matter is just compiled and edited in nature, taken from the various sources which are in public domain.

This book contains the fundamental and basic information of subject and the selection of contents makes it an appropriate book for the students.

—Editor

1

Buddhist Philosophy

Buddhist philosophy is the branch of Eastern philosophy based on the teachings of Gautama Buddha, a.k.a. Siddhartha Gautama (c. 563 BCE-c. 483 BCE). Buddhist philosophy deals extensively with problems in metaphysics, phenomenology, ethics, and epistemology.

Some have asserted that Buddhism as a whole is a practical philosophy rather than a religion. It is "practical" in that it has a specific method of application known as the Noble Eightfold Path (from which notions of divinity are entirely absent) of a particular set of philosophical principles (the Four Noble Truths). Proponents of such a view may argue that (a) Buddhism is non-theistic (i.e., it has no special use for the existence or non-existence of a god or gods) or atheistic and (b) religions necessarily involve some form of theism. Others might contest either part of such an argument. Other arguments for Buddhism "as" philosophy may claim that Buddhism does not have doctrines in the same sense as other religions; the Buddha himself taught that a person should accept a teaching only if one's own experience verifies it and it is praised by the wise.

HISTORICAL DEVELOPMENT OF BUDDHIST PHILOSOPHY

The philosophical outlook of Earliest Buddhism was primarily negative, in the sense that it focused on what doctrines to *reject* more than on what doctrines to *accept*. This dimension has been preserved by the Madhyamaka school. It includes critical rejections of all views, which is a form of philosophy, but it is reluctant to posit its own.

Only knowledge that is useful in achieving enlightenment is valued. The cycle of philosophical upheavals that in part drove the diversification of Buddhism into its many schools and sects only began once Buddhists began attempting to make explicit the implicit philosophy of the Buddha and the early Suttas.

After the death of the Buddha, attempts were made to gather his teachings and transmit them in a commonly agreed form, first orally, then also in writing (The Tripitaka). In addition to collecting the Buddha's speeches and rules for monastic life (Vinaya), monks soon undertook to condense what they considered the essential elements of Buddhist doctrine into lists of categories, provided with extensive commentary. This process took shape from about the 2nd century BCE to probably the 2nd century CE.

Later Developments

Very soon after, additional teachings began to be added to the list of important Buddhist texts. Many of these altered and refined Buddhist philosophy.

Comparison with other Philosophies

- Baruch Spinoza, though he argued for the existence of a permanent reality, asserts that all phenomenal existence is transitory. In his opinion sorrow is conquered "by finding an object of knowledge which is not transient, not ephemeral, but is immutable, permanent, everlasting." Buddhism teaches that such a quest is bound to fail.
- David Hume, after a relentless analysis of the mind, concluded that consciousness consists of fleeting mental states. Hume's Bundle theory is a very similar concept to anatta.
- Arthur Schopenhauer's philosophy was very similar to Buddhism.

- Ludwig Wittgenstein's "word games" map closely to the warning of intellectual speculation as a red herring to understanding, such as the *Parable of the Poison Arrow*.
- Friedrich Nietzsche, although himself dismissive of Buddhism as yet another nihilism, developed his philosophy of accepting life-as-it-exists and self-cultivation as extremely similar to Buddhism as better understood in the West today.

EASTERN PHILOSOPHY

Eastern philosophy refers very broadly to the various philosophies of China, Japan, Korea, India, Iran (Persia), and to an extent, the Middle East (which overlaps with Western philosophy due to being the origin of the Abrahamic religions).

The usefulness of dividing philosophy into Western philosophy and other philosophies, in contrast to a notion that there can be one philosophy, not many, is open to challenge, partly because some see it as condescending to non-Western philosophies. To say this is not to deny that there are important traditions in philosophy that are intimately bound up with historical and geographical circumstances. At the same time however, there are examples of philosophers who are persecuted by the majority in their geographical circumstances and stand against the common opinions and practices of their specific time and place. Many claim that geographical and time notions of "Western" and "Eastern" philosophy is too vague and imprecise, committing the fallacy of over generalization.

When the term "philosophy" is used in an academic context, it typically refers to the philosophical tradition begun with the ancient Greeks that provided us with an abundance of manuscripts and archeological sites to study and research. The "Eastern philosophical" manuscripts and archeological sites are often overlooked in many North American and European universities, just as ancient "Western" and monotheistic claims are also overlooked in the last few decades, unlike in the early 1900's.

Philosophical and Religious Traditions

The following is an overview of the Eastern philosophic traditions listed in alphabetical order. Each tradition has a separate article with more detail on sects, schools, etc. rencyism.

Ayyavazhi

Ayyavazhi is the system of beliefs and philosophical system which is based on the teachings of Ayya Vaikundar and the scriptures Akilattirattu Ammanai and Arul Nool. The philosophy of this religion applies a common formula for the creationism of Human beings and Universe. It also says that what ever exists externally to human beings exist also internally. The dharma concept applied to Ayyavazhi primarily deviates into two. The social as well as spiritual conception. The format of mixing exclusivism and inclusivism in Ayyavazhi is unique and not found else where in the world. Unlike other dharmic religions the time conception in Ayyavazhi is linear projecting into a world of bliss, Dharma Yukam. The concept of personifying a foremost evil as Kroni, and the personification of the evil of the age as Kaliyan in Ayyavazhi were in contrast to other dharmic systems of philosophy.

The primary commandments (virtues) of Ayyavazhi is stated as Neetham.

1. Manu Neetham: How an individual should personify him or herself.
2. Raja Neetham: How an individual should be to the society or Nation.
3. Deiva Neetham: How an individual should be before God.

Buddhism

Buddhism is a system of beliefs based on the teachings of Siddhartha Gautama, an Indian prince later known as the Buddha, or *one who is Awake*-derived from the Sanskrit 'bud', 'to awaken'. Buddhism is a non-theistic religion, one whose tenets are not especially concerned with the existence or nonexistence of a God or gods. The Buddha himself expressly disavowed any special divine status or inspiration, and said that anyone, anywhere could achieve all the insight that he had. The question of God is largely irrelevant in Buddhism, though some sects (notably Tibetan Buddhism) do venerate a number of gods drawn in from local indigenous belief systems.

The Buddhist soteriology is summed up in the Four Noble Truths:

1. *Dukkha*: All worldly life is unsatisfactory, disjointed, containing suffering.
2. *Samudaya*: There is a cause of suffering, which is attachment or desire (*tanha*) rooted in ignorance.
3. *Nirodha*: There is an end of suffering, which is Nirvana.
4. *Marga*: There is a path that leads out of suffering, known as the Noble Eightfold Path.

However, Buddhist philosophy as such has its foundations more in the doctrines of:

- anatta, which specifies that all is without substantial metaphysical being,
- pratitya-samutpada, which delineates the Buddhist concept of causality, and
- Buddhist phenomenological analysis of dharmas, or phenomenological constituents.

Most Buddhist sects believe in karma, a cause-and-effect relationship between all that has been done and all that will be done. Events that occur are held to be the direct result of previous events. One effect of karma is rebirth. At death, the karma from a given life determines the nature of the next life's existence. The ultimate goal of a Buddhist practitioner is to eliminate karma (both good and bad), end the cycle of rebirth and suffering, and attain Nirvana, usually translated as *awakening* or *enlightenment*.

Chan/Zen Buddhism

Chan (*Chinese*) or Zen (*Japanese*) is a fusion of the Dhyana school of Mahayana Buddhism with Taoist principles.

Bodhidharma was a semi-legendary Indian monk who travelled to China in the 5th century. There, at the Shaolin temple, he began the Ch'an school of Buddhism, known in Japan and in the West as Zen Buddhism.

Zen philosophy places emphasis on existing in the moment, right now. Zen teaches that the entire universe is a manifestation of mind, and encourages the practictioner to confirm this for themselves through direct insight satori. Zen schools have been historically divided between those which encourage the pursuit of enlightenment as a sudden event (Rinzai), or as a fruit of "gradual cultivation" (Soto).

Zen practitioners engage in zazen (*sitting*) meditation, as other schools do, but Zen is noted for shikantaza (*just sitting*) as opposed to following the breath or mantra use. The Rinzai school is noteworthy for the use of koans, riddles designed to force the student to abandon futile attempts to understand the nature of the universe through logic.

Carvaka

Carvaka, also frequently transliterated as Charvaka or Carvaka, and also known as Lokayata or Lokyata, was a materialist and atheist school of thought with ancient roots in India. It proposed a system of ethics based on rational thought. However, this school has been dead for more than a thousand years.

Confucianism

Confucianism, developed around the teachings of Confucius and is based on a set of Chinese classic texts. It was the mainstream ideology in China and the sinosphere since the Han dynasty and may still be considered a major underlying element of Far-East culture. It could be understood as a social ethic and humanist system focusing on human beings and their relationships. Confucianism emphasizes formal rituals in every aspect of life, from quasi-religious ceremonies to strict politeness and deference to one's elders, specifically to one's parents and to the state in the form of the Emperor.

Neo-Confucianism

Neo-Confucianism is a later further development of Confucianism but also went much more differently from the origin of Confucianism. It started developing from the Song Dynasty and was nearly completed in late Ming dynasty. Its root can be found as early as Tang Dynasty. It has a great influence on the East Asia including such as China, Japan and Korea. Zhu Xi is considered as the biggest master of Song Neo-confucianism and Wang Yangming is the one of Ming's. But there are conflicts between Zhu's school and Wang's.

Daoism

Daoism, whose essence is centered around letting things take their natural course, is the traditional foil of Confucianism. Daoism's central books are the Dao De Jing, traditionally attributed to Laozi (Lao Tzu), and the Zhuangzi (Chuang Tzu). The core concepts of Daoism are traced far in Chinese History, incorporating elements of mysticism dating back to prehistoric times, linked also with the Book of Changes (Yi Jing or I Ching), a divinatory set of 64 geometrical figures describing states and evolutions of the world. Daoism emphasizes Nature, individual freedom, refusal of social bounds, and was a doctrine professed by those who "retreated in mountains". At the end of their lives-or during the night-Confucian officers often behaved as Daoists, writing poetry or trying to "reach immortality". Yet Daoism is also a government doctrine where the ruler's might is ruling through "non-action" (Wu wei).

Ancient Egyptian Religion

The Egyptian religion, embodied in Egyptian mythology, is a succession of beliefs held by the people of Egypt, as early as predynastic times and all the way until the coming of Christianity and Islam in the Greco-Roman and Arab eras. These were conducted by Egyptian priests or magicians. Every animal portrayed and worshipped in ancient Egyptian art, writing and religion is indigenous to Africa, all the way from the predynastic until the Graeco-Roman eras, over 3000 years.

The Dromedary, domesticated first in Arabia, first appears in Egypt (and North Africa) beginning in the 2nd millennium BC. The temple was a sacred place where only priests and priestesses were allowed. On special occasions people were allowed into the temple courtyard.

Hinduism

Hinduism is generally considered to be the oldest major world religion and first among Dharma faiths. Hinduism is characterized by a diverse array of belief systems, practices and scriptures. It has its origin in ancient Vedic culture at least as far back as 3000 BC. It is the third largest religion with approximately 1.05 billion followers worldwide, 96% of whom live in the Indian subcontinent.

Hinduism rests on the spiritual bedrock of the Vedas, hence Veda Dharma, and their mystic issue, the Upanishads, as well as the teachings of many great Hindu gurus through the ages.

Many streams of thought flow from the six Vedic/Hindu schools, Bhakti sects and Tantra Agamic schools into the one ocean of Hinduism, the first of the Dharma religions. Also, the sacred book Bhagavad Gita is one of the most revered texts among Hindus.

What can be said to be common to all Hindus is belief in Dharma, reincarnation, karma, and moksha (liberation) of every soul through a variety of moral, action-based, and meditative yogas. Still more fundamental principles include ahimsa (non-violence), the primacy of the Guru, the Divine Word of Aum and the power of mantras, love of Truth in many manifestations as gods and goddessess, and an understanding that the essential spark of the Divine (Atman/Brahman) is in every human and living being, thus allowing for many spiritual paths leading to the One Unitary Truth.

ISLAMIC PHILOSOPHY

The rise of Islam led to emergence of various philosophical schools of thought. Amongst them sufism established esoteric philosophy, mu'tazilah (inspired from Greek Philosophy) reconstructed rationalism while asharites cast significant impact on the non-reliability of reason and reshaped logical and rational interpretation of God, justice, destiny and universe.

Sufism is a school of esoteric philosophy in Islam, which is based on the pursuit of spiritual truth as a definite goal to attain. In order to attain this supreme truth, Sufism has marked *Lataif-e-Sitta* (the six subtleties), *Nafs*, *Qalb*, *Sirr*, *Ruh* (spirit), *Khafi* and *Akhfa*. Apart from conventional religious practices, they also perform Muraqaba (meditation), Dhikr (Zikr or recitation), Chillakashi (asceticism) and Sama (esoteric music and dance).

Al-mu'tazilah or Mu'tazilite is another controversial theological school of philosophy in early Islam. They called themselves Ahl al-'Adl wa al-Tawhid ("People of Justice and Monotheism").

They were the first who advocated free will and expanded the (western) rationalism in Islamic society. They also developed Kalam based on Greek dialectic. They ascended dramatically during 8th and 9th century due to support of intellectual and elites, but could not appeal to the masses. Later in the 13th century, they lost official support and most of their valuable works were destroyed.

Jainism

Jainism was founded by Mahavira, a teacher and religious leader who lived around the same time as the Buddha. The word *Jaina* comes from the title *Jina*, or victorious one, referring to those who have achieved victory over their own passions. Jainism teaches asceticism-acts of self-discipline, self-deprivation, and self-denial-as the way to enlightenment.

The original Jains were among the world's first monks, retreating from ordinary life to devote themselves to fasting and meditation. The Jain population is concentrated in India and has crossed 10 million. Jains are among the most prosperous of business communities in India.

JEWISH PHILOSOPHY

Jewish philosophy is continually shaped by the Torah, Tanakh, Talmud, Midrash and Kabbalistic traditions. Much of philosophy (Hashkafa) is also considered in reference to mussar: self-improvement and education to attain a higher purpose-to become close to the Creator.

Philosophical discussions in the Talmud usually centre around legal issues, and the legal implications of having a particular philosophy. Midrash and Kabbalah follow a more overarching philosophical style which deal with issues such as ein sof-without end. The main feature is that the Eternal Creator is a given and that he is One and unique. Rambam (Maimonides) in is classic: Moreh Nevuchim (*Guide to the Perplexed*), clarifies this principal in Greco terms.

Legalism

Legalism advocated a strict interpretation of the law in every respect. Morality was not important; adherence to the letter of the law was paramount. Officials who exceeded expectations were as liable for punishment as were those who underperformed their duties, since both were not adhering exactly to their duties. Legalism was the principal philosophic basis of the Qin Dynasty in China. Confucian scholars were persecuted under Legalist rule.

Maoism

Maoism is a Communist philosophy based on the teachings of 20th century Communist Party of China revolutionary leader Mao Zedong. It is based partially on earlier theories by Marx and Lenin, but rejects the urban proletariat and Leninist emphasis on heavy industrialization in favour of a revolution supported by the peasantry, and a decentralized agrarian economy based on many collectively worked farms.

Many people believe that though the implementation of Maoism in Mainland China led to the victory of communist revolution, it also contributed to the widespread famine, with millions of people starving to death. Chinese Communist leader Deng Xiaoping reinterpreted Maoism to allow for the introduction of market economics, which eventually enabled the country to recover. As a philosophy, Deng's chief contribution was to reject the supremacy of theory in interpreting Marxism and to argue for a policy of seeking truth from facts.

Despite this, Maoism has remained a popular ideology for various Communist revolutionary groups around the world, notably the Khmer Rouge in Cambodia, Sendero Luminoso in Peru, and an ongoing (as of early 2005) Maoist insurrection in Nepal.

Shinto

Shinto is the indigenous religion of Japan, a sophisticated form of animism that holds that spirits called kami inhabit all things. Worship is at public shrines, or in small shrines constructed in one's home. According to Shinto practice, relationship with the kami that inhabit this world is foremost in a person's duties. The kami are to be respected, and in turn, they will return our respect. Shinto further holds that the "spirit" and "mundane" worlds are but one in the same. Purity is the most stressed of its tenants, with acts that create harmony pure, and those that are disharmonious to in the scheme of the universe considered impure. Shinto, as a faith, bears heavy influences from Chinese philosophies, such as Taoism, not to mention Buddhism.

Sikhism

- Simran and Sewa: These are the Foundation of Sikhism. It is the duty of every Sikh to practise Naam Simran (meditation on the Lord's name) daily and engage in Sewa (Selfless Service) whenever there is a possibility- in Gurdwara (Sikh place of worship); in community centre; old people's homes; care centres; major world disasters, etc
- The Three Pillars of Sikhism: Guru Nanak formalised these three important pillars of Sikhism:

- Naam Japna: – A Sikh is to engage in a daily practise of meditation and Nitnem (a daily prayer routine) by reciting and chanting of God's Name.
- Kirat Karni:-To live honestly and earn by ones physical and mental effort while accepting Gods gifts and blessings. A Sikh has to live as a householders carrying out his or her duties and responsibilities to the full.
- Vand Chakna:-The Sikhs are asked to share their wealth within the community and outside by giving Dasvand and practising charity (Daan). To "Share and consume together".
- Kill the Five Thieves: The Sikh Gurus tell us that our mind and spirit are constantly being attacked by the Five Evils – Kam (Lust), Krodh (Rage), Lobh (Greed), Moh (Attachment) and Ahankar (Ego). A Sikh needs to constantly attack and overcome these five vices; be always vigilant and on guard to tackle these five thieves all the time!
- Positive Human Qualities: The Sikh Gurus taught the Sikhs to develop and harness positive human qualities which lead the soul closer to God and away from evil. These are: Sat (Truth); Daya (Compassion); Santokh (Contenment); Nimrata (Humility); and Pyare (Love).
- Sikhism-Brief account of this religion.
- Sikh Beliefs-Brief outline of Sikh beliefs.
- Basic Tenets of the Sikhism:-A Summary of the most Important Beliefs and Tenets of Sikhism.
- Sikhism Primary Beliefs and Principles A more detailed account of Sikh beliefs with quotations from SGGS.

Zoroastrianism and Dualism

Zoroastrianism is the earliest known monotheistic religion, which originated in Iran. Zoroastrianism has a dualistic nature (Ahura Mazda and Angra Mainyu), with an additional series of six important angel-like entities called the Amesha Spentas. In modern Zoroastrianism they are interpreted as aspects or emanations of Ahura Mazda (the Supreme Being), who form a heptad that is good and constructive. They are opposed to another group of seven who are evil and destructive. It is this persistent conflict between good and evil that distinguishes Zoroastrianism from monotheistic frameworks that have only one power as supreme. By requiring its adherents to have faith and belief in *equally opposing* powers Zoroastrianism characterizes itself as dualistic.

Zoroastrianism may also be known as Mazdayasna ("Worship of Wisdom") by some of its followers after the Zoroastrian name of God, Ahura Mazda ("Divine Wisdom"). A modern Persian form is *Behdin* ("Good Religion/Law," see below for the role of *daena* Law). Zoroastrians may refer to themselves as *Zartoshti* ("Zoroastrians"), *Mazdayasni* ("Wisdom-Worshippers") and *Behdini* ("Followers of the Good Religion"), and *Zarathustrian*.

Arguments against the "Eastern Philosophy" Designation

Many have argued that the distinction between Eastern and Western schools of philosophy is arbitrary and purely geographic and to certain extent, Eurocentric. It crosses over three distinct philosophical traditions, Indian, Chinese and Persian philosophy which are as distinct from each other as they are from Western philosophy. It could be argued that the idea of some distinct "Eastern" philosophy as opposed to Western Philosophy is simplistic to the point of absurd inaccuracy. Moreover, this artificial distinction does not take into account the tremendous amount of interaction within Eurasian philosophical tradition, and that the distinction is more misleading than enlightening. For example, Indian and Western schools of thought, with their robust mind-body conceptual dualism, share consequent tendencies to subjective idealism or dualism. Formally, they share the rudiments of Western "folk psychology" —a sentential psychology and semantics; for example, belief and (propositional) knowledge, subject-predicate grammar (and subject-object metaphysics) truth and falsity, and inference.

These concepts underwrote the emergence (or perhaps spread) of logic in Greece and India (In contrast to pre-Buddhist China). Other noticeable similarities include structural features of related concepts of time, space, objecthood and causation — all concepts hard to isolate within ancient Chinese conceptual space. It has also been suggested that the ancient Greek philosophers Pythagoras and Heraclitus were both influenced by ideas that originated in China.

The Perception of God and the Gods

Because of the influence of monotheism and especially the Abrahamic religions, Western philosophies have been faced with the question of the nature of God and His relationship to the universe. This has created a dichotomy among Western philosophies between secular philosophies and religious philosophies which develop within the context of a particular monotheistic religion's dogma regarding the nature of God and the universe.

Eastern philosophies have not been as concerned by questions relating to the nature of a single God as the universe's sole creator and ruler. The distinction between the religious and the secular tends to be much less sharp in Eastern philosophy, and the same philosophical school often contains both religious and philosophical elements. Thus, some people accept the metaphysical tenets of Buddhism without going to a temple and worshipping. Some have worshipped the Taoist deities religiously without bothering to delve into the philosophic underpinnings, while others embrace Taoist philosophy while ignoring the religious aspects. On the other hand, the followers of *Hare Krishna* sect in western countries give more emphasis to meditation and yoga and tend to ignore other traditional Hindu rituals.

This arrangement stands in marked contrast to most philosophy of the West, which has traditionally enforced either a completely unified philosophic/religious belief system (for example, the various sects and associated philosophies of Christianity, Judaism, and Islam), or a sharp and total repudiation of religion by philosophy (for example, Nietzsche, Marx, Voltaire, etc.).

Gods' Relationship with the Universe

Another common thread that often differentiates Eastern philosophy from Western is the belief regarding the relationship between God or the gods and the universe. Western philosophies typically either disavow the existence of God, or else hold that God or the gods are something separate and distinct from the universe.

The obvious exception here is the Greek and Roman pantheon of gods and goddesses during ancient times, which is very distinct from the influence of the Abrahamic religions, which teach that this universe was created by a single all-powerful God who existed before and only partially separately from this universe. Some aspects of the true nature and properties of this God would be incomprehensible to us as creations.

Eastern philosophic traditions generally tend to be less concerned with the existence or non-existence of God or gods. Although some Eastern traditions have supernatural spiritual beings and even powerful gods, these are generally not seen as separate from the universe, but rather as a part of the universe, just as Greek and Roman supernatural beings. Conversely, most Eastern religions teach that ordinary actions can affect the supernatural realm.

The Role and Nature of the Individual

It has been argued that in most Western philosophies, the same can be said of the individual: Many Western philosophers generally assume as a given that the individual is something distinct from the entire universe, and many Western philosophers attempt to describe and categorize the universe from a detached, objective viewpoint.

Eastern philosophers, on the other hand, typically hold that people are an intrinsic and inseparable part of the universe, and that attempts to discuss the universe from an objective viewpoint as though the individual speaking was something separate and detached from the whole are inherently absurd.

Syntheses of Eastern and Western Philosophy

There have been many modern attempts to integrate Western and Eastern philosophical traditions.

German philosopher Georg Wilhelm Friedrich Hegel was very interested in Taoism. His system of dialectics is sometimes interpreted as a formalization of Taoist principles, but it also has similarities to the dialectical method used by Socrates as described by Plato.

Hegel's rival Arthur Schopenhauer developed a philosophy that was essentially a synthesis of Hinduism and Buddhism with Western thought. He anticipated that the *Upanishads* (primary Hindu scriptures) would have a much greater influence in the West than they have had. However, Schopenhauer was working with heavily flawed early translations (and sometimes second-degree translations), and many feel that he may not necessarily have accurately grasped the Eastern philosophies which interested him.

Recent attempts to incorporate Western philosophy into Eastern thought include the Kyoto School of philosophers, who combined the phenomenology of Husserl with the insights of Zen Buddhism. Watsuji Tetsuro, a 20th century Japanese philosopher attempted to combine the works of Soren Kierkegaard, Nietzsche, and Heidegger with Eastern philosophies. Some have claimed that there is also a definite eastern element within Heidegger's philosophy. For the most part this is not made explicit within Heidegger's philosophy, apart from in the dialogue between a Japanese and inquirer. Heidegger did spend time attempting to translate the Tao Te Ching into German, working with his Chinese student Paul Hsaio. It has also been claimed that much of Heidegger's later philosophy, particularly the sacredness of Being, bears a district similarity to Taoist ideas. It may even be that Heidegger's philosophy might be read ultimately as an attempt to 'turn eastwards' in response to the crisis in Western civilisation. This however is only an interpretation. There are clear parallels between Heidegger and the work of Kyoto School.

The Twentieth century Hindu guru Sri Aurobindo was influenced by German Idealism and his Integral yoga is regarded as a synthesis of Eastern and Western thought. The German phenomenologist Jean Gebser's writings on the history of consciousness referred to a new planetary consciousness that would bridge this gap. Followers of these two authors are often grouped together under the term Integral thought.

Swiss psychologist Carl G. Jung's idea of synchronicity moves towards an Oriental view of causality, as he states in the forward to Richard Wilhelm's translation of the I Ching (Book of Changes). He explains that this Chinese view of the world is bases not on science as the west knows it, but on chance.

PHILOSOPHICAL AREAS ADDRESSED IN BUDDHISM

Epistemology

Decisive in distinguishing Buddhism from what is commonly called Hinduism is the issue of epistemological justification. The schools of Indian logic recognize a certain set of valid justifications for knowledge, while Buddhism recognizes a smaller set. Both accept perception and inference, for example, but for the orthodox schools (of Hinduism), the received textual tradition (e.g., the Vedas) is in itself an epistemological category equal to perception and inference (although this is not necessarily true for some of the non-orthodox schools, like Vedanta).

Thus, in the orthodox schools, if a claim was made that could not be substantiated by appeal to the textual canon, it would be considered as ridiculous as a claim that the sky was green. Buddhism, on the other hand, rejected an inflexible reverence of accepted doctrine. As the Buddha said:

Do not accept anything by mere tradition... Do not accept anything just because it accords with your scriptures... Do not accept anything merely because it agrees with your preconceived notions... But when you know for yourselves — these things are moral, these things are blameless, these things are praised by the wise, these things, when performed and undertaken, conduce to well-being and happiness — then do you live acting accordingly. — the Kalama Sutta, Anguttara Nikaya III.65

METAPHYSICS AND PHENOMENOLOGY

Issues Arising from the Doctrine of Anatta

In earliest Buddhism and today still in Theravada and the Madhyamaka, any metaphysical essence or being underlying the play of phenomenal experience is rejected. No "soul" or permanent self was recognized, and the perception of a continuous identity was held to be an illusion.

Any feeling whatsoever, any perception whatsoever, any mental processes whatsoever, any consciousness whatsoever — past, future, or present; internal or external; blatant or subtle, common or sublime, far or near; every consciousness — is to be seen as it actually is with right discernment as "This is not mine. This is not my self. This is not what I am."

— the Anattalakkhana Sutta, Samyutta Nikaya XXII.59

From within the context of the Madhyamaka, we find Candrakirti:

"Self is an essence of things that does not depend on others; it is an intrinsic nature. The non-existence of that is selflessness".

— Bodhisattvayogacaryacatuhsatakamika 256.1.7

This anti-essentialist teaching, known as anatta, brought up many questions. If there is no atman or Brahman underlying the objects and events of the universe, how *could* they be explained? What gave them their existence? And if there was no "self", who makes the decisions we think we make, and what gets reincarnated? Early Buddhist philosophers and exegetes created a pluralist metaphysical and phenomenological system in which all experiences of people, things, and events, can be broken down into smaller and smaller perceptual or perceptual-ontological units called dharmas. These dharmas (roughly synonymous with "phenomena") were interpreted differently by different schools: some held they were real, some held only some were real, some held all were illusory, some held they were empty, some held they were intrinsically associated with suffering, etc. Other debates in metaphysics and phenomenology include the issue of the Pudgala, or "person", which was inserted by the Pudgalavada school to replace the atman as that which transmigrates and that which carries the burden of karma from one life to another. Other schools made unsurprising objection to this. There were further sub-debates regarding whether the pudgala was real or illusory or something in between.

The Yogacara school, somewhat later, would later elevate the mind to act as a substitute for Brahman, much as the Pudgala replaces the atman.

And the Tathagatagarbha (Buddha Essence) doctrine of Mahayana Buddhism would see the Buddha of those Tathagatagarbha sutras insisting that the *atman* (Self) lies at the very heart of the Buddha himself and of Nirvana (the two being One), as well as being concealed within the mass of mental/moral contaminants which blight all beings. In what claim to be the final Mahayana teachings of the Buddha, the eternal Self is distinguished from the five impermanent skandhas (constituents) which make up the non-Self or worldly ego, and the True Self is identified as the Dharmakaya of the Buddha in deathless Nirvana. Such doctrines saw a shift from a largely apophatic (negative) philosophical trend within Buddhism to a decidedly more cataphatic (positive) modus.

In many or all of these debates, some would point out the irony of pursuing questions which the Buddha of the *agamas*/ Pali suttas was often prone to refuse to answer, on the grounds that they were non-conducive to enlightenment. The Buddha of the Mahayana, however, would on occasion take a different stand and speak of allegedly higher doctrines sui for the more advanced of his monks.

Dependent Origination

The original positive Buddhist contribution to the field of metaphysics is *pratityasamutpada*, which arises from the Buddhist critique of Indian theories of causality. It states that events are not predetermined, nor are they random, and it rejects notions of direct causation owing to the need for such theories in the Indian context to be undergirded by a substantialist metaphysics. Instead, it posits the arising of events under certain conditions which are inextricable, such that the units in question at no time have independent existence.

This being, that becomes.

From the arising of this, that arises.

This not being, that does not become.

From the ceasing of this, that ceases.
— Samyutta Nikaya ii.

Pratitya-samutpada goes on to posit that certain specific events, concepts, or realities are always dependent on other specific things. Craving, for example, is always dependent on, and caused by, emotion. Emotion is always dependent on contact with our surroundings. This chain of causation purports to show that the cessation of decay, death, and sorrow is indirectly dependent on the cessation of craving, and ultimately dependent on an all-encompassing stillness. Nagarjuna, one of the most influential Buddhist philosophers, asserted a direct connection between, even identity of, dependent origination, anatta, and sunyata. He pointed out that implicit in the early Buddhist concept of dependent origination is the lack of any substantial being (anatta) underlying the participants in origination, so that they have no independent existence, a state identified as emptiness, or emptiness of a nature or essence (sva-bhava). This element of Nagarjuna's thought is relatively uncontroversial, but it opens the way for his identification of samsara and nirvana, which was revolutionary.

Interpenetration

This doctrine comes from the Avatamsaka Sutra and its

associated schools. It holds that all phenomena are intimately connected. Two images are used to convey this idea. The first is known as Indra's net. The net is set with jewels which have the extraordinary property that they reflect all of the other jewels. The second image is that of the world text. This image portrays the world as consisting of an enormous text which is as large as the universe itself. The 'words' of the text are composed of the phenomena that make up the world. However, every atom of the world contains the whole text within it. It is the work of a Buddha to let out the text so that beings can be liberated from suffering. This idea was enormously influential on the Japanese monk Kukai in founding the Shingon school of Buddhism.

Ethics

Although there are many ethical tenets in Buddhism that differ depending on whether one is a monk or a layman, and depending on individual schools, the Buddhist system of ethics can always be summed up in the Eightfold Path.

> *And this, monks, is the noble truth of the way of practice leading to the cessation of suffering — precisely this Noble Eightfold Path — right view, right resolve, right speech, right action, right livelihood, right effort, right mindfulness, right concentration.*
>
> — Samyutta Nikaya LVI.11

The purpose of living an ethical life is to escape the suffering inherent in (unenlightened) worldly life. Although early Buddhism (Hinayana) is contrasted with later Buddhism (Mahayana) in that the latter emphasizes striving for the enlightenment of all (apparent) beings rather than simply oneself, in neither case can the motivation for ethical living be called 'selfish', because Buddhist doctrine holds the notion of a 'self' to be illusory.

Buddhist teachings claim that there is no real difference between ourselves and others; therefore one should attempt to increase the happiness of all living things as eagerly as one's own. This is why some Buddhists choose to be vegetarians.

2

Teaching of Theravada

Theravada literally, "the Teaching of the Elders" or "the Ancient Teaching", is the oldest surviving Buddhist school. It was founded in India. It is relatively conservative, and generally closest to early Buddhism, and for many centuries has been the predominant religion of Sri Lanka (about 70% of the population) and most of continental Southeast Asia (Cambodia, Laos, Burma, Thailand).

Theravada is also practiced by minorities in parts of southwest China (by the Shan and Tai ethnic groups), Vietnam (by the Khmer Krom), Bangladesh (by the ethnic groups of Baruas, Chakma, and Magh), Malaysia and Indonesia, while recently gaining popularity in Singapore and the Western World. Today Theravada Buddhists number over 100 million worldwide, and in recent decades Theravada has begun to take root in the West and in the Buddhist revival in India.

FUNDAMENTALS OF THERAVADA

One thing that should be expressed first and foremost is that the Theravada philosophy is a continuous analytical process of life, not a mere set of ethics and rituals. The ultimate theory of Theravada uses the Four Noble Truths, also known as the Four Sublime Truths. In the simplest form these can be described as the problem, the cause, the solution and the pathway to solution (implementation).

The Four Noble Truths

The Four Noble Truths (or The Four Truths of the Noble Ones) is one of the most fundamental Buddhist teachings. This Dharma Enlightenment makes ordinary person become the Buddha (Khun Weera Boontanorm, 2000). In broad terms, these truths relate to suffering (or dukkha), its nature, its origin, its cessation and the path leading to its cessation. They are among the truths Siddhartha Gautama is said to have realized during his experience of enlightenment.

The Four Noble Truths appear many times, throughout the most ancient Buddhist texts, the Pail Canon. The early teaching and the traditional understanding in Theravada is that the Four Noble Truths are an advanced teaching for those who are ready for them. Mahayana Buddhism regards them as a preliminary teaching for people not ready for its own teachings.

Some may see "truths" as a mistranslation (one author cites "realities" as a possibly better choice: these are *things*, not statements, in the original grammar). However, the original Tibetan Lotsawas, who studied Sanskrit grammar thoroughly, did translate the term from Sanskrit into Tibetan as "bden pa" which has the full meaning of "truth".

Background

Why the Buddha is said to have taught in this way is illuminated by the social context of the time in which he lived. The Buddha was a Sramana – a wandering ascetic whose "aim was to discover the truth and attain happiness." He is said to have achieved this aim while under a bodhi tree near the River Neranjana; the Four Noble Truths are a formulation of his understanding of the nature of "suffering", the fundamental cause of all suffering, the escape from suffering, and what effort a person can go to so that they themselves can "attain happiness."

These truths are not expressed as a hypothesis or tentative idea; rather, the Buddha says:

These Four Noble Truths, monks, are actual, unerring, not otherwise. Therefore, they are called noble truths.

The Buddha says that he taught them......because it is beneficial, it belongs to the fundamentals of the holy life, it leads to disenchantment, to dispassion, to cessation of suffering, to peace, to direct knowledge, to enlightenment, to Nirvana. That is why I have declared it.

This teaching was the basis of the Buddha's first discourse after his enlightenment. In early Buddhism this is the most advanced teaching in the Buddha's Gradual Training.

A formal description of the Four Noble Truths follows:

1. Dukkha (suffering)- This can be somewhat broadly classified into three categories. Inherent suffering, or the suffering one undergoes in all the worldly activities, what one suffers in day-to-day life: birth, aging, diseases, death, sadness, etc. In short, all that one feels from separating from 'loving' attachments and/or associating with 'hating' attachments is encompassed into the term. The second class of suffering, called Suffering due to Change, implies that things suffer due to attaching themselves to a momentary state which is held to be 'good'; when that state is changed, things are subjected to suffering. The third, termed 'Sankhara Dukkha', is the most subtle. Beings suffer simply by not realizing that they are mere aggregates with no definite, unchanging identity.
2. Dukkha Samudaya (cause of suffering)-Craving, which leads to Attachment and Bondage, is the cause of suffering. Formally, this is termed 'Tanha'. It can be classified into three instinctive drives. 'Kama Tanha' is the Craving for any pleasurable sense object (which involves sight, sound, touch, taste, smell and mental perceptives). 'Bhava Tanha' is the Craving for attachment to an ongoing process, which appears in various forms, including the longing for existence. 'Vibhava Tanha' is the Craving for detachment from a process, which includes non-existence and causes the longing for self-annihilation.

3. Dukkha Nirodha (cessation of suffering)-One cannot possibly adjust the whole world to one's taste in order to eliminate suffering and hope that it will remain so forever. This would violate the chief principle of Change. Instead, one adjusts one's own mind through detachment so that the Change, of whatever nature, has no effect on one's peace of mind. Briefly stated, the third Noble Truth implies that elimination of the cause (craving) eliminates the result (suffering). This is inferred in the scriptural quote by The Buddha, 'Whatever may result from a cause, shall be eliminated by the elimination of the cause'.
4. Dukkha Nirodha Gamini Patipada (pathway to freedom from suffering)-This is the Noble Eightfold Pathway towards freedom or Nirvana. The path can roughly be rendered into English as right view, right intention, right speech, right actions, right livelihood, right effort, right mindfulness and right concentration.

HISTORY

Origin of the School

The Theravada school is ultimately derived from the Vibhajjavada (or 'doctrine of analysis') grouping which was a continuation of the older Sthavira (or 'teaching of the Elders') group at the time of the Third Buddhist Council around 250 BC, during the reign of Emperor Asoka in India. Vibhajjavadins saw themselves as the continuation of orthodox Sthaviras and after the Third Council continued to refer to their school as the Sthaviras/There's ('The Elders'), their doctrines were probably similar to the older Sthaviras but were not completely identical. After the Third Council geographical distance led to the Vibhajjavadins gradually evolving into four groups: the Mahiuasaka, Kauyapa, Dharmaguptaka and the Tamraparniya. The Theravada is descended from the Tamraparniya, which means 'the Sri Lankan lineage'. Some sources claim that only the Theravada actually evolved directly from the Vibhajjavadins.

According to Buddhist scholar A.K. Warder, the Theravada "spread rapidly south from Avanti into Maharastra and Andhra and down to the Chola country (Kanchi), as well as Ceylon. For sometime they maintained themselves in Avanti as well as in their new territories, but gradually they tended to regroup themselves in the south, the Great Vihara (Mahavihara) in Anuradhapura, the capital of Ceylon, become the main centre of their tradition, Kanchi a secondary centre and the northern regions apparently relinquished to other schools." There is little information about the later history of Theravada Buddhism in India, and it is not known when it disappeared in its country of origin.

The name of Tamraparniya was given to the Sri Lankan lineage in India but there is no indication that this referred to any change in doctrine or scripture from the Vibhajjavadins, since the name points only to geographical location. The Theravadan accounts of its own origins mention that it received the teachings that were agreed upon during the Third Buddhist Council, and these teachings were known as the Vibhajjavada. In the 7th century, Chinese pilgrims Xuanzang and Yi Jing refer to the Buddhist school in Sri Lanka as 'Sthavira'. In ancient India, those schools that used Sanskrit as their religious language referred to this school as the 'Sthaviras', but those that use Pail as their religious language referred to this school as the 'Theres'. Both 'Sthaviras' (Sanskrit) and 'There's' (Pail) both literally mean 'The Elders'. The school has been using the name 'Theravada' for itself in a written form since at least the fourth century CE when the term appears in the *Dipavamsa*.

The Theravada school had also reached Burma around the time it arrived in Sri Lanka and something of a synergy gradually developed. Around the end of the tenth century C.E, for example, war in Sri Lanka had extinguished the Theravadan ordination lineage, and a contingent of Burmese monks had to be imported to rekindle it. Burmese and Sri Lankan Theravada reinforced each other sufficiently, so that by the time Buddhism died out in India in the eleventh century, it had established a stable home in these countries. Gradually the Theravada form of Buddhism spread to Thailand, Laos, and Cambodia. Although the Theravada tradition was always reputed to be one of the more conservative schools, like the other Nikaya Buddhist schools in India at one point it included Mahayana practioners ("Mahayana-Theravada" or "Mahayana-Sthaviravada"), according to reports of Chinese pilgrims such as Xuanzang. Royal houses in Sri Lanka and Southeast Asia associated themselves closely with Buddhism. States in those areas strictly enforced orthodoxy, and ensured that Theravada remained traditionalist. This contrasts with the relationship of Buddhism to states throughout most of Buddhism's history in India.

HISTORY OF THE TRADITION

According to Sinhalese tradition, Buddhism was first brought to Sri Lanka by Mahinda, who is believed to have been the son of the Mauryan emperor Asoka, in the third century BCE, as a part of the missionary activities of the Asokan era. In Sri Lanka, Mahinda established the Mahavihara Monastery of Anuradhapura. Later it became divided into three subgroups, known after their monastic centres as the Mahavihara, the Abhayagiri Vihara, and the Jetavanavihara. In 1164, with the guidance of two monks from a forest branch of the Mahavihara, the Sri Lankan King reunited all bhikkhus in Sri Lanka into the orthodox Mahavihara school.

A few years after the arrival of Sthavira Mahinda, Sanghamitta, who is also believed to be the daughter of Emperor Asoka, came to Sri Lanka. She started the first nun order in Sri Lanka, but the nun order died out in Sri Lanka in the 11th century and in Burma in the 13th. In 429 CE, by request of China's emperor, nuns from Anuradhapura were sent to China to establish the Nun Order. The order was then spread to Korea. In 1996, 11 selected Sri Lankan nuns were ordained fully as Bhikkhunis by a team of Theravada monks in concert with a team of Korean Nuns in India. There is disagreement among Theravada vinaya authorities as to whether such ordinations are valid. In the last few years the head of the

Dambulla chapter of the Siyam Nikaya in Sri Lanka has carried out ordination ceremonies for hundreds of nuns. This has been criticized by some other leading figures in the Siyam Nikaya and Amarapura Nikaya, and the governing council of Burmese Buddhism has declared that there can be no valid ordination of nuns in modern times, though some Burmese monks disagree with this.

According to Mahavamsa the Sri Lanka chronical, after the conclusion of the Third Buddhist Council, a missionary was also sent to Suvannabhumi where two monks Sona and Uttara, are said to have proceeded. Scholar opinions differ as to where exactly this land of Suvannabhumi is located, but Suvannabhumi is believed to be located somewhere in the area which now includes lower Burma, Thailand, Malay Peninsula and Sumatra Island.

The Mon and Pyu were among the earliest people to inhabit Burma. Recent archaeological research at a Pyu settlement in the Samon Valley (around 100 km south-east of Bagan) has shown that they had trade links with India from 500-400 BC and with China around 200 BC. Chinese sources which have been dated to around 240 A.D. mention a Buddhist kingdom by the name of Lin-Yang, which some scholars have identified as the ancient Pyu kingdom of Beikthano 300 km north of Yangon. The Burmese slowly became Theravadan when they came into contact with the Pyu and Mon civilization. The Thais also slowly became Theravadan as they came into contact with the Mon civilization.

Despite its success in Southeast Asia, Theravada Buddhism in China has generally been limited to areas bordering Theravada countries.

Modern Developments

The following modern trends or movements have been identified.

- modernism: attempts to adapt to the modern world and adopt some of its ideas; includes among other things.
  * green movement

  * syncretism with other Buddhist traditions
  * women's rights
  * gay rights.
- reformisms: attempts to restore a supposed earlier, ideal state of Buddhism; includes in particular the adoption of Western scholars' theories of original Buddhism (in recent times the "Western scholarly interpretation of Buddhism" is the official Buddhism prevailing in Sri Lanka and Thailand.)
- ultimatism: tendency to concentrate on advanced teachings such as the Four Noble Truths at the expense of more elementary ones
- neo-traditionalism; includes among other things.
  * revival of ritualism
  * remythologization.
- insight meditation
- social action
- devotional religiosity
- reaction to Buddhist nationalism
- renewal of forest monks
- revival of samatha meditation.

Buddhist revivalism has also reacted against changes in Buddhism caused by colonialist regimes. Western colonialists and Christian missionaries deliberately imposed a particular type of Christian monasticism on Buddhist clergy in Sri Lanka and colonies in Southeast Asia, restricting monks' activities to individual purification and temple ministries.

Prior to British colonial control, monks in both Sri Lanka and Burma had been responsible for the education of the children of lay people, and had produced large bodies of literature. After the British takeover, Buddhist temples were strictly administered and were only permitted to use their funds on strictly religious activities. Christian ministers were given control of the education system and their pay became state funding for missions.

Foreign, especially British rule had an enervating effect on the sangha. According to Walpola Rahula, Christian missionaries displaced and appropriated the educational, social, and welfare activities of the monks, and inculcated a permanent shift in views regarding the proper position of monks in society through their institutional influence upon the elite.

Many monks in post-colonial times have been dedicated to undoing this paradigm shift. Movements intending to restore Buddhism's place in society have developed in both Sri Lanka and Burma.

Overview of Philosophy

Theravada promotes the concept of Vibhajjavada (Pail), literally "Teaching of Analysis." This doctrine says that insight must come from the aspirant's experience, critical investigation, and reasoning instead of by blind faith; however, the scriptures of the Theravadan tradition also emphasize heeding the advice of the wise, considering such advice and evaluation of one's own experiences to be the two tests by which practices should be judged.

In Theravada, the cause of human existence and suffering is identified as craving, which carries with it the defilements (*kilesas*). Those defilements that bind human to the cycle of rebirth are classified into a set of ten "Fetters", while those defilements that impede concentration are presented in a fivefold set called the "Five Hindrances". The level of defilement can be coarse, medium, and subtle. It is a phenomenon that frequently arises, remains temporarily and then vanishes. Theravadans believe defilements are not only harmful to oneself, but also harmful to others. They are the driving force behind all inhumanities a human being can commit.

Theravadian's believe these defilements are the habits born of ignorance (*avijja*) which afflict the minds of all unenlightened beings. It is believed that unenlightened beings are under the influence of the defilements, unenlightened beings cling to them through ignorance of the truth. But in reality, those mental defilements are nothing more than taints that have afflicted the mind and create suffering and stress. It is also believed that unenlightened beings cling to the body, assuming it as their own "*Self*", but in reality the body is an impermanent phenomenon formed from the four basic elements. Often characterized by earth, water, fire and air, in the early Buddhist texts these are defined to be abstractions representing the sensorial qualities solidity, fluidity, temperature, and mobility, respectively. The mental defilements' frequent instigation and manipulation of the mind is believed to have prevented the mind from seeing the true nature of reality. Unskillful behaviour in turn can strengthen the defilements, but following the Noble Eightfold Path can weaken or eradicate them.

It is also believed that unenlightened beings experience the world through their imperfect six sense doors (eye, ear, nose, tongue, tactile sense, and mind) and then use the mind clouded by defilements to form their own interpretation, perception and conclusion.

In such a condition the perception or conclusion made will be based on that being's own illusion of reality. In the state of *jhana* (deep concentration), the five physical sense doors will fade, the mental defilements will be suppressed, and wholesome mental traits will become strengthened. The mind can then be used to investigate and gain insight into the true nature of reality.

There are three stages of defilements. During the stage of passivity the defilements lies dormant at the base of the mental continuum as latent tendencies (*anusaya*), but through the impact of sensory stimulus it will manifest (*pariyutthana*) itself to the surface of consciousness in the form of unwholesome thoughts, emotions, and volitions. If they gather additional strength, the defilement will reach the dangerous stage of transgression (*vitikkama*), which will then involve physical or vocal actions. It is believed that in order to be free from suffering and stress these defilements need to be permanently uprooted. Initially the defilements are restrained through mindfulness to prevent them from taking over the mind and bodily action. They are then uprooted through internal investigation, analysing, experiencing and understanding the true nature of those defilements by using *jhana*. This process needs to be repeated for each and every defilement. The practice will then lead the meditator to realize the Four Noble Truths, Enlightenment, and Nirvana. Nirvana is the ultimate goal of Theravadans. *Nirvana* is said to be the perfect bliss and the person is liberated from the repeated cycle of birth, illness, aging and death.

Theravadans believe that every individual is personally responsible for their own self-awakening and liberation, as they are the ones that were responsible for their own actions and consequences (Sanskrit: *karma*; Pail: *kamma*). Simply learning or believing in the true nature of reality as expounded by the Buddha is not enough, the awakening can only be achieved through direct experience and personal realization. An individual will have to follow and practice the Noble Eightfold Path as taught by the Buddha to discover the reality for themselves. In Theravada belief, Buddhas, gods or deities are incapable of giving a human being the awakening or lifting them from the state of repeated cycle of birth, illness, aging and death (*samsara*). For Theravadans, Buddha is only a Teacher of the Noble Eightfold Path, while gods or deities are still subject to anger, jealousy, hatred, vengeance, craving, greed, delusion, and death.

It is believed that some people who practice with earnestness and zeal can attain Nirvana within a single lifetime, as did many of the first few generations of Buddha's disciples. For others, the process may take multiple lifetimes, with the individual reaching higher and higher states of realization. One who has attained Nirvana is called an *Arahant*. It is believed that the Nirvana is most quickly attained as a disciple of Buddha, since Lord Buddha is believed to have possessed the ultimate knowledge on how to guide a person through the process of enlightenment.

According to the early scriptures, the Nirvana attained by *Arahants* is identical to that attained by the Buddha himself, as there is only one type of Nirvana. Buddha was superior to

Arahants because the Buddha had discovered the path all by himself, and has taught it to others (i.e., metaphorically turning the wheel of Dhamma). *Arahants*, on the other hand, attained Nirvana due in part to the Buddha's teachings. Theravadans revere the Buddha as a single supremely gifted person but do recognize the existence of other such Buddhas in the distant past and future. Maitreya (Pail: Metteyya), for example, is mentioned very briefly in the Pail Canon as a Buddha who will come in the distant future.

Traditionally Theravadans can either have the conviction (or "faith") in the Buddha's teaching and practice the minor precepts in the hope of gaining some minor benefits or they can investigate and verify by direct experience the truth of the Buddha's teaching by practicing the *jhana* which is part of the Noble Eightfold Path for their own Enlightenment.

BUDDHIST DOCTRINE AND TERMINOLOGY

Is Buddhism a Religion or a Philosophy?

The Buddha referred to his teachings simply as *Dhamma-vinaya* — "the doctrine and discipline" — but for centuries people have tried to categorize the teachings in various ways, trying to fit them into the prevailing molds of cultural, philosophical, and religious thought. Buddhism is an ethical system — a way of life — that leads to a very specific goal and that possesses some aspects of both religion and philosophy:

It is a Philosophy: Like most philosophies, Buddhism attempts to frame the complexities of human existence in a way that reassures us that there is, in fact, some underlying order to the Universe.

In the Four Noble Truths the Buddha crisply summarizes our predicament: there is suffering, it has a cause, it has an end, and there is a way to reach the end. The teachings on kamma provide a thorough and logically self-consistent description of the nature of cause-and-effect. And even the Buddhist view of cosmology, which some may at first find farfetched, is a logical extension of the law of kamma. According to the Dhamma, a deep and unshakable logic pervades the world.

It is not a Philosophy: Unlike most philosophical systems, which rely on speculation and the power of reason to arrive at logical truths, Buddhism relies on the direct observation of one's personal experience and on honing certain skills in order to gain true understanding and wisdom. Idle speculation has no place in Buddhist practice.

Although studying in the classroom, reading books, and engaging in spirited debate can play a vital part in developing a cognitive understanding of basic Buddhist concepts, the heart of Buddhism can never be realized this way. The Dhamma is not an abstract system of thought designed to delight the intellect; it is a roadmap to be *used,* one whose essential purpose is to lead the practitioner to the ultimate goal, nibbana.

It is a Religion: At the heart of each of the world's great religions lies a transcendent ideal around which its doctrinal principles orbit. In Buddhism this truth is nibbana, the hallmark of the cessation of suffering and stress, a truth of utter transcendence that stands in singular distinction from anything we might encounter in our ordinary sensory experience.

Nibbana is the *sine qua non* of Buddhism, the guiding star and ultimate goal towards which all the Buddha's teachings point. Because it aims at such a lofty transcendent ideal, we might fairly call Buddhism a religion.

It is not a Religion: In stark contrast to the world's other major religions, however, Buddhism invokes no divinity, no supreme Creator or supreme Self, no Holy Spirit or omniscient loving God to whom we might appeal for salvation.

Instead, Buddhism calls for us to hoist ourselves up by our own bootstraps: to develop the discernment we need to distinguish between those qualities within us that are unwholesome and those that are truly noble and good, and to learn how to nourish the good ones and expunge the bad. This is the path to Buddhism's highest perfection, nibbana. Not even the Buddha can take you to that goal; you alone must do the work necessary to complete the journey:

> *"Therefore, Ananda, be islands unto yourselves, refuges unto yourselves, seeking no external refuge; with the Dhamma as your island, the Dhamma as your refuge, seeking no other refuge."— DN 16*

Despite its non-theistic nature, however, Buddhist practice does call for a certain kind of faith. It is not blind faith, an uncritical acceptance of the Buddha's word as transmitted through scripture. Instead it is *saddha,* a confidence born of taking refuge in the Triple Gem; it is a willingness to trust that the Dhamma, when practiced diligently, will lead to the rewards promised by the Buddha. Saddha is a provisional acceptance of the teachings, that is ever subject to critical evaluation during the course of one's practice, and which must be balanced by one's growing powers of discernment.

For many Buddhists, this faith is expressed and reinforced through traditional devotional practices, such as bowing before a Buddha statue and reciting passages from the early Pali texts.

Despite a superficial resemblance to the rites of many theistic religions, however, these activities are neither prayers nor pleas for salvation directed towards a transcendent Other. They are instead useful and inspiring gestures of humility and respect for the profound nobility and worth of the Triple Gem.

Is Vipassana the same as Theravada?

The Pali word *vipassana* — often translated as "insight"— has a variety of meanings. First, it refers to the flash of liberating intuitive understanding that marks the culmination of Buddhist meditation practice. In the Pali discourses *vipassana* also refers to the mind's ability to witness clearly as events unfold in the present moment. In this sense it is a skill that a meditator develops using a broad arsenal of meditative tools and techniques. With practice, this skill can bring the meditator to the threshold of liberating insight.

In its third meaning, one that has become especially popular in the West in recent years, "Vipassana" (usually with a capital "V") refers to a system of meditation — *vipassana bhavana,* or "Insight Meditation" — that is based on an interpretation of the Satipatthana Sutta (MN 10), the Buddha's concise "how-to" guide to the development of mindfulness *(sati).* Followers of the popular Vipassana movement often cite the Satipatthana Sutta as the essence of the Buddha's teachings; some even claim that the instructions it contains are the *only* ones necessary for achieving liberating insight.

Theravada Buddhism, by contrast, embraces the thousands of discourses of the Pali canon, each highlighting a different aspect of the Buddha's teachings. In Theravada each discourse supports, depends upon, reflects, and informs all the others; even a discourse as important as the Satipatthana Sutta is seen as but a single thread in the Buddha's complex tapestry of teachings.

Although many students do find all they want in Vipassana, some have a nagging sense that something fundamental is missing. This reaction is hardly surprising, as the Satipatthana discourse itself was delivered to a group of relatively advanced students who were already quite experienced and well established in the path of Dhamma practice.

Happily, all those missing pieces can be found in the Pali canon. In the Canon we find the Buddha's teachings on generosity and virtue, the twin pillars upon which all spiritual practice is built. His teachings on the recollection of the Buddha, Dhamma, and Sangha serve to strengthen the development of *saddha* (faith, confidence), which provides a potent fuel to sustain Dhamma practice long after we return home from that meditation retreat.

In the Canon we also find his teachings on the drawbacks of sensuality and the value of renunciation; on developing *all* the factors in the Eightfold Path, including those that are seldom explored during organized Vipassana retreats: right speech, right livelihood, right effort, and right concentration (meaning jhana). And there is much, much more.

In Theravada, the path to liberating insight does not boil down to a single meditation technique or to being continuously mindful. The path to Awakening is full of surprising twists and turns but, thankfully, the Buddha left for us an assortment of tools to use and skills to learn to help us safely make the journey. If we're all reborn when we die, how does Buddhism explain the world's increasing population?

According to Buddhist cosmology, when a living being passes away he or she is reborn into one of thirty-one distinct "planes" or "realms" of existence, of which the human realm is just one. An increase in the human population simply implies that creatures from other planes are being reborn into the human realm at a rate faster than humans are dying. Likewise, a decline in the human population would imply that humans, upon death, are taking rebirth in other planes (or exiting samsara altogether) at a rate faster than other creatures are taking rebirth as humans. These sorts of population shifts have been occurring for countless eons and in themselves hold little cosmic significance.

If there's no self, then who gets enlightened?

If there's no self, then what gets reborn?

If there's no self, then why...?

Nowhere in the Pali canon does Buddha categorically declare, without qualification, "There is no self." Any question that begins along the lines of, "If there's no self..." is thus inherently misleading, dooming the questioner to a hopeless tangle of confusion — "a thicket of [wrong] views" [MN 2]. Such questions are best put aside altogether in favour of more fruitful lines of questioning. I hear the word "sangha" used a lot these days in Buddhist circles. What does it really mean?

The Pali word "sangha" literally means "group" or "congregation," but when it is used in the suttas, the word usually refers to one of two very specific kinds of groups: either the community of Buddhist monastics *(bhikkhus* and *bhikkhunis),* or the community of people who have attained at least the first stage of Awakening.

In recent decades, a new usage of the word has emerged in the West, one that seems to have no basis in classical Theravada Buddhist teachings: the usage of the word "sangha" to describe a meditation group or any sort of spiritual community. It sounds innocent enough, but this particular usage can — and often does — lead to profound confusion concerning one of the most fundamental underpinnings of the Buddha's teachings, the going for refuge in the Triple Gem.

The act of going for refuge in the Buddha, Dhamma, and Sangha marks a major turning point in one's spiritual development, the real start of the journey down the Buddhist path. It helps foster a healthy attitude towards Buddhist practice by encouraging the development of right view, and serves as a constant reminder both of the goal of practice and of the means to achieve that goal. It is therefore crucial to be clear and precise about the meaning of the refuges, lest we end up heading down a road quite different from the one the Buddha had in mind.

In taking refuge in the Sangha, we set our inner sights on the ideal community of Noble Ones *(ariya-sangha)* — those monks, nuns, laywomen, and laymen who, throughout history, have by their own diligent efforts successfully carried out the Buddha's instructions and gained at least a glimpse of the supreme happiness of nibbana. If this is the direction in which we also wish to go, then it is to these individuals that we should turn for refuge:

> *The Sangha of the Blessed One's disciples who have practiced well... who have practiced straight-forwardly... who have practiced methodically... who have practiced masterfully — in other words, the four types [of noble disciples] when taken as pairs, the eight when taken as individual types — they are the Sangha of the Blessed One's disciples: worthy of gifts, worthy of hospitality, worthy of offerings, worthy of respect, the incomparable field of merit for the world. — AN 11.12*

But going for refuge doesn't stop there. We are also asked to turn to the monastic community *(bhikkhu-sangha)* for refuge, for it is thanks to the unbroken lineage of this 2,600-year-old institution that we are fortunate enough today to be able to hear the teachings. Moreover, the living example of the monastic community serves to remind us of the immense value of generosity, of living a morally upright life, of renunciation — in short, it reminds us that it is indeed possible to live a life fully in tune with every aspect of the Buddha's teachings.

In reality, of course, not every monk or nun necessarily lives up to the Buddha's high standards of conduct. For this reason it is to the *institution* of the Sangha that we turn to refuge, not to the individual members themselves. This is the Sangha to which lay people have turned since the time of the Buddha: *I go to Master Gautama for refuge, to the Dhamma, and to the Sangha of monks. May Master Gautama remember me as a lay follower who has gone to him for refuge, from this day forward, for life. — DN 2, MN 72, SN 51.15, AN 4.184, etc.]*

So it is these exceptional groups of people — the *ariya-sangha* and the *bhikkhu-sangha* — that define the Third Gem and Refuge; it is to *these* groups that we are asked to turn for refuge, not to some vaguely defined community of like-minded Dhamma friends and fellow meditators. In which group would you rather put your trust?

In an effort to resolve this confusion, some writers have proposed various alternatives to the word "sangha" to describe gatherings and communities of Dhamma companions. But this still leaves me wondering why we must invoke the Pali language here at all. Does a meditation group really need a special name? Why not simply call it a "meditation group" and leave it at that? "Sangha" is an important term with a rich and precise meaning. It stands for something truly extraordinary and brilliant that can constantly remind us of the highest and most excellent possibilities the Path has to offer. Let's use it well.

What's the Difference between a Buddha and an Arahant? The attainment of arahantship and Buddha-hood are identical: the attainment of the Deathless (Nibbana) and the complete and irreversible eradication of the defilements, the underlying cause of suffering. It is the Buddha who (re-)discovers the Dhamma on his own; it is the arahant who puts his teachings into practice and follows in his footsteps.

Here is the Buddha's answer to this very question:

> [The Buddha:] *"So what difference, what distinction, what distinguishing factor is there between one rightly self-awakened and a monk discernment-released?"*
>
> A group of monks: *"For us, lord, the teachings have the Blessed One as their root, their guide, & their arbitrator. It would be good if the Blessed One himself would explicate the meaning of this statement. Having heard it from the Blessed One, the monks will remember it."*
>
> *"In that case, monks, listen & pay close attention. I will speak."*
>
> *"As you say, lord," the monks responded.*

The Blessed One said, "The Tathagata — the worthy one, the rightly self-awakened one — is the one who gives rise to the path (previously) unarisen, who engenders the path (previously) unengendered, who points out the path (previously) not pointed out. He knows the path, is expert in the path, is adept at the path. And his disciples now keep following the path and afterwards become endowed with the path.

> *"This is the difference, this the distinction, this the distinguishing between one rightly self-awakened and a monk discernment-released." — SN 22.58*

THERAVADA BUDDHISM

Theravada (pronounced — more or less — "terra-VAH-dah"), the "Doctrine of the Elders," is the school of Buddhism that draws its scriptural inspiration from the Tipitaka, or Pali canon, which scholars generally agree contains the earliest surviving record of the Buddha's teachings. For many centuries, Theravada has been the predominant religion of continental Southeast Asia (Thailand, Myanmar/Burma, Cambodia, and Laos) and Sri Lanka. Today Theravada Buddhists number well over 100 million worldwide. In recent decades Theravada has begun to take root in the West.

Many Buddhisms, One Dhamma-vinaya

The Buddha — the "Awakened One" — called the religion he founded *Dhamma-vinaya* — "the doctrine and discipline." To provide a social structure supportive of the practice of Dhamma-vinaya (or *Dhamma* for short [Sanskrit: *Dharma]),* and to preserve these teachings for posterity, the Buddha established the order of *bhikkhus* (monks) and *bhikkhunis* (nuns) — the *Sangha* — which continues to this day to pass his teachings on to subsequent generations of laypeople and monastics, alike.

As the Dhamma continued its spread across India after the Buddha's passing, differing interpretations of the original teachings arose, which led to schisms within the Sangha and the emergence of as many as eighteen distinct sects of Buddhism. One of these schools eventually gave rise to a reform movement that called itself *Mahayana* (the "Greater Vehicle") and that referred to the other schools disparagingly as *Hinayana* (the "Lesser Vehicle"). What we call Theravada today is the sole survivor of those early non-Mahayana schools. To avoid the pejorative tone implied by the terms Hinayana and Mahayana, it is common today to use more neutral language to distinguish between these two main branches of Buddhism. Because Theravada historically dominated southern Asia, it is sometimes called "Southern" Buddhism, while Mahayana, which migrated northwards from India into China, Tibet, Japan, and Korea, is known as "Northern" Buddhism.

The Language of Theravada Buddhism

The language of the Theravada canonical texts is Pali (lit., "text"), which is based on a dialect of Middle Indo-Aryan that was probably spoken in central India during the Buddha's time. Ven. Ananda, the Buddha's cousin and close personal attendant, committed the Buddha's sermons *(suttas)* to memory and thus became a living repository of these teachings. Shortly after the Buddha's death *(ca.* 480 BCE), five hundred of the most senior monks — including Ananda — convened to recite and verify all the sermons they had heard during the Buddha's forty-five year teaching career. Most of these sermons therefore begin with the disclaimer, *"Evam me sutam"* — "Thus have I heard." After the Buddha's death the teachings continued to be passed down orally within the monastic community, in keeping with an Indian oral tradition that long predated the Buddha. By 250 BCE the Sangha had systematically arranged and compiled these teachings into three divisions: the Vinaya Pitaka (the "basket of discipline" — the texts concerning the rules and customs of the Sangha), the Sutta Pitaka (the "basket of discourses" — the sermons and utterances by the Buddha and his close disciples), and the Abhidhamma Pitaka (the "basket of special/higher doctrine" — a detailed psycho-philosophical analysis of the Dhamma). Together these three are known as the Tipitaka, the "three baskets." In the third century BCE Sri Lankan monks began compiling a series of exhaustive commentaries to the Tipitaka; these were subsequently collated and translated into Pali beginning in the fifth century CE. The Tipitaka plus the post-canonical texts (commentaries, chronicles, etc.) together constitute the complete body of classical Theravada literature.

Pali was originally a spoken language with no alphabet of its own. It wasn't until about 100 BCE that the Tipitaka was first fixed in writing, by Sri Lankan scribe-monks, who wrote the Pali phonetically in a form of early Brahmi script. Since then the Tipitaka has been transliterated into many different scripts (Devanagari, Thai, Burmese, Roman, Cyrillic, to name a few). Although English translations of the most popular Tipitaka texts abound, many students of Theravada find that learning the Pali language — even just a little bit here and there — greatly deepens their understanding and appreciation of the Buddha's teachings.

No one can prove that the Tipitaka contains any of the words actually uttered by the historical Buddha. Practicing Buddhists have never found this problematic. Unlike the scriptures of many of the world's great religions, the Tipitaka is not regarded as gospel, as an unassailable statement of divine truth, revealed by a prophet, to be accepted purely on faith. Instead, its teachings are meant to be assessed firsthand, to be put into practice in one's life so that one can find out for oneself if they do, in fact, yield the promised results. It is the truth towards which the words in the Tipitaka point that ultimately matters, not the words themselves. Although scholars will continue to debate the authorship of passages from the Tipitaka for years to come (and thus miss the point of these teachings entirely), the Tipitaka will quietly continue to serve— as it has for centuries — as an indispensable guide for millions of followers in their quest for Awakening.

THERAVADA COMES WEST

Until the late 19th century, the teachings of Theravada were little known outside of southern Asia, where they had flourished for some two and one-half millennia. In the past century, however, the West has begun to take notice of Theravada's unique spiritual legacy in its teachings of Awakening. In recent decades this interest has swelled, with the monastic Sangha from various schools within Theravada establishing dozens of monasteries across Europe and North America. Increasing numbers of lay meditation centres, founded and operated independently of the monastic Sangha, strain to meet the demands of lay men and women — Buddhist and otherwise — seeking to learn selected aspects of the Buddha's teachings.

The turn of the 21st century presents both opportunities and dangers for Theravada in the West: Will the Buddha's teachings be patiently studied and put into practice, and allowed to establish deep roots in Western soil, for the benefit of many generations to come? Will the current popular Western climate of "openness" and cross-fertilization between spiritual traditions lead to the emergence of a strong new form of Buddhist practice unique to the modern era, or will it simply lead to confusion and the dilution of these priceless teachings? These are open questions; only time will tell.

Spiritual teachings of every description inundate the media and the marketplace today. Many of today's popular spiritual teachings borrow liberally from the Buddha, though only rarely do they place the Buddha's words in their true context. Earnest seekers of truth are therefore often faced with the unsavory task of wading through fragmentary teachings of dubious accuracy. How are we to make sense of it all?

Fortunately the Buddha left us with some simple guidelines to help us navigate through this bewildering flood. Whenever you find yourself questioning the authenticity of a particular teaching, heed well the Buddha's advice to his stepmother:

> *The teachings that promote] the qualities of which you may know, 'These qualities lead to passion, not to dispassion; to being fettered, not to being unfettered; to accumulating, not to shedding; to self-aggrandizement, not to modesty; to discontent, not to contentment; to entanglement, not to seclusion; to laziness, not to aroused persistence; to being burdensome, not to being unburdensome': You may definitely hold, 'This is not the Dhamma, this is not the Vinaya, this is not the Teacher's instruction.'*
>
> *As for the teachings that promote] the qualities of which you may know, 'These qualities lead to dispassion, not to passion; to being unfettered, not to being fettered; to shedding, not to accumulating; to modesty, not to self-aggrandizement; to contentment, not to discontent; to seclusion, not to entanglement; to aroused persistence, not to laziness; to being unburdensome, not to being burdensome': You may definitely hold, 'This is the Dhamma, this is the Vinaya, this is the Teacher's instruction.' [AN 8.53]*

The truest test of these teachings, of course, is whether they yield the promised results in the crucible of your own heart. The Buddha presents the challenge; the rest is up to you.

3

Buddhist Monasteries

LONGXING MONTHARPA CHOLING MONASTERY

The Tharpa Choling Monastery is a Buddhist monastery near Kalimpong in West Bengal, India. Built atop Tirpai Hill in 1937, the monastery belongs to the Gelukpa sect (Yellow Hat) of Tibetan Buddhism. The monastery has a collection of rare Buddhist manuscripts and thangkas (images of deities on cloth). It also imparts religious training to young Buddhist monks.

WAT FLORIDA DHAMMARAM

Wat Florida Dhammaram is a Buddhist monastery in Kissimmee, Florida, established by Lung-po Chaokhun Phra Tepvaraporn (Im Arindhamo) in the mid-1990s.

Over a decade ago, Lung-po visited lay-devotees in Florida and perceived the lack of a Buddhist monastery in the Central Florida area.

With approval from the late abbot of Wat Sommanat Vihara, Chaokhun Somdej Phra Wannarat Chop Thitadhammamahathera, he began fund raising in Thailand. In 1993, three monks were sent with Prakrupalad Sunnan (now Chaokhun Phra Vijitrdhammapani, the present abbot) to establish and further the development of Wat Florida Dhammaram.

ZAṄG DHOK PALRI PHODANG

The Zang Dhok Palri Phodang is a Buddhist monastery in Kalimpong in West Bengal, India. The monastery is located atop Durpin Hill, one of the two hills of the town. It was consecrated in 1976 by the visiting Dalai Lama.

The monastery houses many rare scriptures that were brought into India after the invasion of Tibet in 1959. It also houses the 108 volumes of the Kangyur.

MAG-DHOG YOLMOWA MONASTERY

Mag-Dhog Yolmowa Monastery is a Buddhist monastery in the town of Darjeeling in the Indian state of West Bengal. The monastery is also known as "Aloobari" monastery after the locality it is located in. The monastery was built under the supervision of Sri Sangay Lama, a highly revered religious head of the Yolmowas-a small ethnic group hailing from north-east of Nepal and later settled in Darjeeling. The construction of the monastery started in 1914, the year World War I started.

The name Mag-Dhog means warding off the war and the monastery was dedicated for world peace. The monastery contains several idols of Lord Buddha and Padmasambhava and varied paintings on the wall which are said to be done with grass and herbs. The monastery also preserves several ancient Buddhist manuscripts. The monastery was built under the supervision of Sri Sangay Lama, a highly revered religious head of the Yolmo or Yolmowas-a small ethnic group hailing from Nepal and later settled in Darjeeling.

MAGNOLIA VILLAGE PRACTICE CENTRE

Magnolia Village Mindfulness Practice Centre is a retreat and practice centre located in Batesville, Mississippi. The 120 acre grounds are located near Memphis, Tennessee. The centre is part of the Order of Interbeing and practices in the tradition of Thich Nhat Hanh, who visited Magnolia Village in October of 2005 and officially accepted Magnolia Village. They are closely in touch with Plum Village for resources and support.

MAHAMEVNAWA BUDDHIST MONASTERY

Mahamevnawa is an organization of monasteries established for the sake of spiritual development of human beings through the teachings of the Sakyamuni Buddha. It has 18 more monastries for meditation through out the Sri Lanka's rural and some in urban areas. The chief Buddhist monk incharge of these monasteries is Venerable Kiribathgoda Gnananada thero is born to a Roman Catholic family converted to be a Buddhist monk. Venerable Kiribathgoda Gnananada Thero learnt buddhism from India and came to Sri Lanka and teaching buddhism to local and international community.

Practice of Meditation: According to Lord Buddha's teachings that birth as a human being is, indeed, a very rare opportunity. Fortunate people who achieve that rare opportunity should develop their minds to reach the ultimate goal of Nibbana. So the Mahamevnawa monastery is teaching the people how to practice meditation to reach the Nibbana.

Four Noble Truths: The meditation is based on the Lord Buddha's doctrine of the Four Noble Truths and this world to make known and explain the four Noble Truths.

1. Suffering (Dukkha Arya Satya)-It incorporates suffering, both mental and physical, dissatisfaction, unpleasant, unsatisfactory and many others.
2. Origin of Suffering (Dukkha Samudaya Arya Satya)
3. Cessation of Suffering (Dukkha Nirodha Arya Satya)
4. Noble Eightfold Path (Marga Arya Satya)

REWALSAR

Rawalsar (also spelled Rewalsar) is a town and a nagar panchayat in Mandi district in the Indian state of Himachal Pradesh.

Demographics: As of 2001 India census GR India, Rawalsar had a population of 1369. Males constitute 54% of the population and females 46%. Rawalsar has an average literacy rate of 76%, higher than the national average of 59.5%: male literacy is 78%

and female literacy is 73%. In Rawalsar, 12% of the population is under 6 years of age.

Geography: Rawalsar is located at an altitude of 1360 m above sea level. It is connected to Mandi by a motorable road and is about 25 km from Mandi. Lying in the Southern Himalayan belt, winters in Rawalsar can be freezing, while summers are generally pleasant.

Religion: Rawalsar is sacred to adherents of three major religions-Hinduism, Buddhism and Sikhism.

Hinduism: Seven mythological lakes associated with the Pandavas of Mahabharata are located above Rawalsar. Also associated with Rawalsar are the legends of Lord Shiva and Lomas Rishi. There is also a famous Krishna temple in the town.

Sikhism: The tenth Guru of Sikhs, Guru Gobind Singh visited Rawalsar to consult with kings of the Hill states seeking support against Aurangzeb. He stayed at Rawalsar for a month. Raja Joginder Sen of Mandi built a gurudwara at Rawalsar in 1930 to commemorate the Guru's visit. The place is particularly sacred to Namdhari Sikhs due to its mention in Sau Sakhi as a sanctuary.

Buddhism: The famous Rawalsar lake is associated with Padmasambhava (also known as Guru Rinpoche), a Buddhist monk. One version of a legend has it that the king of Mandi had Padmasambhava burnt alive after rumours that the monk had flirted with the king's daughter. The lake appeared at the spot where the monk was burnt and Padmasambhava manifested himself from within a lotus in the middle of the lake.

The king, repenting his actions, married his daughter with Padmasambhava. It was from Rawalsar that Padmasambhava went to Tibet to spread Mahayana Buddhism. The Tsechu fair was held in Rawalsar in 2004 to commemorate the birthday of Padmasambhava.

The fair was inaugurated by the Dalai Lama and was attended by Urgyen Trinley Dorje Karmapa along with 50,000 other Buddhist pilgrims. The fair was held after a gap of 12 years. There are other versions that mention that the lake associated with Padmasambhava's birth was located in Pakistan or Afghanistan. However, Rawalsar came to be known as a sacred place for Buddhists and two monasteries-the Drikung Kadyud Gompa and Tso-Pema Ogyen Heru-kai Nyingmapa Gompa are located here.

Rawalsar Lake: The lake around which the town of Rawalsar is established has a maximum depth of 6.5 metres. The lake is oligotrophic in nature. It is rectangular in shape, with the catchment area situated to its north and west.

MONASTERIES IN BHUTAN

Taktshang

Taktshang is the most famous of monasteries in Bhutan. It hangs on a cliff at 3,120 metres (10,200 feet), some 700 metres (2,300 feet) above the bottom of Paro valley. Famous visitors include Ngawang Namgyal in the 17th century and Milarepa. The name means "Tiger's nest", the legend being that Padmasambhava (Guru Rinpoche) flew there on the back of a tiger. The monastery includes seven temples which can all be visited. The monastery suffered several blazes and is a recent restoration. Climbing to the monastery is on foot or mule.

Kurjey Lhakhang

Kurjey Lhakang, also known as Kurjey Monastery, is located in the beautiful Bumthang valley in the Bumthang district of Bhutan. This is the final resting place of the remains of the first three kings of Bhutan. As well, a large tree behind one of the temple buildings is believed to be a terma (Buddhism) that was left there by Padmasambhava.

Tamshing Lhakhang

Tamshing Lhakang (temple) in the Bumthang District of central Bhutan is the most important Nyingmapa temple in Bhutan. The temple and monastery are remarkable for their direct connection to the Bhutanese saint Pema Lingpa. It is now a seat of Lama Sungtrul Rinpoche the current speech incarnation of Pema Lingpa. Tamshing consists of a deteriorating temple and cramped monks quarters. The monastery supports a body of over 95 monks.

History: From an interview of Lopen Kharma, teacher and administrator of Tamshing Lhakang, conducted by Friends of Tamshing in December 2005:

The temple was built by Pema Lingpa himself in 1501.

Before 1960 Tamshing was a privately owned temple (like many other temples in Bhutan). After Pema Lingpa died in the temple at the age of seventy-two in 1521, his descendants took over care of the temple. Gradually, over many years, Tamshing fell into a state of disrepair and neglect. The temple courtyard was used as a granary and local people came less and less, except for special days.

In 1959, when many Tibetans (including the present Dalai Lama) fled their country for fear of being killed quite a few came to the Bumthang region, which is the cradle of Buddhism in Bhutan. In his time, Pema Lingpa received a vision to travel to Tibet where he revealed a treasure hidden by Guru Rinpoche (Padmasambhava) many centuries before. He was given land in the Longti area of the Siti valley and built a temple there which is called Lhalung. This temple was later enlarged by his third (Tibetan) incarnation. Pema Lingpa travelled frequently to Tibet and most of his incarnations were Tibetan.

The 10th incarnation of Pema Lingpa died in Tibet shortly before the Tibetan diaspora. In 1960, a group of three monks from Lhalung monk body headed by Lhalung's second in command, Thinley Kuenchap (d. 1975) came to Tamshing to reestablish the Lhalung monk body at Tamshing.

Lopen Thinley Kuenchap was well known to the exiled Tibetan monks in Bhutan. Hearing of his arrival at Tamshing, many gathered there in late 1960 and established the current monk body. Over time, this group has grown from 10 or 15 monks to over 95.

When the Khudun, Lopen Kharma, came to Tamshing as a young boy in 1980, most of the senior monks from Tibet had passed on, however, Lopen Tseten who came from Tibet to Tamshing as a 10 year old monk in 1960 was still there. Today, Lopen Tseten is the head of the monastery organization and its senior teacher.

The present spiritual head of Tamshing is the 11th incarnation of Pema Lingpa, the Lama Sungtrul Rinpoche (speech incarnation) he was born in the Chumi Valley of Bumthang, Bhutan in 1967.

Tamshing Today: The core missions of Tamshing are teaching the Dharma, performing religious services for the community and educating the young monks under its care. Since Tamshing is not government supported it faces increasing challenges posed by supporting 95 monks while maintaining the ancient physical structures.

Mostly under the age of 15, the monks are either orphans or from very poor families who can't afford to send their children to a state school. As the economy of the country changes and as the culture becomes more outward looking, it is inevitable that some of the old ways of supporting the temples and monasteries, (which are the repositories of traditional wisdom), are being tested.

Tamshing has no endowment; no mission to make money, its only mission is to meet the needs of the community. Currently, the monastery runs at a loss.

Tamshing and Bhutanese Dance: Tamshing is the original home of sacred dances that are celebrated at traditional Tsechus (festivals) throughout Bhutan. According to Joseph Houseal, director of Core of Culture Dance Preservation:

"Dance...is the living tradition of their founding identity and the means by which Pema Lingpa sought to teach the world Buddhism-and the treasure he specifically left the Tamshing monks. It is the life of the order, the Buddhist truth they maintain. That is one reason we have focused on Tamshing: their dances were revealed by the most famous Bhutanese saint and Tamshing alone performs the dances correctly..."

HALLS OF THE TASHILHUNPO MONASTERY

Jamba Chyenmu 'The Maitreya Temple': The Maitreya Temple known as (Jambu Chyenmu)) on the west side is the tallest building of the monastery. It was erected in 1914 by the Ninth Panchen Lama to house a gigantic statue of the Maitreya Buddha and is 26.2 metres (86 feet) in height. The staue sits on a splendid lotus throne in the 'European' posture with its hands in the symbolic teaching pose. A single finger of the giant figure is almost 4 feet in length. The statue contains 279kg (614lbs) of gold and 150,000kg (330,000lb) of copper and brass moulded on a solid wooden frame by Tibetan and Nepalese craftsmen. Small versions of the Maitreya are positioned in all four corners of the chamber and the murals on either side of the door show a more active, antic style than any to be seen in Lhasa.

Gudong: The Panchen Lama's Palace: On the east side of the monastery is the old living quarters of the Panchen lama, the Panchen Lama's Palace known as Gudong. Within, a narrow courtyard gives access to the temple containing the Fourth Panchen Lama's tomb. The temple vestibule has very large inscriptions at either end praising his holiness. Inside, the silver and gold stupa tomb rivals any in the Potala Palace in Lhasa for the splendour of its craftsmenship and jewels. Measuring 11 metres (36ft) in height it contains 85kg (187lb) of gold and countless semi-precious stones. On the left is three statues representing Amitabha, the Buddha of Infinite Light, whom the Panchen Lams are thought to embody. An upper level has a number of long chapels embroidered in silk thangka's that relate the lives and events surrounded the Panchen Lamas. Most were made in Hangzou as indeed many throughout Tibet were during the 1920s. The old living quarters of the Panchen Lama are no longer open to the public but the rooms are more modest and human that any of the rooms at the Potala.

Main Chanting Hall: The main chanting hall contains the throne of the Panchen Lama and two connected chapels. The left-one is devoted to an elaborately ensconced Sakyamuni with eight Bodhisattva robed in bocade. The right hand one is dedicated to Tara the goddess who sanctifies the mountain above and whose image is depicted throughout the temple. A White Tara goddess occupies the centre of the altar with a Jade Green Tara on either side.

Sutra Hall: Sutra Hall is the repository chamber of the monastery containing some 10,000 hand-carved wooden blocks used for printing the Buddhist scriptures. These are all Tibetan translations of the original Sanskrit text. Visitors to the temple can buy coloured prayer flags and Tibetan lunar calendars as souvenirs which are printed in the chamber.

Gyeni Chanting Hall: The Gyeni Chanting Hall is a chanting chamber of the Tashilhunpo Monastery on the south-east side where Tibetan Buddhism is practised. It has a debating garden in its courtyard with many fine trees. The roof of the chanting hall has a chapel on the north side where two very tall guardians are formed from its structural columns by the use of masks and ancient armour. Outside it are some extraordinary colourful Buddha murals and animal murals which have emerged from folklore and animism It is situated near the smaller chanting hall of the Ngagang college on the west side.

Ngang College: Ngang College is a smaller chanting chamber of the monastery on the west side of the main path upstairs of the Deyangshar courtyard. A Ngang a morning chanting ceremony with musical instruments usually takes place between the few remaining monks of the temple. Pilgrims may circumambulate the hall but tourists, particularly photographers are asked to be extremely sensitive to the religious atmosphere.

Chuajing Duogang: The Great Courtyard: The great flagstoned courtyard of Tashilhunpo, known as (Chuajing Duogang) has walls which are covered by over 1000 repeated Sakyamuni, with their hands gesturing the five symbolic poses (mudras).

The Great Gallery: The gallery of the monastery surrounds the Deyangshar courtyard and leads to the chapels on the east side housing many hundreds of tiny Buddha statues.

The Roof Chapels: The roof of Tashilhunpo has several bronze-gated chapels located on two-tiered levels. On the north side, above the chapels of the chanting hall is the funerary stupa of the First Dalai Lama, the only one not entombed in Lhasa. On the east side is a small 'chamber of horrors' chapel. Painted demons, considered now to be defenders of Buddhism betray their origins as the terrifying gods of the old animist Bon faith who only later were absorbed by Buddhism. On the south side is a charming Tara chapel with blue and gold murals on the walls depicting Tibetan history.

Tsurphu Monastery

Tsurphu is a Tibetan Buddhist monastery which served as the traditional seat of the Karmapa. It is located in the Tolung area of Central Tibet in the Dowo Lung valley, 70 km from Lhasa. It is 14000 feet above sea level and built in the middle of the valley facing south, with high mountains surrounding the monastery complex. Tsurphu is a 300m2 complex with walls up to 4 metres thick.

Tsurphu was founded by the first Karmapa, Dusum Khyenpa in 1159 after he visited the site and laid the foundation for an establishment of a seat there by making offerings to the local protectors. In 1189 he revisited the site and founded his main seat there. The monastery grew to hold 1000 monks. It was totally destroyed in 1966 during the Chinese Cultural Revolution and began to be rebuilt in 1980 by the 16th Karmapa, Rangjung Rikpai Dorje. Following the recognition of Urgyen Trinley Dorje by Tai Situpa and the Chinese government, Urgyen Trinley was enthroned at Tsurphu. He resided there until he escaped from Tibet to India in 2000.

LABRANG MONASTERY

Labrang Monastery is one of the six great monasteries of the Geluk (Yellow Hat) school of Tibetan Buddhism, of which the Dalai Lama is a member. Labrang is located in Xiahe County in Gansu province and also in the traditional Tibetan province of Amdo. Labrang Monastery is home to the largest number of monks outside of Tibet Autonomous Region. Xiahe is located about 8 hours from the city of Lanzhou, the capital of Gansu.

Labrang Monastery is located in the town of Xiahe, which belongs to the Gannan Tibetan Autonomous Prefecture. The town is reflection of the different minorities that can be found in China, such as Tibetans about 70% of the population), Hui Chinese (20%) and Han Chinese (10%).

Although the region is mostly rural and pastoral (including yak and other animal rearing), tourism is growing rapidly mainly due to the monastery. The monastery was founded in 1709 by the first Jamyang Zhaypa, Ngawang Tsondru. It is Tibetan Buddhism's most important monastery town outside the Tibetan Autonomous Region.

The monastery complex dominates the northern village. The white walls and golden roofs feature a blend of Tibetan and Han architectural styles. The monastery contains 18 halls, six institutes of learning, a golden stupa, a sutra debate and nearly 60,000 sutras. There are more than 2000 monks in residence. It has a Buddhist museum with a large collection of Buddha statues, sutras and murals. In addition, a large amount of Tibetan language books, including history is available for purchase, together with medicines, calendars, music and art objects.

The monastery today is an important place for Buddhist ceremonies and activities. From 4 to 17 January and 26 June to 15 July (these dates may change according to the lunar calendar), the great Buddhist ceremony will be held with Buddha-unfolding, sutra enchanting, praying, sutra debates, etc. The monks are extremely friendly to foreigners and used every opportunity to practice their basic English which in most cases is self-taught. Accommodation is easy to find and a great variety of articles and souvenirs are available.

Lamayuru

Lamayuru is a Tibetan Buddhist Gompa in Kargil District, Western Laddakh, situated on the Srinagar-Kargil-Leh road

15km east of the Fatu La pass, at a height of 3510m. Founded by the Indian scholar Mahasiddhacarya Naropa in the 11th century (alledgedly on the site of a dried-up lake) after spending many years meditating, Lamayuru is the largest and oldest gompa in Laddakh with a population of around 150 permanent monks resident. It has, in the past, housed up to 400 monks, many of which are now based in gompas in surrounding villages. Lamayuru is host to two yearly masked dance festivals, in the second and fifth months of the Tibetan lunar calendar, when all the monks from these surrounding gompas gather together to pray.

Rumtek Monastery

Rumtek, also called the Dharmachakra Centre, is a Tibetan Buddhist monastery located in the Indian state of Sikkim near the capital Gangtok. Originally built by the 9th Karmapa Wangchuk Dorje in 1740, Rumtek served as the main seat of the Karma Kagyu lineage in Sikkim for some time. But when the 16th Karmapa arrived in Sikkim in 1959, after fleeing before the Chinese occupation of Tibet, it was in ruins. Despite being offered other sites, the Karmapa decided to rebuild Rumtek. To him, the site possessed many auspicious qualities and was surrounded by the most favourable attributes. For example, flowing streams, mountains behind, a snow range in front and a river below. With the generosity and help of the Sikkim royal family and the Indian government, it has been built by the 16th Karmapa as his main seat in exile.

After four years, construction of the monastery was completed. The sacred items and relics brought out from Tsurphu, the Karmapa's seat in Tibet, were installed. On Tibetan New Year's day (Losar) in 1966 the 16th Karmapa officially inaugurated the new seat called, "The Dharmachakra Centre, a place of erudition and spiritual accomplishment, the seat of the glorious Karmapa."

The monastery is currently the largest in Sikkim. It is home to the community of monks and where they perform the rituals and practices of the Karma Kagyu lineage. A Golden

Stupa contains the relics of the 16th Karmapa. Opposite that building is a college, Karma Shri Nalanda Institute for Higher Buddhist Studies.

Rumtek is located 24 km from Gangtok, the capital of the Sikkim, at an altitude of about 1500 m.

Rumtek is currently at the centre of the Karmapa controversy with a lengthy battle being played out in the Indian courts. Two rival organisations, both supporting different candidates for the 17th Karmapa claim stewardship of the monastery and its contents. The two organisations are the Karmapa Charitable Trust (supporting Thaye Dorje) and the Tsurpu Labrang (supporting Urgyen Trinley Dorje). Currently neither Karmapa candidate resides at Rumtek.

Shechen Monastery

The Shechen Monastery is one of the primary Nyingma monasteries in Tibet. It was founded in 1695. There are also now Shechen monasteries in Nepal and India.

Yonghe Temple

The Yonghe Temple, also known as the "Palace of Peace and Harmony Lama Temple", the "Yonghe Lamasery", or-popularly-the "Lama Temple" is a temple and monastery of the Geluk School of Tibetan Buddhism located in the northeastern part of Beijing, China. It is one of the largest and most important Tibetan Buddhist monasteries in the world. The building and the artworks of the temple combine Han Chinese and Tibetan styles.

History: Building work on the Yonghegong Temple started in 1694 during the Qing Dynasty. It originally served as an official residence for court eunuchs. It was then converted into the court of the Prince Yong (Yin Zhen), a son of the Kangxi Emperor and himself the future Yongzheng Emperor. After Yongzheng's ascension to the throne in 1722, half of the building was converted into a lamasery, a monastery for monks of Tibetan Buddhism. The other half remained an imperial palace.

After Yongzheng's death in 1735, his coffin was placed in the temple. The Qianlong Emperor, Yongzheng's successor, gave the temple imperial status signified by having its turquoise tiles replaced with yellow tiles which were reserved for the emperor. Subsequently, the monastery became a residence for large numbers of Tibetan Buddhist monks from Mongolia and Tibet and so the Yonghe Lamasery became the national centre of Lama administration. The temple is said to have survived the Cultural Revolution due to the intervention of Prime Minister Zhou Enlai. It was reopened to the public in 1981.

Architecture and Artworks: The Yonghe Temple is arranged along a north-south central axis, which has a length of 480m. The main gate is at the southern end of this axis. Along the axis, there are five main halls which are separated by courtyards: the Hall of the Heavenly Kings (Tian Wang Dian or Devaraja Hall), the Hall of Harmony and Peace (Yonghegong), the Hall of Everlasting Protection (Yongyoudian), the Hall of the Wheel of the Law (Falundian) and the Pavilion of Ten Thousand Happinesses (Wanfuge).

The Hall of the Heavenly Kings is the southernmost of the main halls, it served originally as the main entrance to the monastery. In the centre of the hall stands a statue of the Maitreya Buddha, along the walls statues of the four Heavenly Kings are arranged.

The Hall of Harmony and Peace is the main building of the temple. It houses three bronze statues of the Buddhas of the Three Ages, the statue of the Gautama Buddha (Buddha of the Present) is in the centre, it is flanked by the statue of Kasyapa Matanga (Buddha of the Past, right) and the Maitreya Buddha (Buddha of the Future, left). Along the sides of the hall, the statues of the 18 Arhats are placed. A mural in the hall shows the bodhisattva Avalokitesvara. The Hall of Everlasting Protection was Emperor Yongzheng's living quarters as a prince and the place where his coffin was placed after his death. Today, a statue of the Bhaisajya-guru (healing Buddha) stands in this hall.

The Hall of the Wheel of the Law functions as a place for reading scriptures and conducting religious ceremonies. It contains a large statue of Je Tsongkhapa, founder of the Geluk School. The hall also contains the Five-Hundred-Arhat-Hill, a carving make of red sandalwood with statues of the arhats made from five different metals (gold, silver, copper, iron and tin). The Pavilion of Ten Thousand Happinesses contains an 18m tall statue of the Maitreya Buddha carved from a single piece of White Sandalwood. The statue is one of three artworks in the Temple which were included in the Guinness Book of Records in 1993.

CHUDAMANI VIHARA

Chudamani Vihara was a Buddhist vihara in Nagapattinam, Tamil Nadu, India. Chudamani Vihara was constructed in 1006 AD by the Indonesian king Sri Vijaya Soolamanivarman with the patronage of Rajaraja Chola. The vihara building survived in dilapidated condition till 1867, when Jesuit missionaries demolished it. Since 1856, about 350 Buddha bronzes have been found at Nagapattinam, dating from the 11th to the 16th century.

History: The heritage of Nagapattinam is mentioned in the Burmese historical text of 3rd century B.C. which mentions of a Budha Vihar built by the great Ashoka. The Chinese traveller Hiuen Tsang also mentioned the vihar. Nagappattinam is mentioned as Padarithitha in the ancient Buddhist literature. The Animangalam Copperplate of Kulothunga Chola mentions that Kasiba Thera (Buddhist Monk) renovated the Buddhist shrine in 6th century AD with the help of monks of "Naganadu" (Nagapattinam). The Pallava King Rajasimha (690-728) permitted a Chinese king to build Buddha Vihar in Nagappattinam. According to the copperplate record of Chola king Rajaraja, the Sailendra king, Sri Mara-vijayottunga-varman constructed the vihara with the support of Rajaraja.

One statue, now at John D. Rockefeller Collection of Asian Art in New York, has an inscription that mentions that this Buddha was created to be carried in a procession during the temple's sacred festival. The inscription has been translated by Vidya Dehejia as: Well-being [and] prosperity. The nayakar [Buddha], of all of the eighteen countries, of the metalworkers. The procession image, for the sacred festival of the alvar temple, which was caused to be taken in procession by the respected one (utaiyar) endowed of the four gunas from Cirutavur; [in] the perum-palli (great place of worship or great vihara) of the metalworkers, [in] the perum-palli of Rajendra Chola.

DEER PARK MONASTERY

Deer Park Monastery in California: Deer Park Monastery is a 400 acre Buddhist sanctuary in Escondido, California. It was founded in July 2000 by monastic and lay practitioners from Plum Village in France.

The monastery is under the direction of the Thich Nhat Hanh's Order of Interbeing in the Vietnamese Zen tradition. Deer Park follows the same practices and schedule as Plum Village and its sister monasteries Maple Forest Monastery and Green Mountain Dharma Centre in Vermont. Since its founding the monastery has grown to be very active. Deer Park hosts an annual retreat when Thich Nhat Hanh travels to North America. Over the years several people have taken novice vows and members of the other monasteries have moved to Deer Park so the ordained sangha has been growing. Lay practitioners also live at the monastery. The monastery is now composed of two hamlets; Solidity Hamlet for monks and laymen and Clarity Hamlet for nuns and laywomen.

Deer Park Monastery in Wisconsin: The Deer Park Monastery in Oregon, WI whch pre-dates the founding of the Deer Park Monastery in Escondido, CA by 25 years, carries the same name and can be confusing to the casual inquisitor. The Wisconsin monastery is headed by Geshe Lhundub Sopa, the first Tibetan tenured professor in an American University who went on to teach Buddhist philosophy, language and culture at the University of Wisconsin-Madison for 30 years. During that time, Geshe Sopa trained many of this country's first generation of respected Buddhist scholars and translators, including Jeffrey Hopkins, Jose Cabezon and John Makransky. The Deer Park Corp. is currently in the process of building a new $2.7M Temple Project to house an extensive collection of Tibetan art and artifacts, provide greater capacity for group meetings and educational sessions, continue the expansion of Tibetan Buddhism in the New World by training a successive string of new Monks and to continue the promotion of the cause of Tibetan freedom from China. Part of the project also includes restoration work that will be done on the current temple, which was originally an open-air pavilion erected to house the first Kalachakra Initiation performed by the Dalai Lama in the western world. That event, performed in 1981, is commemorated by the stupa that was erected the following year near the current temple.

Geshe Sopa founded Deer Park Buddhist Centre in 1975, after students began requesting instruction outside the formal academic setting. Deer Park today remains the only full-scale monastic and teaching centre upholding the Dalai Lama's tradition in the Midwest, attracting students from around the world to its annual programmes. Geshe Sopa has facilitated an ongoing relationship between His Holiness the Dalai Lama and the University of Wisconsin, Madison, which His Holiness has visited five times and from which he has received an honourary doctoral degree.

GHOOM MONASTERY

Ghoom Monastery is the popular name of the Yiga-Choling Monastery located at Ghoom near the town of Darjeeling in the state of West Bengal, India. The monastery belongs to the Yellow Sect of Buddhists. There is a famed statue of "Coming Buddha" (Maitreya Buddha) in the monastery. It was built in 1875 by Lama Sherab Gyatso. Rare scripts on Buddhism have been kept in the monastery for decades.

Green Mountain Dharma Centre

Green Mountain Dharma Centre (GMDC) was founded in April 1998 and is located in Hartland-Four-Corners, VT. As of

2006, 6 nuns and 3 monks are in residence there. Recently, the GMDC has been developing in a new direction by becoming a Fourfold (monks, nuns, laymen, laywomen) Retreat and Practice Centre for the teachings of Thich Nhat Hanh. They are closely in touch with Plum Village and share the same practice. During a stay at the GMDC, retreatants are encouraged to practice and observe the monastic way of life. Retreatants are invited to help in communal activities such as preparing meals, general cleaning, washing dishes, etc. as a way of continuing mindfulness practice while performing everyday tasks.

The Abbess of the centre is Annabel Laity, Sister True Virtue (Vietnamese: Chan Duc) a senior Dharma Teacher of the Order of Interbeing. She has been a disciple of Thich Nhat Hanh since 1986, became a Dharma Teacher in 1990 and was Director of Practice at Plum Village. Since 1997, she has been Director of the Maple Forest Monastery and was installed as Abbess at the Green Mountain Dharma Centre in 1998. She has travelled widely, leading meditation retreats and giving talks in many different countries of the world. She has translated many of Thich Nhat Hanh's books into English.

During a Retreat

A sample daily schedule:

- 5:00 a.m.-Wake up
- 6:00 a.m.-Sitting Meditation/Chanting
- 8:00 a.m.-Breakfast
- 9:00 a.m.-Mindful Work or Monastic Classes
- 11:15 a.m.-Walking Meditation
- 12:30 p.m.-Lunch
- Rest & Personal Time after lunch
- 3:30 p.m.-Sitting Meditation & Chanting
- 5:15 p.m.-Exercise & Sports Time
- 6:00 p.m.-Dinner
- 7:30 p.m.-Personal Study or Misc. Classes
- 9:30 p.m.-Noble Silence

The Dharma Centre believes that because the Buddhist teachings emphasize practising with the Sangha, the retreatants should participate fully in all scheduled activities. All guests are asked to refrain from smoking and drinking alcohol. Meals are vegetarian.

JETAVANA

Jetavana was one of the most famous of the Buddhist monasteries in India. It was the second monastery donated to Buddha, after the Veluvana in Rajagaha. Jetavana is located just outside the old city of Savatthi. Jetavana was the place where Buddha gave many teachings and discourses, more than in any other place. Mainly, this is because Buddha spent 19 (out of 45) rainy-seasons (also pansah or vassa) at Jetavana, more than in any other monastery. The remains of Jetavana and Savatthi were locally known as Sahet-Mahet. Alexander Cunningham used the ancient (6th century AD) accounts of Chinese pilgrim-monks to determine that Sahet-Mahet actually referred to Jetavana and Savatthi.

The site of Jetavana was donated by Anathapindaka to Buddha himself. Originally it was owned by Prince Jeta, a son of King Pasenadi. Anathapindaka covered the ground by gold coins in order to buy the land. This event is frequently portrayed in Buddhist art, such as the art of Sanchi. Jetavana is currently a historical park, with remains of many ancient buildings such as monasteries, huts (such as the Gandhakuti and the Kosambakuti) and stupas. In Jetavana is also located the second-holiest tree of Buddhism: the Anandabodhi Tree. A visit to Savatthi and Jetavana is part of the Buddhist pilgrim route in North-India. The most revered place in Jetavana is the Gandhakuti, where Buddha used to stay.

BUDDHIST MONASTERIES IN RUSSIA

Datsan

Datsan is the term used for Buddhist university monasteries in the Tibetan tradition of Gelukpa located throughout Russia, but concentrated in Eastern Siberia. As a rule, in a datsan there are two departments-philosophical and medical. Sometimes to them is added the department of the tantric practices where the monks studied only after the finishing education of the philosophical department. In pre-20th century Russia, datsans traditionally existed only in Buryatia and Transbaikalia.

Datsans were officially acknowledged in the Imperial Russia in 1734. By statute of 1853 were recognized 34 datsans: two in the Irkutsk governorate and others in Zabaykalsky Governorate. The first datsan in Europe was Gunzechoyney datsan. It was built in St. Petersburg between 1903 and 1913 and started to operate on February 21, 1913.

Between 1927 and 1938 all 47 datsans, existed in Buryatia and Transbaikalia were closed or destroyed. In 1945 Ivolginsky datsan was opened, several years later Aginsky datsan resume operations. The following ten datsans were not opend until 1991.

List of Datsans in Russia

- Khambyn Khure datsan in Ulan-Ude
- Aginsky datsan in Aginskoye
- Kurumkansky datsan in Kurumkan
- Sartuul Gegetuy datsan in Gegetuy
- Egituysky datsan in Egituy
- Sanaginsky datsan in Sanaga
- Ivolginsky datsan in Verkhnyaya Ivolga
- Kizhinginsky datsan in Kizhinga
- Baldan Breybun datsan in Murochi
- Tugnuysky datsan in Mukhorshibir
- Okinsky datsan in Orlik
- Tamchinsky datsan in Gusinoozyorsk
- Kyrensky datsan in Kyren
- Khoymorsky datsan in Arshan
- Ugdansky datsan
- Ust-Ordynsky datsan in Ust-Ordynsky

- Aninsky datsan in Ana
- Chesansky datsan in Chesan
- Tsugolsky datsan in Tsugol
- Gunzechoyney datsan in Saint Petersburg

Ivolginsky Datsan

Ivolginsky datsan is the Buddhist Temple located in Buryatia 23 km from Ulan Ude, near Verkhnyaya Ivolga village.

History: The datsan was opened in 1945 as the only Buddhist spiritual centre of USSR. In the course of time the little "Khambin's sume" changed into the Monastic centre with a residence of Pandido Khambo lama, the leader of all Russian Lamas.

Buddhist Centre: It was just here located the residence of the Central Spiritual Buddhist Board of the Soviet Union (Buddhist Traditional Sangkha of Russia since 1995) and Pandido Khambo lama-head of Buddhist church. Spiritual activity of the datsan is manifested in temple rites, medical practice, Buddhist education traditional system. Buddhist university "Dashi Choinkhorling" was opened in 1991 attached to the datsan.

Treasures of Culture: Wonderful samples of old Buryat art-picturesque thangkas, sculptures, ritual subjects are gathered and preserved in the Ivolginsky datsan. One of the monastery's treasures is a rare collection of old Buddhist manuscripts written in Tibetan language on natural silk and a greenhouse with a holly Bodskhva tree. Being a cultural and religion monument the Datsan is protected by the State. The Datsan Centre consists of such temples as Sockshin-gugan, Maidrin-sume, Devazhin and Sackhjusan-sume. There are also a library, hotel, the philosophic faculty-Choyra, building of the Buddhistic University-Dashy Choinhorlin, museum of monuments of Buryat art, sacred tumbs-suburgans, some service buildings and houses for lamas there.

Itigelov: In 1927, the 12th Pandito Hambo Lama of the Ivolginsky Datsan, Dashi-Dorzho Itigelov, told his students and fellow monks to bury his body after his death and to check on it again in 30 years. According to the story, Itigelov then sat in the lotus position, began chanting the prayer of death and died, mid-meditation.

The monks followed Itigilov's directions, but when they exhumed his body 30 years later, they were amazed to find none of the usual signs of decay and decomposition. On the contrary, Itigilov looked as if he had been dead only a few hours, rather than three decades. Fearful of the Soviet response to their "miracle", the monks reburied Itigilov's body in an unmarked grave.

Itigelov's story was not forgotten over the years and on 11 September of 2002 the body was finally exhumed and transferred to Ivolginsky Datsan where it was closely examined by monks and, which is now more important, by scientists and pathologists. The official statement was issued about the body-very well preserved, without any signs of decay, whole muscles and inner tissue, soft joints and skin. The interesting thing is that the body was never embalmed or mummified.

TIBETAN BUDDHIST MONASTERIES

Ani Tsankhung Nunnery

Ani Tsankhung Monastery is a Buddhist nunnery in Lhasa the administrative centre of Tibet. It was built in the 7th century by Songsten Gampo who used its meditation chamber.

The monastery is a yellow building which lies on the street parallel and north of Chingdol Dong Lu in Lhasa.

Since the 12th century the monastery has been used chiefly by Buddhist nuns.

The nunnery's main hall contains a beautiful image of Chenrezi, the multi-armed bodhisattva of Compassion. The sacred meditation chamber lies behind it.

An air of quiet serenity pervades the ancient place with its flower bushes and spotless compound and is one of the quieter tourist locations in the Tibetan capital.

Barkhor

The Barkhor is an area of narrow streets and a public square located around Jokhang Temple in the Lhasa, Tibet. Other nearby small monasteries include Muru Ningba Monastery.

Buchasergyi Lakang Monastery

Buchasergyi Lakang Monastery is a Buddhist temple that was built by King Songsten Gampo near the town of Nyingchi in eastern Tibet, China. The monastery was built in the eight century by the great Tibetan King to apparently subdue the great she-demon. Only ruins remain at the site.

Changzhu Temple

Changzhu Temple is an ancient Buddhist monastery located in Changzhu village 5km south of Tsedang on the road to Yumbi Lakang in Tibet. Very little remains of the temple which was thought to have been founded in the 7th century, during the reign of King Songtsen Gampo. The original temple was made from wood and thatch but in the 14th century it was rebuilt and enlargened and turned into a monastery that supported 300 monks.

Changzhu monastery contained numerous halls including a Great Hall which closely resembled that of the Jokhang Temple in Lhasa. The hall was famous for its grand bell and sublime statuary. In the forecourt of the temple the immense pillars and massive beams of the 14th century entrance can still be seen and one small temple still remains in the inner courtyard. Its centrepiece is a splendid old banner embroidered in almost 30,000 pearls representing Chenrezi in repose. Restored in the 1980s, Changzhu Temple is now a repository for ancient religious objects of value that have been found throughout Tibet.

Drepung Monastery

Drepung Monastery is one of the "great three" Gelukpa university monasteries of Tibet. The other two are Ganden and

Sera. Drepung is the largest of all Tibetan monasteries and indeed at its peak was the largest monastery of any religion in the world. It was founded in 1416 by Jamyang Chojey, a direct disciple of Je Tsongkhapa, the founder of the Gelukpa school. It is located on the Gambo Utse mountain, 5 kilometres from the western suburb of Lhasa. At its largest, before the Chinese invasion of Tibet in 1959, the monastery housed fifteen thousand celibate monks. It was known for the high standards of its academic study and was called the "Nalanda" of Tibet, a reference to the great Buddhist monastic university of Nalanda.

Drepung is divided into what are known as the seven great colleges-Gomang (sGo-mang), Loseling (Blo-gsal gling), Deyang (bDe-dbyangs), Shagkor (Shag-skor), Gyelwa (rGyal-ba) or Tosamling (Thos-bsam gling), Dulwa ('Dul-ba) and Ngagpa (sNgags-pa).

Today the population at the monastery located in Tibet is much smaller with merely a few hundred monks, due to population capping enforced by the Chinese government. However the institution has continued its tradition in exile within South India, relocated to land in Karnataka given to the Tibetan community in exile by Prime Minister Nehru. The monastery in India today houses over five thousand celibate monks, with around 3,000 at Drepung Loseling and some 2,000 at Drepung Gomang. Hundreds of new monks are admitted each year, many of them refugees from Tibet.

Drigung Monastery

Drigung Monastery is a notable monastery in Tibet, known for performing sky burials.

The monastery is named after its location in a valley about 150 km east from Lhasa, in Drigung district and is the mother monastery of the Drigung Kagyu (Drikung Kargyu) tradition.

It was founded in 1179 by the founder of that tradition, Drigung Kyobpa Jigten-gonpo-rinchenpel. The tradition emphasizes on its founders tantric meditation and Phowa practices.

After destructions by the Chinese, after 1959, reconstruction works began in 1980. Drigung Kagyu traditions are nowadays also kept at the Jangchubling Drikung Kargyu Institute at Dehra Dun, Uttar Pradesh, India, founded in 1985.

Dzogchen Monastery

Dzogchen Monastery is one of the six great monasteries of the Nyingma tradition, the original Buddhist tradition in Tibet. It is located in Eastern Tibet in the Chinese province of Sichuan.

It is the main monastery for over three hundred branch monasteries in the Kham, Amdo and Central regions of Tibet. Since the early eighties the monastery has been undergoing reconstruction and it is currently home to around two hundred and fifty monks. About one kilometre from Dzogchen Monastery is the prestigious Buddhist University of Dzogchen Shira Sing. It is one of the main centres of learning in Tibet and enjoys a reputation for scholarly excellence. The university is famous in Tibet and world-wide for the standard of education it provides and students come from all over Tibet to study at Shira Sing University. Pema Tung, or the Lotus Ground, is a newly built retreat centre and temple complex situated deep in the Dzogchen valley. The centre is dedicated to the teaching and practice of the Dzogchen tradition and is a natural haven for peaceful reflection and meditation.

Ganden Monastery

Ganden Monastery is one of the 'great three' Gelukpa university monasteries of Tibet, located on Wangbur Mountain, Tagtse County, 47 kilometres from Lhasa. The other two are Sera Monastery and Drepung Monastery. Being the furthest from Lhasa of the three university monasteries, Ganden traditionally had a smaller population with some 6,000 monks in the early 20th century. However, it was the original monastery of the Geluk order, founded by Tsongkhapa himself in 1409 and traditionally considered to be the seat of Geluk administrative and political power. The Ganden Tripa or 'throne-holder of Ganden' is the head of the Gelukpa school (and not the Dalai Lama as is widely misunderstood).

Ganden Monastery consisted of two colleges, Jangtse and Shartse, meaning North Peak and East Peak respectively. The monastery was completely destroyed following the Chinese invasion of Tibet and since the 1980s, a small part is being re-built and in use. Ganden has been re-established on a much larger scale in Karnataka, India by the Tibetan population in exile.

Jokhang

The Jokhang, also called the Jokhang Temple or the Jokhang Monastery, is a famous Buddhist temple located on Barkhor Square in Lhasa, Tibet. Along with the Potala Palace, it is probably the most popular tourist attraction in Lhasa. It is part of the UNESCO World Heritage Site "Historic Ensemble of the Potala Palace" and a spiritual centre of Lhasa.

Jokhang temple was constructed by King Songtsen Gampo starting in the year 639. This temple has remained a centre of Buddhist pilgrimage for centuries. In the past several centuries the temple complex was expanded and now covers an area of about 25,000 sq. metres. Jokhang temple is a four-story construction, with roofs covered with gilded bronze tiles. The architectural style is based on the Indian vihara design and was later extended resulting in a blend of Indian, Nepalese and Tang Dynasty styles. The rooftop statues of two golden deer flanking a Dharma wheel is iconic.

Jokhang temple complex has several decorated shrines and rooms. The main hall of the temple houses the Jowo Shakyamuni Buddha statue, perhaps the single most venerated object in Tibetan Buddhism. There are also statues of King Songtsan Gambo and his two famous foreign brides, Princess Wen Cheng (daughter of Emperor Taizong of Tang China) and Princess Bhrikuti of Nepal.

Menri Monastery

The Menri Monastery is a Buddhist monastery in Tibet. It was established in 1405 by Nyammey Sherab-gyeltsen (1356-1416) and became the main Bon monastery in Tibet.

Muru Ningba Monastery

Muru Ningba Monastery is a small Buddhist monastery located between the larger monasteries of Jokhang and Barkhor in the holy city of Lhasa, Tibet.

Namgyal Monastery

Namgyal Monastery is any of several Tibetan Buddhist institutions associated with the Dalai Lama(s).

(1) The monastery (dratsang) historically housed within the Potala Palace, to which the Dalai Lama traditionally belongs. It was founded by the Third Dalai Lama, Sonam Gyatso, in 1575 and has focused on ritual duties associated with the Dalai Lama in his religious role. Whether the Peoples Republic of China has maintained an institution with this name is unclear.

(2) The same institution in exile in Dharamsala. For several decades its monks have accompanied the fourteenth Dalai Lama overseas and demonstrated such things as lama dances and Tibetan sand painting or sand Mandalas at various venues.

(3) An American branch of the above, founded 1992 in Ithaca, New York. Its several monks (rotated in and out from Dharamsala) teach a several-year curriculum in "sutra and tantra," including Tibetan language, to a clientele consisting predominantly of Western dharma students. In addition it sponsors various lectures, short courses and retreats. Its full name is "Namgyal Monastery Institute of Buddhist Studies." Also one third of Nirvana lead singer Kurt Cobains ashes were scattered here.

Narthang Monastery

Narthang Monastery is a monastery 15km west of Shigatse in Tibet. Founded in 1153 by one of the disciples of Atisha, Nathang was the fourth great monastery of Tsang with Shalu Monastery, Sakya and Tashilhunpo. Narthang was first famous for its scriptual teaching and monastic discipline. After the fourteenth century it gained great eminence as the oldest of Tibet's three great printing centres (the other being the Potala and the Derge).

The Fifth Panchen Lama took control of the monastery and it continued printing the Buddhist scriptures the Kangyur and the Tengyur up until 1959. Narrthang's five main buildings and large chanting hall were razed to the ground by the Chinese in 1966. They had contained priceless 14th century murals possibly painted by the artist scholars of nearby Shalu Monastery. Today only the mud-brick foundations can be discerned although parts of the Mongolian styled high-fortress walls are still standing.

Palcho Monastery

The Palcho Monastery or Pelkor Chode Monastery is the main monastery in Gyantse, Tibet. It is most notable for its Kumbum, which has 108 chapels in its four floors. The monastery was founded in 1418 by the first Panchen Reldrup. In the early 20th century, the town and monastery were attacked by British soldiers and bullet holes remain in the monastery to this day.

Pyenzhangling Monastery

Pyenzhangling Monastery is a small Tibetan Buddhist monastery in a tiny village called Zhonggang, Tibet that is consecrated to the eleventh century Tibetan legend, Milarepa. It is built around the cave where he once lived.

Ralung Monastery

Ralung Monastery, located in the Tsang region of western Tibet, is the traditional seat of the Drukpa Kagyu order of Tibetan Buddhism. It was founded in 1180 by Tsangpa Gyare who was the First Gyalwang Drukpa and the founder of the Drukpa order.

The monastery is located in present-day Gyantse county several kilometres south of the road connecting Nakartse and Lungmar, immediately north of the Gasa district of Bhutan.

In previous times, trade could be conducted across the Yak La pass across the high Himalayas, extending the influence of Ralung to the south.

The monastery is surrounded by the towering peaks and glacier fields of Gyetong Soksum (6,244m), Jangzang Lhamo (6,324m) and Nojin Gangzang (7,191m). From the beginning the location was recognized as especially auspicious:

> *"The eight auspicious symbols adorned the surrounding: The mountain in front of the monastery appeared in the form of a white conch turning clock-wise; the peak of Rala pass appeared like a precious open parasol; the peak behind Pokya appeared like a brimming vase; the Tsenchu peak appeared like a victory banner hoisted high; the Yangon hill appeared like a pair of golden fish; the ground at Gormo appeared like a golden wheel; the hill in the direction of Penthang appeared like an open lotus stem with the twin streams appearing like two birds facing each other; and Gyamo meadow appeared like an auspicious knot."*

The founder of Bhutan, the first Shabdrung, Ngawang Namgyel, was the 18th abbott of Ralung monastery. In 1616 he fled Tibet when his recognition as the reincarnation of renowned scholar Pema Karpo was challenged by the governor of Tsang province. Ngawang Namgyel proved to be a worthy incarnation of Pema Karpo, as he far surpassed the accomplishments of his tormentors by unifying the warring valleys of Bhutan, fending off attacks from Tibet, forming a national identity and establishing a Drukpa theocracy that continues to this day in modified form as the Royal Government of Bhutan.

Other names for Ralung monastery include Shedrub Chokhar Ling Gompa (the original name), Druk Ralung and Ralung Gompa.

Ramoche Temple

Ramoche Temple is a Buddhist monastery situated in the northwest of the Tibetan capital of Lhasa, covering a total area of 4000 square metres (one acre). This temple is one of the key cultural relic protection sites of the Tibet Autonomous Region as well as a popular attraction in Lhasa. The original building complex has a strong Tang architecture influence, for it was first built by Han Chinese architects in the middle of the 7th century (during the Tang Dynasty). Han Princess Wencheng took charge of this project and ordered the temple be erected facing east to show her homesickness.

Erroneously referred to as Little Jokhang it stands in the northern older part of the holy city and originally housed Wen Cheng's statue of Sakyamuni, now the Holy of Holies of Jokhang Monastery. In the 8th century an exchange was made and a Nepalese Chizun princess's small bronze statue of Sakyamuni aged eight was enshrined at Ramoche instead, brought by the Wencheng Princess from the capital Chang'an during the Tang Dynasty. As one of the precious cultural relics of Tibet, the statue is now placed in Jokhang Temple (Da Zhao Si), 500 metres (0.31mile) south of Ramoche Monastery. The temple was gutted and partially destroyed in the 1960s and the bronze statue disappeared. Years later it was found and is now housed in the Ramoche Temple which was restored in the 1986.

Following the large restoration of 1986, the main building in the temple now has three stories. The first story includes an atrium, a scripture hall and a Buddha palace with winding corridors. The third story was the bedroom once reserved for Dalai Lama. Upon entering the main building, one can see the ten pillars holding some of the remaining Tibetan relics such as the encased lotus flowers, coiling cloud, jewellery and particular Tibetan Characters. The golden peak of the temple with the Han-style upturned eave can be seen from any direction in Lhasa city. Needless to say, the temple is a wonderful example of the combination of Han and Tibetan architectural styles.

Nowadays, the temple has become the very place for the Tibetan monks to study the Mi Zong (one of the sects of Buddhism).

Sakya Monastery

Sakya Monastery is an important old Buddhist monastery of the Sakya school 128 kilometres west of Shigatse in the Tibet

Autonomous Region of China. Founded in 1071, by the powerful noble family of the Tsang its strong abbots governed Tibet during the whole of the 13th century after the downfall of the kings I.

Its medieval Mongolian architecture is quite different from that of temples in Lhasa and Yarlong. Originally built as a cave into the mountainside, it was funded in 1268 by Kublai Khan to be developed into a new magnificent monastery across the river, a site which remained a secular and religious centre in Tibet for almost a century.

SHALU MONASTERY

Shalu Monastery is small monastery 22km south of Shigatse in Tibet. Founded in 1040 by Chetsun Sherab Jungnay, for centuries it was renowned as a centre of scholarly learning and psychic training and its mural paintings were considered to be the most ancient and beautiful in Tibet. Shalu was the first of the major monasteries to be built by noble families of the Tsang Dynasty during Tibet's great revival of Buddhism.

History: In 1329 a devastating earthquake demolished the temple of Shalu but was later rebuilt in 1333 by local lords under the command of the Mongol Emperor of China. The new architectural framework of the monastery was dominated by Mongolian styles with massive inward-sloping walls around a main courtyard and strong woodwork and glazed roof tiles from Qinghai.

At the time of the new establishment in the 1330s Shalu Temple was under the command of the 11th Abbot Buton Rinchen Drub who lived 1290-1364. Buton was not merely a capable administrator but he is still remembered to this very day as a prodigious scholar and writer and is Tibet's most celebrated historian. Buston catalogued all of the Buddhist scriptures at Shalah, some 4,569 religious and philosophical works and formatted them in a logical, coherent order. He wrote the famous book the History of Buddhism in India and Tibet at Shalu which many Tibetan scholars utilize into their study today.

Buton's activity inevitably attracted a great deal of attention to the monastery and brought in other Buddhist interllectuals around Tibet and India to study in the grounds amounting to some 3000 by 1360. After his death the monastery became an important epicentre of esoteric studies and psychic training for centuries.

The avowed purpose of lamas who cultivated paranormal abilities were not to become magicians or miracle workers but to attain philosophical enlightenment, a belief that all earthly phenomena are a state of the mind. Shalu Temple became known throughout the far east for its dedication to these philosophies and its enlightenment of the Buddhist faith.

However by the 1800s the monastery had become less influential and Tibetan scholars chose to study at the Samye monastery which had grown to be one of the most politically powerful in the Tibetan lands by this time. The monastery fell into ruin and little of the original 1330 structure remains, although the outer wall and the main building with damaged roofs still stands and a number of 14th century murals on the outer walls of the temple still follow an iconographic scheme developed by the great Buton himself.

One of the murals is an allegory in which an elephant representing a human soul evolves through many steps and earthly trials to Nirvana becoming progressively white and purer in the cleansing process.

Precise rules are still imbedded into the walls on what the monks should wear, place their robes and how to behave in the central courtyard Deyangshar. Remnants of former Mandala murals are concealed by over 100 Thanka most of which were emboidered in Hangzou in eastern China in the 1920s. Only two chapels of the Shalu temple are open to tourists although funds were allocated in 1995 for roof repair and the eventual restoration of the fine 14th century structure by 2005.

Inside Shalu Monastery: Shalu Lakhang temple is in the centre of the monastery. On the ground floor, in the Tshomchen, Sakyamuni and his disciples are enshrined. The chapels flanking it house the Tanjur and the Kanjur books respectively. Chapels on the roof floor are typical Chinese blue tiled structures, housing Sakyamuni, Buton and Arhats Buddhas. Massive delicate and old murals cover the walls of the monastery, mostly depicting stories from the life of the Buddha. Restoration and preservation are badly needed to protect those arts.

Inside Treasures: Shalu has four treasures which are of notable value. One is a sutra board, which is 700 years old and cannot be reassembled once broken apart, a piece of sutra printed against the board is regarded as good luck. Another is a brass urn, which is usually covered with a piece of red cloth and sealed; the holy water may clean 108 filths and is changed every 12 years. Another is a stone basin, which was the washbasin of the builder Chetsun Sherab Jungnay dating back to 1040; and another is a stone tablet, which was uncovered in the first construction of Shalu. The tablet displays a mantra which reads "om mani Padme Hum" and has four dagoba carved into it.

Tashilhunpo

Tashilhunpo Monastery, built in 1447, is a historic and culturally important monastery in Shigatse, Tibet. The monastery is the traditional seat of successive Panchen Lamas, the second highest ranking tulku lineage in the Gelukpa tradition.

Located on a hill in the centre of the city, the full name in Tibetan of the monastery means "all fortune and happiness gathered here" or "heap of glory".

History: This monastery was originally built by Gedun Drub the First Dalai Lama, financed by donations from local nobles. Later Lobsang Chokyi Gyalsten, the Fourth Panchen Lama and the first Panchen Lama to be recognized as such by the rulers of Mongolia, made major expansions to the monastery. Since then all Panchen Lamas have resided at Tashilhunpo and have managed to expand it gradually. Choekyi Gyalpo, the 11th Panchen Lama according to the government of the People's Republic of China, has been enthroned there, while Gedhun Choekyi Nyima, the 11th Panchen Lama recognised by the

Dalai Lama, has been held under "protective custody" by the Chinese authorities since 1995.

In 1791 the monastery was attacked and looted by an army of Nepalese Gurkha warriors but were driven out by the Chinese who at the same time strengthened their control, over the temple and Tibet. Tashilhunpo in its prime had over 4,000 monks and had four Tantric colleges each with its own Abbot. After the death of a Panchen Lama, these four abbots led the search for his infant incarnation and one of them always acted as a Prime Minster of Tsang under the control of the Dalai Lama in Lhasa.

In 1960 however the monastery was disbanded by the Chinese army whilst the Panchen Lama was absent although less damage was inflicted on the monastery as on others around Tibet.

During the 1960s many senior lamas and monastics left Tibet and helped re-establish new monasteries in India, Nepal and Bhutan. The late Panchen Lama did not leave Tibet and consequently many of the senior lamas from Tashilhunpo Monastery remained inside Tibet. Therefore, while other monasteries-in-exile have expanded and developed under the guidance of senior lamas, Tashilhunpo has remained at a disadvantage, although in 1972 a new campus of Tashilhunpo Monastery was built by Tibetan exiles at a settlement in Bylakuppe, Karnataka in southern India. Since the early 1980s parts of the Tashilhunpo monastery have been open to the public and it is an important tourist attraction in Tibet today.

4

Disciples of the Buddha

ANANDA

Ananda was one of many principal disciples and a devout attendant of the Buddha. He was renowned as the *Guardian of the Dharma*. The word 'Ananda' means 'bliss' in Sanskrit and is quite often part of Hindu monastic names.

Ananda was the first cousin of the Buddha, and was devoted to him. In the twentieth year of the Buddha's ministry, he became his personal attendant, accompanying him on most of his wanderings and taking the part of interlocutor in many of the recorded dialogues. He is the subject of a special panegyric delivered by the Buddha just before his death (the Mahaparinibbana Sutta (Digha Nikaya 16)); it is a panegyric for a man who is kindly, unselfish, popular, and thoughtful toward others.

In view of the abundance of praise, recognition and privileges Ananda received, mutterings of envy and resentment might have been expected, but this was not the case at all. Ananda was so occupied subordinating his entire life to the Dhamma that fame had no influence over him.

He knew that all that was good in him was due to the influence of the Teaching, and so avoided pride. One who is never proud has no enemies and is not the subject of envy. If someone turns inward completely and keeps away from any social contact, as Ananda's brother Anuruddha did, then it is also easy to be without enemies. But Ananda had daily contact with a large number of people with regard to diverse matters, yet he had no enemies or rivals, and his relationships with others were without conflict or tension.

In the long list of the disciples given in the Anguttara where each of them is declared to be the chief in some quality, Ananda is mentioned five times (more often than any other). He was named chief in conduct, in service to others, and in power of memory. The Buddha sometimes asked him to substitute for him as teacher and then later stated that he himself would not have presented the teachings in any other way.

Because he attended the Buddha personally and often travelled with him, Ananda overheard and memorized many of the discourses the Buddha delivered to various audiences. Therefore, he is often called the disciple of the Buddha who "heard much". At the First Buddhist Council, convened shortly after the Buddha died, Ananda was called upon to recite many of the discourses that later became the Sutta Pitaka of the Pali Canon.

Despite his long association with and close proximity to the Buddha, Ananda was only a stream-winner prior to the Buddha's death. During the period he was the Buddha's attendant, though he was still a "learner" and "one in the higher training", no thoughts of lust or hate arose in him; this is seen as implying that his close connection with the Buddha and his devotion to him gave no room for these.

Prior to the First Buddhist Council, it was proposed that Ananda not be permitted to attend on the grounds that he was not yet an arahant. According to legend, this prompted Ananda to focus his efforts on the attainment of nibbana and he was able to reach the specified level of attainment before the calling of the conclave.

In contrast to most of the figures depicted in the Pali Canon, Ananda is presented as an imperfect, if sympathetic. He mourns the deaths of both Sariputta, with whom he enjoyed a close friendship, and the Buddha. A verse of the Theragatha reveals his loneliness and isolation following the parinirvana of the Buddha.

In the Zen tradition, Ananda is considered to be the second Indian patriarch. He is often depicted with the Buddha alongside Mahakashyapa, the first Indian patriarch.

UPALI

Upali was a monk in the order of Buddha. Before joining the order, its interesting to note he worked as a barber. He asked if a person of "low birth" such as he could join the order, Buddha on purpose ordained him before the princes and asked the princes to pay homage to Upali, who by then had become an Arhant with Buddha's sermons while Buddha was getting a hair cut. He became the Chief disciple in knowing the rules of the order and the foremost disciple in keeping precepts.

Upali Thera One of the most eminent of the Buddha's immediate disciples. He belonged to a barber's family in Kapilavatthu and entered the service of the Sakiyan princes. When Anuruddha and his cousins left the world and sought ordination from the Buddha at Anupiya Grove, Upali accompanied them.

They gave him all their valuable ornaments, but, on further consideration, he refused to accept them and wished to become a monk with them. The reason given for his refusal is that he knew the Sakyans were hot-headed, and feared that the kinsmen of the princes might suspect him of having murdered the young men for the sake of their belongings.

At the request of the Sakiyan youths, the Buddha ordained Upali before them all, so that their pride might be humbled.

Upali's upajjhaya was Kappitaka. When Upali went to the Buddha for an exercise for meditation, he asked that he might be allowed to dwell in the forest. But the Buddha would not agree, for if Upali went into the forest he would learn only meditation, while, if he remained amongst men, he would have knowledge both of meditation and of the word of the Dhamma.

Upali accepted the Buddha's advice and, practising insight, in due course won arahantship. The Buddha himself taught Upali the whole of the Vinaya Pitaka.

In the assembly of the Sangha, the Buddha declared him to be the most proficient of those who were learned in the Vinaya (vinayadharanam). He is often spoken of as having reached the pinnacle of the Vinaya, or as being its chief repository (Vinaye agganikkhitto), and three particular cases-those of Ajjuka, the Bharukacchaka monk (Vin.iii.39) and Kumara-Kassapa-are frequently mentioned in this connection as instances where Upali's decisions on Vinaya rules earned the special commendation of the Buddha. In the Rajagaha Council, Upali took a leading part, deciding all the questions relative to the Vinaya, in the same way as Ananda decided questions regarding the Dhamma.

In accordance with this tradition, ascribing to Upali especial authority regarding the rules of the Order, various instances are given of Upali questioning the Buddha about the Vinaya regulations. Thus we find him consulting the Buddha as to the legality or otherwise of a complete congregation performing, in the absence of an accused monk, an act at which his presence is required. Again, he wishes to know if, in a matter which has caused altercations and schisms among members of the Order, the Sangha declares re-establishment of concord without thorough investigation, could such a declaration be lawful?. When a monk intends to take upon himself the conduct of any matter that has to be decided, under what conditions should he do so? What qualities should a monk possess in himself before he takes upon himself to warn others?. In what case can there be an interruption of the probationary period of a monk who has been placed on probation?

A whole list of questions asked by Upali and answers given by the Buddha on matters pertaining to the Vinaya rules is found in the chapter called Upali-Pancaka in the Parivara.

It is not possible to determine which of these and other questions were actually asked by Upali, and which were ascribed to him on account of his traditional reputation.

It is said that even in the Buddha's lifetime monks considered it a great privilege to learn the Vinaya under Upali. The monks seem to have regarded Upali as their particular friend, to whom they could go in their difficulties. Thus, when certain monks had been deprived by thieves of their clothes, it is Upali's protection that they seek.

The canon contains but few records of any discourses connected with Upali, apart from his questions on the Vinaya. In the Anguttara Nikaya he is mentioned as asking the Buddha for a brief sermon, the Buddha telling him that if there were anything that did not conduce to revulsion and detachment, Upali could be sure that such things did not form part of the Buddha's teaching. There is a record of another sermon which the Buddha is stated to have preached when Upali expressed the desire to retire into the solitude of the forest. The Buddha tells him that forest-life is not for the man who has not mastered his mind or attained to tranquillity.

Three verses are ascribed to Upali in the Theragathawhere he admonishes the brethren to seek noble friends of unfaltering character, to learn the monks' code of discipline and to dwell in solitude.

In the time of Padumuttara, Upali was a very rich brahmin named Sujata. When the Buddha came to his father's city in order to preach to him the Dhamma, Sujata saw him, and in the assembly be noticed an ascetic named Sunanda, holding over the Buddha for seven days a canopy of flowers. The Buddha declared that Sunanda would, in the time of Gautama Buddha, become famous as the Elder Punna Mantani-putta. Sujata, too, wished to seethe future Buddha Gautama, and having heard Padumuttara praise the monk Patika as chief of the Vinayadharas, he wished to hear, regarding himself, a similar declaration from Gautama. With this end in view he did many deeds of merit, chief of which was the erection of a monastery named Sobhana, for the Buddha and his monks, at an expense of one hundred thousand.

As a result he was born in heaven for thirty thousand kappas and was one thousand times king of the devas. One thousand times, too, he was cakkavatti. Two kappas ago there was a Khattiya named Anjasa, and Upali was born as his son Sunanda. One day he went to the park riding an elephant named Sirika, and met, on the way, the Pacceka Buddha Devala, whom he insulted in various ways. Sunanda was, thereupon, seized with a sensation of great heat in his body, and it was not till he went with a large following to the Pacceka Buddha and asked his pardon that the sensation left him. It is said that if the Buddha had not forgiven him, the whole country would have been destroyed. This insult paid to the Pacceka Buddha was the cause of Upali having been born as a barber in his last birth.

Buddhaghosa says that while the Buddha was yet alive Upali drew up certain instructions according to which future Vinayadharas should interpret Vinaya rules, and that, in conjunction with others, he compiled explanatory notes on matters connected with the Vinaya.

In direct pupillary succession to Upali as head of the Vinayadharas was Dasaka, whom Upali had first met at the Valikarama, where Upali was staying. Upali taught him the whole of the Vinaya.

ANGULIMALA

Angulimala is an important early figure in Buddhism, particularly within the Theravada school. Depicted in the suttas as a ruthless killer who is redeemed by conversion to Buddhism, his story is seen as an example of the redemptive power of the Buddha's teaching and the universal human potential for spiritual progress.

Textual Sources

Two texts in the Pali canon concern themselves with Angulimala's initial encounter with the Buddha and his conversion. The first is the Theragatha, verses 866-91, and the second is the Angulimala Sutta in the Majjhima Nikaya. Both offer a fairly short description of Angulimala's encounter with the Buddha, and omit much of the background information later incorporated into the story (such as Angulimala being placed under an oath by a jealous teacher). These later additions-which appear in the sutta commentaries attributed to Buddhaghosa and Dhammapala (the Majjhima Nikaya commentary known as the Papancasudani (*Ps*) and the Therigatha commentary Paramattha-dipani (*Pad*), respectively)-may represent attempts by later commentators to "rehabilitate" the character of Angulimala-making him appear as a fundamentally good human being entrapped by circumstance, rather than as a vicious killer. The sutta texts themselves do not provide for any motive for Angulimala's actions, other than pure sadism.

The Story

Early Life

A robber who was converted by the Buddha in the twentieth year of his ministry, and who, later, became an arahant. He was born under the thieves' constellation, and on the night of his birth all the armour in the town shone, including that belonging to the king. Because this omen did no harm to anyone the babe was named Ahimsaka. The Thag. Cy. says he was first called Himsaka and then Ahimsaka. At Takkasila (Taxila) he became a favourite at the teacher's house, but his jealous fellow-students poisoned his teacher's mind, and the latter, bent on his destruction, asked as his Guru-Dakshina (honorarium) a thousand human right-hand fingers. Thereupon Ahimsaka waylaid travellers in the Jalini forest in Kosala and killed them, taking a finger from each. The finger-bones thus obtained he made into a garland to hang round his neck, hence the name Angulimala (*Anguli*-Finger, *Mala*-Garland).

According to the sutta and commentarial texts, omens seen at the time of Angulimala's birth (the flashing of weapons in the city, and the appearance of the 'constellation of thieves' in the sky) indicated that Angulimala would become a robber. Angulimala's father, the Brahmin chaplain to the king of Kosala, named him Ahimsaka ("harmless"-derived from the Sanskrit and Pali word Ahimsa), as an attempt to deter the dark fate predicted at his birth (*Pad* indicates that he was initially named Himsaka ("harmful"), but that the name was later changed).

Angulimala was sent to Taxila to study under a well-known Brahmin guru. There he excelled in his studies and became the teachers' favourite student, enjoying special privileges in his teachers' house. However, the other students grew jealous of Ahimsaka's speedy progress and sought to turn his master against him. To that end, they made it seem as though Ahimsaka had seduced the master's wife and boasted that he was wiser than the guru. Unwilling or unable to attack Ahimsaka directly (*Pad* states that Ahimsaka was as "strong as seven elephants", while *Ps* states that the teacher worried that his business would suffer if he was found to have murdered a student, the teacher said that Ahimsaka's training was complete, but that he must provide the traditional final gift offered to a guru before the teacher would grant his approval. As his payment, the teacher demanded 1,000 fingers, each taken from a different victim, thinking that Angulimala would be killed in the course of seeking this grisly prize (*Pad* states that Angulimala was required to fetch 1,000 fingers from right hands, seemingly unaware that this could be achieved by killing 200 people. *Ps* states, even more strangely, that he was told to "kill a thousand legs", and gathered fingers only as an aid to keeping an accurate count).

Sources indicate that one of his motivations may have been the unquestioning obedience to the guru-an echo of the higher principles governing his earlier life. But tradition reports that it was probably his innate disposition to violence. In his previous life, he was a Yakkha-a man-eating spirit with superhuman strength. The guru's instructions may have also aroused a strange attraction for killing, or could be seen as a challenge to his manly prowess. It was reported that in all his past lives, two traits were prominent: his physical strength and his lack of compassion.

It is also suggested that he was in fact cast out of his Guru's house, branding him an outcast among Brahmins. Being unable to find acceptance anywhere, he turned to brigandry, murdering pilgrims and traders passing through the wilderness, and collecting a finger each from their right hands.

Life as a Highway Murderer

Ahimsaka became a highwayman, killing travellers who passed through the forest. When the people of the kingdom began to avoid the roads, he entered the villages and dragged people from their homes. He never took clothes or jewels from his victims, only fingers. To keep count of the number of victims that he had taken, he strung them on a thread and hung them on a tree. However because birds began to eat the flesh from the fingers, he started to wear them around his neck as a garland. Thus he came to be known as *Angulimala* ("garland (or necklace) of fingers"). As a result of his deeds whole villages were deserted, and the king ordered a detachment of men to seize the bandit, whose name nobody knew. But Angulimala's mother, guessing the truth, started off to warn him. By now he lacked but one finger to complete his thousand, and seeing his mother coming he determined to kill her. But the Buddha, seeing his upanissaya, went himself to the wood, travelling thirty yojanas, and intercepted Angulimala on his way to slay his mother. Angulimala was converted by the Buddha's power and received the "ehi bhikkhu pabbajja" while the populace were yelling at the king's palace for the robber's life. Later, the Buddha presented him before King Pasenadi when the latter came to Jetavana, and Pasenadi, filled with wonder, offered to provide the monk with all requisites. Angulimala, however, had taken on the dhutangas and refused the king's offer.

Meeting the Buddha

Villagers petitioned the king of Kosala, who vowed to hunt down Angulimala. Fearing for her son's life, Angulimala's mother set out to find him and warn him of the king's intent. The Buddha perceived with his "divine eye" (faculty of clairvoyance) that Angulimala had slain 999 victims, and was desperately seeking a thousandth. If the Buddha encountered Angulimala that day, he would become a monk and subsequently attain Nirvana. If Angulimala encountered his mother instead, he would slay her as his thousandth victim and fall into hell for millennia as a matricide.

The Buddha set off to intercept Angulimala, despite being warned by the people of the village in which he was staying. On the road through the forest of Kosala, Angulimala first saw his mother who came to warn him of the impending arrival of the kings' army. Angulimala, after some deliberation, decided to make her his 1000th victim. But then when Buddha also arrived, he chose to kill him instead. He drew his sword, and started running towards the Buddha. But although Angulimala was running as fast as he could, he couldn't catch up with the Buddha who was walking calmly, but who also was using his psychic powers to stay ahead of Angulimala. This bewildered Angulimala so much that he stopped in his tracks, and told the Buddha to stop. The Buddha said that he himself had already stopped, and that Angulimala should stop also. Angulimala asked for further explanation, after which the Buddha said that he had stopped harming living beings a long time ago, and that Angulimala was still harming and hurting living beings. After hearing this, Angulimala changed his ways, vowed to cease his life as a brigand and joined the Buddhist order.

Angulimala the Monk

Later, King Pasenadi (the king of Kosala) set out to find and kill Angulimala. He stopped first to pay a visit to the Buddha and his followers at the monastery where they dwelled. He explained to the Buddha his purpose, and the Buddha asked how the king would respond if he were to discover that Angulimala had given up the life of a highwayman and become a monk. The king said that he would salute him and offer to provide for him in his monastic vocation. The Buddha then revealed that Angulimala sat only a few feet away, his hair and beard shaven off, a member of the Buddhist order. The king, astounded, offered to donate robe materials to Angulimala, and then returned to his palace.

Later, Angulimala came across a young woman undergoing a difficult labour. He went to the Buddha and asked him what he could do to ease her pain. The Buddha told Angulimala to go to the woman and say:

'Sister, since I was born I do not recall intentionally killing a living being. Through this truth may there be wellbeing for you, wellbeing for your fetus.'

Angulimala pointed out that it would be untrue for him to say this (it is unclear why the Buddha even suggested this course of action; it seems unlikely that the Buddha did not realise to whom he was speaking. Perhaps he was testing Angulimala's honesty.) The Buddha offered a revised stanza to recite to the woman:

'Sister, since I was born with the noble birth (became a monk), I do not recall intentionally killing a living being. Through this truth may there be wellbeing for you, wellbeing for your fetus.'

After Angulimala delivered this benediction, the woman safely gave birth to her child. This verse, commonly called the *Angulimala paritta*, continues to be recited at the blessings of houses or pregnant women in Theravada countries.

This helped Angulimala focus his mind on his basic meditation subject. Before, there would always appear in his mind's eye, the place in the jungle where he had slain so many people. After performing the Act of Truth, he was seen to bring safety to people and people started to approach him and provide him with almsfood.

At last, his earlier name Ahimsaka fully befitted him. Most of the people had gained full confidence in his inner transformation and there was no lack of support for him.

However a resentful few could not forget that he was responsible for the deaths of their loved ones. Unable to win revenge through the law, they took matters into their own hands. With sticks and stones, they attacked him as he walked for alms.

With a bleeding head, torn outer robe and a broken alms bowl, Angulimala managed to return to the monastery. The Buddha encouraged Angulimala to bear his torment with equanimity; he indicated that Angulimala was experiencing the fruits of the karma that would otherwise have condemned him to hell. This illustrates the Buddhist belief that while the effects of karma are inescapable, the form that they take and the schedule on which they occur can be modified by later actions — in this case, Angulimala experienced physical suffering during the course of his last life, rather than experiencing torment in another birth for a much longer period of time.

Being an arahant, Angulimala remained firm and invulnerable in mind and heart. But his body, the symbol and fruit of previous kamma was still exposed to the effects of his former evil deeds. As an arahant, he needed no words of consolation, but a reminder of the kammic concatenation of cause and effect, which still has to be endured until the end.

When he entered Savatthi for alms, he was attacked by the mob, but on the admonition of the Buddha, endured their wrath as penance for his former misdeeds.

According to the Dhammapadatthakatha he appears to have died soon after he joined the Order.

There is a story of how he eased a woman's labour pains by an act of truth. The words he used in this saccakiriya have come to be regarded as a paritta to ward off all dangers and constitute the Angulimala Paritta. The water that washed the stone on which he sat in the woman's house came to be regarded as a panacea. In the Angulimala Sutta he is addressed by Pasenadi as Gagga Mantaniputta, his father being a Gagga. The story is evidently a popular one and occurs also in the Avadana Sataka (No.27).

At the Kosala king's Asadisadana, an untamed elephant, none other being available, was used to bear the parasol over Angulimala. The elephant remained perfectly still-such was Angulimala's power.

The conversion of Angulimala is often referred to as a most compassionate and wonderful act of the Buddha's, e.g. in the Sutasoma Jataka which was preached concerning him. The story of Angulimala is quoted as that of a man in whose case a beneficent kamma arose and destroyed former evil kamma.

It was on his account that the rule not to ordain a captured robber was enacted.

Meanings and Interpretations

To the Theravada and Mahayana, Angulimala's story serves as an example that even the worst of people can undo the faults in their beings and return to the right path. The Theosophical viewpoint on this story is similar, and also includes that Karma must be repaid, but it is up to the individual as to how they react to their karma that will determine the change in their character. Even though Angulimala had repented and was enlightened, he still had to pay the karma of killing so many. He was peaceful and accepted what was done, and was therefore liberated from the Wheel of Rebirth.

Angulimala's story also illustrates the Buddhist belief that individuals can be reformed more readily through compassion than through punishment. As Angulimala says, "Some prisoners are tamed with punishment of a stick, or a hook or a whip. I was tamed without a stick or a weapon. I was tamed by the kind words of the Compassionate Buddha."

Richard F. Gombrich, in his paper *Who was Angulimala?*, has postulated that the story of Angulimala may represent an encounter between the Buddha and a follower of an early form of Saivite or Shakti tantra. Gombrich reaches this conclusion on the basis of a number of inconsistencies in the sutta text that indicate possible corruption (particularly the failure of the verses in the Theragatha to conform to accepted Pali metrical schemes), and the fairly weak explanations for Angulimala's behaviour provided by the commentators. He notes that there are several other references in the early Pali canon that seem to indicate the presence of devotees of Siva, Kali, and other divinities associated with sanguinary tantric practices, and that Angulimala's behaviour would not be inconsistent with certain violent practices that were observed in India by Thuggee-like transgressive cults into recent times. If Gombrich's thesis could be conclusively proven, it would establish the Angulimala Sutta as likely being the earliest known documentation of tantric practices in South Asia, about which very little is known before the 7th century CE.

Modern Influences

In 1985, the British-born Theravada monk Venerable Ajahn Khemadhammo Mahathera founded ANGULIMALA: The Buddhist Prison Chaplaincy in England. It has been recognized by the British government as the official representative of the Buddhist religion in all matters concerning the British prison system, and provides chaplains, counselling services, and instruction in Buddhism and meditation to prisoners throughout England, Wales, and Scotland.

In 2002, Thai director Suthep Tannirat attempted to release a film entitled 'Ongkulimal' (the Thai pronunciation of Angulimala) that re-told the story of the famous monk. Conservative Buddhist organizations in Thailand launched a protest, claiming that the movie distorted Buddhist teachings, and introduced Hindu and theistic influences not found in the source material.

The Thai film censorship board rejected appeals to ban the film, but insisted that the director cut some violent material, and re-title the film to distance it further from its scriptural sources. Interestingly, what seemed to be most offensive to many was the fact that the director omitted commentarial information that depicted Angulimala as a hapless victim of the actions of others, and instead portrayed him (as the sutta does) as engaging in his violent behaviour of his own free choice.

MAHAPAJAPATI GOTAMI

Mahapajapati Gotami (in Pali; Mahaprajapati Gautami in Sanskrit) was the first woman to request ordination from the Buddha and to join the Sangha. She was both the Buddha's aunt and adoptive mother, raising him after her sister, Queen Maya (Mahamaya), the Buddha's birth mother, died.

Early Life

An eminent Theri, Mahaprajapati (Pajapati) was born at Devadaha, in the family of Suppabuddha, as the younger sister of Mahamaya. Mahapajapati was so called because, at her birth, augerers prophesied that she would have a large following; Gotami was her gotta name. She was predicted by sages to be the one who causes Buddha to allow women to join his holy order. Ap.ii.538 says her father was Anjana Sakka and her mother Sulakkhana. Mhv.ii.18 says her father was Anjana and her mother Yasodhara. Dandapani and Suppabuddha were her brothers. At the birth of each sister, interpreters of bodily marks prophesied that the children would be cakkavattins. Both sisters married King Suddhodana, leader of the Uakya. When Mahamaya died, seven days after the birth of the Buddha, Pajapati looked after the Buddha and nursed him. She was the mother of Nanda, but it is said that she gave her own son to nurses and herself nursed the Buddha. She raised Buddha and had her own children, Siddhartha's step brother Nanda and step sister Sundari Nanda.

Ordination of the First Woman

When her husband, Suddhodana, died, Pajapati decided to renounce the world. The Buddha was at Vesali and she waited for an opportunity to ask permission of him. Pajapati was already a sotapanna. She attained this eminence when the Buddha first visited his father's palace and preached the Mahadhammapala Jataka. She was predicted by sages to be the one who causes Buddha to allow women to join his holy order. Her opportunity came when the Buddha visited Kapilavatthu to settle the dispute between the Sakiyans and the Koliyans as to the right to take water from the river Rohini. When the dispute had been settled, the Buddha preached the Kalahavivada Sutta, and five hundred young Sakiyan men joined the Order. The Sakiyan wives, led by Pajapati, went to the Buddha and asked leave to also be ordained. The Buddha refused and went on to Vesali. But Pajapati and her companions, nothing daunted, had barbers cut off their hair, and donning yellow robes, followed the Buddha to Vesali on foot. They arrived with wounded feet at the Buddha's monastery and repeated their request to ordain as monastics. The Buddha again refused, But, Ananda interceded on their behalf and Buddha granted their request, subject to eight strict conditions. There was some question, which arose later, as to the procedure of Pajapati's ordination, which was not formal. When the nuns discovered this some of them refused to hold the uposatha with her. But the Buddha declared that he himself had ordained her and that all was in order. Her upasampada consisted in acquiescing in the eight conditions laid down for nuns.

Mahapajapati's Monastic Life

After her ordination, Pajapati came to the Buddha and worshipped him. The Buddha preached to her and gave her a subject for meditation. With this topic she developed insight and soon after won arahantship, while her five hundred companions attained the same after listening to the Nandakovada Sutta. Later, at an assembly of monks and nuns in Jetavana, the Buddha declared Pajapati "Chief of Those Who had Experience (rattannunam)". Not long after, while at Vesali, she realized that her life had come to an end. She was one hundred and twenty years old; she took leave of the Buddha, performed various miracles, and then died, her five hundred companions dying with her. It is said that the marvels which attended her cremation rites were second only to those of the Buddha.

Other Lives

In the time of Padumuttara Buddha Pajapati resolved to gain eminence. In that rebirth, she belonged to a clansman's family in Hamsavati, and, hearing the Buddha assign the foremost place in experience to a certain nun, wished for similar recognition herself, doing many good deeds to that end. After many births she was born once more at Benares, forewoman among five hundred slave girls. When the rains drew near, five Pacceka Buddhas came from to Isipatana seeking lodgings. Pajapati saw them after the Treasurer had refused them any assistance, and, after consultation with her fellow slaves, they persuaded their several husbands to erect five huts for the Pacceka Buddhas during the rainy season and they provided them with all requisites. At the end of the rains they gave three robes to each Pacceka Buddha. After that she was born in a weaver's village near Benares, and again ministered, this time to five hundred Pacceka Buddhas, sons of Padumavati.

It is said that once Pajapati made a robe for the Buddha of wonderful material and marvellously elaborate. But when it came to be offered to the Buddha he refused it, and suggested it should be given to the Order as a whole. Pajapati was greatly disappointed, and Ananda intervened. But the Buddha explained that his suggestion was for the greater good of Pajapati, and also as an example to those who might wish to make similar gifts in the future. This was the occasion for the preaching of the Dakkhinavibhanga Sutta. The Buddha had a great love for Pajapati, and when she lay ill, as there were no monks to visit her and preach to her-that being against the rule-the Buddha amended the rule and went himself to preach to her.

Pajapati's name appears several times in the Jatakas. She was the mother monkey in the Cula Nandiya Jataka, Canda in the Culla Dhammapala (J.iii.182), and Bhikkhudayika (or Bhikkhudasika) daughter of Kiki, king of Benares.

There is a story related of a nurse employed by Pajapati and born in Devadaha. She renounced the world with Pajapati, but for twenty five years was harassed by thoughts of lust till, at last, she heard Dhammadinna preach. She then practiced meditation and became an arahant. Thiga.75f.

Two of the most powerful nuns:

ANATHAPINDIKA

Anathapindika-Chief lay disciple of Buddha, and his name means "feeder of the orphans or helpless". His given name was Sudatta. He was extremely wealthy and a patron of the Buddha. He gave Jeta Park to the Buddha having purchased it from Prince Jeta. He honored the Buddha with laying out 1.8 million gold pieces in the grove. Anathapindika upon death entered Tusita heaven, or the heaven of the Bodhisattvas. Anathapindika was known as the "foremost disciple in generosity" as well as character.

A banker (setthi) of Savatthi who became famous because of his unparalleled generosity to the Buddha. His first meeting with the Buddha was during the first year after the Enlightenment, in Rajagaha, whither Anathapindika had come on business.

His wife was the sister of the setthi of Rajagaha, and when he arrived he found the setthi preparing a meal for the Buddha and his monks on so splendid a scale that he thought that a wedding was in progress or that the king had been invited. On learning the truth he became eager to visit the Buddha, and did so very early the next morning. He was so excited by the thought of the visit that he got up three times during the night. When, at last, he started for Sitavana, the road was quite dark, but a friendly Yakkha, Sivaka, sped him on with words of encouragement. By force of his piety the darkness vanished.

The Buddha was staying in the Sitavana, and when Anathapindika reached there spirits opened the door for him. He found the Buddha walking up and down, meditating in the cool air of the early dawn. The Buddha greeted him and talked to him on various aspects of his teaching. Anathapindika was immediately converted and became a Sotapanna. He invited the Buddha to a meal the next day, providing everything himself, although the setthi, the Mayor of Rajagaha and King Bimbisara asked to be allowed to help. After the meal, which he served to the Buddha with his own hand, he invited the Buddha to spend the rainy season at Savatthi, and the Buddha accepted, saying "the Tathagatas, o householder, take pleasure in solitude." "I understand, o Blessed One, I understand," was the reply.

When Anathapindika had finished his business at Rajagaha he set out towards Savatthi, giving orders along the way to his friends and acquaintances to prepare dwellings, parks, rest-houses and gifts all along the road to Savatthi in preparation for the Buddha's visit. He had many friends and acquaintances and he was Adeyyavaco (his word was held to be of weight), where it is said that Anathapindika bore all the expenses of these preparations. Viharas were built costing 1,000 pieces each, a yojana apart from each other.

Understanding the request implied in the Buddha's words when he accepted the invitation, Anathapindika looked out for a quiet spot near Savatthi where the Buddha and the monks might dwell, and his eye fell on the park of Jetakumara. He bought the park at great expense and erected therein the famous Jetavanarama. As a result of this and of his numerous other benefactions in the cause of the Sasana, Anathapindika came to be recognised as the chief of alms-givers.

Anathapindika's personal name was Sudatta, but he was always called Anathapindika (feeder of the destitute) because of his munificence; he was, however, very pleased when the Buddha addressed him by his own name. He spent eighteen crores on the purchase of Jetavana and a like sum on the construction of the vihara; another eighteen crores were spent in the festival of dedication. He fed one hundred monks in his house daily in addition to meals provided for guests, people of the village, invalids, etc. Five hundred seats were always ready in his house for any guests who might come.

Anathapindika's father was the setthi Sumana (AA. loc. cit). The name of Anathapindika's brother was Subhuti.

Anathapindika married a lady called Punnalakkhana; he had a son Kala and three daughters, Maha-Subhadda, Cula-Subhadda and Sumana. (Besides Kala, Anathapindika had another son, who joined the Order under Subhuti Thera; AA.ii.865). Mention is also made of a daughter-in law, Sujata by name, daughter of Dhaṇanjaya and the youngest sister of Visakha. She was very haughty and ill-treated the servants.

The son, in spite of his father's efforts, showed no piety until he was finally bribed to go to the vihara and listen to the Buddha's preaching. The daughters, on the other hand, were most dutiful and helped their father in ministering to the monks. The two elder ones attained to the First Fruit of the Path, married, and went to live with the families of their husbands. Sumana obtained the Second Fruit of the Path, but remained unmarried. Overwhelmed with disappointment because of her failure in finding a husband, she refused to eat and died; she was reborn in Tusita.

The Bhadraghata Jataka tells us of a nephew of Anathapindika who squandered his inheritance of forty crores. His uncle gave him first one thousand and then another five hundred with which to trade. This also he squandered. Anathapindika then gave him two garments. On applying for further help the man was taken by the neck and pushed out of doors. A little later he was found dead by a side wall.

The books also mention a girl, Punna, who was a slave in Anathapindika's household. On one occasion when the Buddha was starting on one of his periodical tours from Jetavana, the king, Anathapindika, and other eminent patrons failed to stop him; Punna, however, succeeded, and in recognition of this service Anathapindika adopted her as his daughter. On uposatha days his whole household kept the fast; on all occasions they kept the pancasila inviolate. A story is told of one of his labourers who had forgotten the day and gone to work; but remembering later, he insisted on keeping the fast and died of starvation. He was reborn as a deva.

Anathapindika had a business village in Kasi and the superintendent of the village had orders to feed any monks who came there. One of his servants bore the inauspicious name of Kalakanni (curse); he and the banker had been playmates as children, and Kalakanni, having fallen on evil days, entered the banker's service. The latter's friends protested against his having a man with so unfortunate a name in his household, but he refused to listen to them. One day when Anathapindika was away from home on business, burglars came to rob his house, but Kalakanni with great presence of mind drove them away.

A similar story is related of another friend of his who was also in his service.

All his servants, however, were not so intelligent. A slave woman of his, seeing that a fly had settled on her mother, hit her with a pestle in order to drive it away, and killed her.

A slave girl of his borrowed an ornament from his wife and went with her companions to the pleasure garden. There she became friendly with a man who evidently desired to rob her of her ornaments. On discovering his intentions, she pushed him into a well and killed him with a stone.

The story of Anathapindika's cowherd, Nanda, is given elsewhere.

All the banker's friends were not virtuous; one of them kept a tavern. As a result of Anathapindika's selfless generosity he was gradually reduced to poverty. But he continued his gifts even when he had only bird-seed and sour gruel. The devata who dwelt over his gate appeared before him one night and warned him of his approaching penury; it is said that every time the Buddha or his monks came to the house she had to leave her abode over the gate and that this was inconvenient to her and caused her to be jealous. Anathapindika paid no attention to her warnings and asked her to leave the house. She left with her children, but could find no other lodging and sought counsel from various gods, including Sakka. Sakka advised her to recover for Anathapindika the eighteen crores that debtors owed him, another eighteen that lay in the bottom of the sea, and yet eighteen more lying unclaimed. She did so and was readmitted.

Anathapindika went regularly to see the Buddha twice a day, sometimes with many friends, and always taking with him alms for the young novices. But we are told that he never asked a question of the Buddha lest he should weary him. He did not wish the Buddha to feel obliged to preach to him in return for his munificence. But the Buddha of his own accord preached to him on various occasions; several such sermons are mentioned in the Anguttara Nikaya:

On the importance of having a well-guarded mind like a well-protected gable in a house; on the benefits the recipient of food obtains (life, beauty, happiness, strength); on the four obligations that make up the pious householder's path of duty (gihisamikiccani-waiting on the Order with robes, food, lodgings, medical requirements. Referred to also in S. v.387, where Anathapindika expresses his satisfaction that he had never failed in these obligations); on the four conditions of success that are hard to win (wealth gotten by lawful means, good report, longevity, happy rebirth); on the four kinds of happiness which a householder should seek (ownership, wealth, debtless ness, blamelessness). on the five kinds of enjoyment which result from wealth rightfully obtained (enjoyment-experienced by oneself and by one's friends and relations, security in times of need, ability to pay taxes and to spend on one's religion, the giving of alms to bring about a happy rebirth); the five things which are very desirable but difficult to obtain (long life, beauty, happiness, glory, good condition of rebirths, A.iii.47-8); the five sinful acts that justify a man's being called wicked; the inadvisability of being satisfied with providing requisites for monks without asking oneself if one also experiences the joy that is born of ease of mind.

The Buddha preached the Velama Sutta to encourage Anathapindika when he had been reduced to poverty and felt disappointed that he could no longer provide luxuries for the monks. On another occasion the Buddha tells Anathapindika that the Sotapanna is a happy man because he is free from various fears: fear of being born in hell, among beasts, in the realm of Peta or in some other unhappy state; he is assured of reaching Enlightenment.

Elsewhere the Buddha tells Anathapindika that it is not every rich man who knows how to indulge in the pleasures of sense legitimately and profitably.

There is, however, at least one sutta preached as a result of a question put by Anathapindika himself regarding gifts and those who are worthy to receive them; and we also find him consulting the Buddha regarding the marriage of his daughter, Cola Subhadda.

Anathapindika died before the Buddha. As he lay grievously ill he sent a special message to Sariputta asking him to come (again, probably, because he did not want to trouble the Buddha). Sariputta went with Ananda and preached to him the Anathapindikovada Sutta. His pains left him as he concentrated his mind on the virtuous life he had led and the many acts of piety he had done. Later he fed the Elders with food from his own cooking-pot, but quite soon afterwards he died and was born in the Tusita heaven. That same night he visited the Buddha at Jetavana and uttered a song of praise of Jetavana and of Sariputta who lived there, admonishing others to follow the Buddha's teaching. In heaven he will live as long as Visakha and Sakka.

Various incidents connected with Anathapindika are to be found in the Jatakas. On one occasion his services were requisitioned to hold an inquiry on a bhikkhuni who had become pregnant.

Once when the Buddha went on tour from Jetavana, Anathapindika was perturbed because there was no one left for him to worship; at the Buddha's suggestion, an offshoot from the Bodhi tree at Gaya was planted at the entrance to Jetavana.

Once a brahmin, hearing of Anathapindika's luck, comes to him in order to find out where this luck lay so that he may obtain it. The brahmin discovers that it lay in the comb of a white cock belonging to Anathapindika; he asks for the cock and it is given to him, but the luck flies away elsewhere, settling first in a pillow, then in a jewel, a club, and, finally, in the head of Anathapindika's wife. The brahmin's desire is thus frustrated. On two occasions he was waylaid by rogues. Once they tried to make him drink drugged toddy. He was at first shocked by their impertinence, but, later, wishing to reform them, frightened them away.

On the other occasion, the robbers lay in wait for him as he returned from one of his villages; by hurrying back he escaped them. Whenever Anathapindika visited the Buddha, he was in the habit of relating to the Buddha various things which had come under his notice, and the Buddha would relate to him stories from the past containing similar incidents. Among the Jatakas so preached are: Apannaka, Khadirahgara, Rohini, Varuni, Punnapati, Kalakanni, Akatannu, Veri, Kusanali, Siri, Bhadraghata, Visayha, Hiri, Sirikalakanni and Sulasa.

Anathapindika was not only a shrewd business man but also a keen debater. The Anguttara Nikaya records a visit he paid to the Paribbajakas when he could think of nothing better to do. A lively debate ensues regarding their views and the views of the Buddha as expounded by Anathapindika. The latter silences his opponents. When the incident is reported to the Buddha, he speaks in high praise of Anathapindika and expresses his admiration of the way in which he handled the discussion.

During the time of Padumattara Buddha Anathapindika had been a householder of Hamsavati. One day he heard the Buddha speak of a lay-disciple of his as being the chief of alms-givers. The householder resolved to be so designated himself in some future life and did many good deeds to that end. His wish was fulfilled in this present life. Anathapindika is sometimes referred to as Maha Anathapindika to distinguish him from Cula Anathapindika.

SCHOOLS OF BUDDHISM

The Schools of Buddhism. An extensive list of historical schools is given below according to lineage. Surviving schools can be roughly grouped under the categories of Theravada, Mahayana, and Vajrayana. Theravada and Mahayana share common methods as sutric schools, while Vajrayana can be seen as a tantric school.

Most of the sects encourage followers to adhere to certain practices and philosophies, some shared, some unique to the particular school.

Nikaya Schools

- Sthaviravada
    - Pudgalavada ('Personalist') (c. 280 BCE)

- o Sarvastivada
  - * Vibhajjavada (prior to 240 BCE; during Ashoka)
  - * Theravada (c. 240 BCE)
  - * Theravada subschools
  - * Mahiuasaka (after 232 BCE)
  - * Dharmaguptaka (after 232 BCE)
  - * Kauyapiya (after 232 BCE)
  - * Vatsiputriya (under Ashoka) later name: Sammitiya
  - * Dharmottariya
  - * Bhadrayaniya
  - * Sannagarika
  - * Mulasarvastivada (third and fourth centuries)
  - * Sautrantika (between 50 BCE and c. 100 CE).

- Mahasamghika ('Majority', c. 380 BCE)
  - o Ekavyaharikas (under Ashoka)
    - * Lokottaravada.
  - o Golulika (during Ashoka)
    - * Bahuurutiya (late third century BCE)
    - * Prajnaptivada (late third century BCE)
    - * Cetiyavada.
  - o Caitika (mid-first century BCE)
    - * Apara Saila
    - * Uttara Saila.

Influences on East Asian Schools

The following later schools used the Vinaya of the Dharmaguptaka:

- Chinese Vinaya School
- Korean Gyeyul
- Japanese Ritsu
- The Japanese Jojitsu is considered an offshoot of Sautrantika
- The Chinese/Japanese Kusha school is considered an offshoot of Sarvastivada, influenced by Vasubandhu.

Theravada Subschools

The different schools in Theravada often emphasize different aspects (or parts) of the Pali Canon and the later commentaries, or differ in the focus on (and recommended way of) practice. There are also significant differences in strictness or interpretation of the Vinaya.

- *Bangladesh*:
  - Sangharaj Nikaya
  - Mahasthabir Nikaya
- *Burma*:
  - Thudhamma Nikaya
    - Vipassana tradition of Mahasi Sayadaw and disciples
  - Shwekyin Nikaya
- *Sri Lanka*:
  - Siam Nikaya
    - Waturawila (or Mahavihara Vamshika Shyamopali Vanavasa Nikaya)
  - Amarapura Nikaya
    - Kanduboda (or Swejin Nikaya)
    - Tapovana (or Kalyanavamsa)
  - Ramanna Nikaya
    - Galduwa (or Kalyana Yogashramaya Samsthava)
    - Delduwa
- *Thailand*
  - Maha Nikaya
    - Vijja Dhammakaya
  - Thammayut Nikaya
    - Thai Forest Tradition
    - Tradition of Ajahn Chah

Mahayana Schools

- Madhyamaka

  - o Prasangaka
  - o Svatantrika
- Yogacara
- Tathagatagarbha
  - o Sanlun (Three Treatise school)
    - * Sanron
- Dauabhumika (absorbed in to Huayan)
- Huayan (AvataCsaka)
  - o Hwaeom
  - o Kegon
- Chan/Zen/Seon/Thien
  - o Caodong
    - * Soto
  - o Linji
    - * Rinzai
    - * Obaku
    - * Fuke
    - * Won Buddhism: Korean Reformed Buddhism
- Pure Land (Amidism)
  - o Jodo
  - o Jodo Shin
  - o Amida-shu
- Tiantai (Lotus Sutra School)
  - o Cheontae
  - o Tendai (also contained Vajrayana elements)
- Nichiren
  - o Nichiren Shu
  - o Nichiren Shoshu
  - o Nipponzan Myohoji
  - o Soka Gakkai
- Vijnanavada.

Tantric Schools

- Tibetan Buddhism

- o Nyingmapa
- o New Bon (synthesis of Yungdrung Bon and Nyingmapa)
- o Kadampa
- o Sakyapa
  - * Jonangpa
- o Gelukpa
- o Kagyupa
  - * Shangpa Kagyu
  - * Rechung Kagyu
  - * Dagpo Kagyu
  - * Karma Kagyu (or Kamtshang Kagyu)
  - * Tsalpa Kagyu
  - * Baram Kagyu
  - * Pagtru Kagyu (or Phagmo Drugpa Kagyu)
  - * Taglung Kagyu
  - * Trophu Kagyu
  - * Drukpa Kagyu
  - * Martsang Kagyu
  - * Yerpa Kagyu
  - * Yazang Kagyu
  - * Shugseb Kagyu
  - * Drikung Kagyu
- o Rime movement (ecumenical movement)

• Japanese Mikkyo
  - o Shingon
  - o Tendai (derived from Tiantai but added tantric practices).

ABHIDHAMMA

Abhidharma (Sanskrit) or Abhidhamma (Pali) is a category of Buddhist scriptures that attempts to use Buddhist teachings to create a systematic, abstract description of all worldly phenomena. The Abhidharma represents a generalization and reorganization of the doctrines presented piecemeal in the narrative *sutra* tradition.

The literal translation of the term Abhidharma is unclear. Two possibilities are most commonly given: 1) *abhi*-higher or special + *dharma*-teaching, philosophy, thus making Abhidharma the 'higher teachings', or 2) *abhi*-about + *dharma* of the teaching, translating it instead as 'about the teaching' or even 'meta-teaching'.

Origins

Scholars generally believe that the Abhidharma emerged *after* the time of the Buddha, as the growth of monastic centres and support for the Buddhist saegha provided the resources and expertise necessary to systematically analyse the early teachings. However, some scholars believe that rather than being wholly created by later thinkers, the Abhidharma represents an expansion of a set of mnemonic lists and categories that were employed by early Buddhists to preserve the oral tradition.

Numerous apparently independent Abhidharma traditions arose in India, roughly during the period from the 2nd or 3rd Century BCE to the 5th Century CE. The 7th Century Chinese pilgrim Xuanzang reportedly collected Abhidharma texts from seven different traditions. In the modern era, only the Abhidharmas of the Sarvastivadins and the Theravadins have survived intact, each consisting of seven books. The Theravada Abhidharma, the Abhidhamma Pitaka, is preserved in Pali, while the Sarvastivadin Abhidharma is mostly preserved only in Chinese-the (likely Sanskrit) original texts having been lost. A small number of other Abhidharma texts of unknown origin are preserved in translation in the Chinese canon.

Traditionally, Theravada Buddhists have been of the belief that the Abhidhamma was not a later addition to the tradition, but rather represented the first, original understanding of the teachings by the Buddha. According to myth, shortly after his awakening the Buddha spent several days in meditation, during which he formulated the Abhidhamma.

Later, he travelled to the heavenly realm and taught the Abhidhamma to the divine beings that dwelled there, including his deceased mother Mahamaya, who reincarnated as a celestial being. The tradition holds that the contents of the teachings given in the heavenly realm were related to the monk Uariputra, who passed them on. The Abhidhamma is thus presented as a pure and undiluted form of the teaching that was too difficult for most practitioners of the Buddha's time to grasp. Instead, the Buddha taught by the method related in the various suttas, giving appropriate, immediately applicable teachings as each situation arose, rather than attempting to set forth the Abhidhamma in all its complexity and completeness. Thus, there is a similarity between the traditions of the Adhidhamma and that of the Mahayana, which also claimed to be too difficult for the people living in the Buddha's time.

Theravada Abhidhamma

The Abhidhamma Pimaka is the third pimaka, or basket, of the Tipimaka (Sanskrit: Tripimaka), the canon of the Theravada school of Buddhism. It consists of the seven sections as described below.

1. Dhamma Saegani ('Enumeration of Factors')-Describes the fundamental phenomena or *dhamma* which constitute human experience.
2. Vibhaga ('Analysis')-An analysis of various topics by a variety of methods, including catechism using material from the Dhamma Sangani.
3. Dhatu Katha ('Discussion of Elements')-Some interrelations between various items from the first two books, formulated as sets of questions and answers.
4. Puggala Pannatti ('Descriptions of Individuals')-An enumeration of the qualities of certain different 'personality types'. These types were believed to be useful in formulating teachings that an individual would respond to positively.
5. Kathavatthu ('Points of Controversy')-A collection of debates on points of doctrine, traditionally said to have

been compiled by Moggaliputta Tissa at the Buddhist Council sponsored by King Ashoka, which took place in the 3rd Century BCE.

6. Yamaka ('The Pairs')-Deals with various questions relating to interrelations within various lists of items; here the items belong to the same list, whereas in the Dhatu Katha they are in different lists.
7. Patthana ('Foundational Conditions' *or* 'Relations')-The laws of interaction by which the *dhamma* described in the Dhamma Sangani operate.

These have all been published in romanized Pali by the Pali Text Society, and most have been translated into English as well. Some scholars date these works from about 400 BCE to about 250 BCE, the first being the oldest and the fifth the latest of the seven. Additional post-canonical texts composed in the following centuries attempted to further clarify the analysis presented in the Abhidhamma texts. The best known such texts are the Visuddhimagga of Buddhaghosa and the Abhidhammavatara of Buddhadatta.

Early Western translators of the Pali canon found the Abhidhamma Pitaka the least interesting of the three sections of the Tipimaka, and as a result this important aspect of Buddhist philosophy was little studied in the West until the latter half of the 20th Century. Caroline Rhys Davids, a Pali scholar and the wife of Pali Text Society founder T. W. Rhys Davids, famously described the ten chapters of the Yamaka as "ten valleys of dry bones". Interest in the Abhidhamma has grown in the West as better scholarship on Buddhist philosophy has gradually revealed more information about its origins and significance. Within the Theravada tradition, the prominence of the Abhidhamma has varied considerably from country to country, with Burma (Myanmar) placing the most emphasis on the study of the Abhidhamma.

Sarvastivada Abhidharma

The Sarvastivada Abhidharma also consists of seven texts. However, comparison of the content of the Sarvastivada texts with that of the Theravada Abhidhamma reveals that it is unlikely that this indicates that one textual tradition originated from the other. In particular, the Theravada Abhidharma contains two texts (the *Katha Vatthu* and *Puggala Pannatti*) that seem entirely out of place in an Abhidharma collection.

The texts of the Sarvastivadin Abhidharma are:

- Sangitiparyaya ('Discourses on Gathering Together')
- Dharmaskandha ('Aggregation of Dharmas')
- Prajnaptiuastra ('Treatise on Designations')
- Dhatukaya ('Body of Elements')
- Vijnanakaya ('Body of Consciousness')
- Prakaranapada ('Exposition')
- Jnanaprasthana ('Foundation of Knowledge').

AGGANNA SUTTA

Agganna Sutta is the 27th Sutta of Digha Nikaya collections. The sutta describes a discourse imparted from the Buddha to two Brahmins, Bharadvaja and Vasettha, who left their family and caste to become monks. The two brahmins are insulted and maligned by their own caste for their intention to become member of Sangha. Buddha firstly explains that the caste system has originated from the Truth (Dhamma). Caste and lineage can not be compared to the achievement of morality practice and the Dhamma, as anyone from four castes can become monk and reached the state of Arahant. Then, he explains about the beginning of the Earth, and the birth of social order and its structure, including the castes. The Buddha emphasizes the message of universality in Dhamma and how Dhamma is the best of all things.

The Beginning

The Sutta begins when the Buddha is staying in Savatthi, in the temple donated by Visakkha, the Mother of Migara. At that time, two brahmins, Bharadvaja and Vasettha are training with the Monks (bhikkhu) and aim to be a member of Sangha. As usual in the evening, the Buddha raises from his meditation and strolls in the open yard nearby his dwelling. Vasettha sees his Teacher strolling, and he tells his friend, Bharadvaja, and suggests to meet Buddha; see if they can hear a Dhamma exposition from the Buddha. They both approach the Buddha and after some formal properieties, the Buddha asks the two if they received insults and denigration when they left their caste and layman's life in order to join the order of Sangha. Vasettha and Bharadvaja answer that they did receive a 'flood of insults'. They say that the other Brahmins maintain that the Brahmin caste is the best, as the Brahmins are of high status and authority, pure-bred, have radiant complexion, born from the mouth of God Brahma, unlike the other lower castes. So, by the opinion of the other Brahmins, how can Vasettha and Bharadvaja leave this good caste and status, thus join together with fraud ascetics with shaven head from other castes, lower in status as they are born from the feet of Brahma.

To this remark, Buddha tell them that the Brahmins have indeed forgotten about their past if they said such things. The fact is that the women in Brahmin caste can get pregnant, give birth, and take care of their children. But the Brahmins still speak that they are born from the Mouth of God Brahma and other (castes) are born from Brahma's feet. Thus the Brahmin's words are untrue. Buddha speaks that the Brahmins are not speaking truthfully and they will reap a bad result from their own deeds.

The Buddha then elaborates that if any of the caste does the following deeds: killing, taking anything which is not given, do sexual misconduct, lying, slandering, speaking rough words or nonsense, greedy, cruel, and practise wrong beliefs (miccha ditthi); people would still see that they do negative deeds and therefore doesn't worthy of respect. They even will get trouble from their own deeds, whatever their caste (Brahmin, Khattiya, Vessa, and Sudda) might be.

While those who refrain themselves from: killing, taking anything which is not given, do sexual misconduct, lying, slandering, speaking rough words or nonsense, greedy, cruel, and practised wrong beliefs (miccha ditthi); will be seen by people as positive and will earn respect from the people and the wise ones. They would be profiting from their deeds, no matter what their caste might be.

Logically, as the four castes can do either the negative (demerit) or positive (merit) deeds, so will the wise reject the statement that only the Brahmins is the best of caste. Why? Because anyone from the four castes; if they left the worldly affairs and become a monk, and due to their discipline and struggle, they become arahant, people who conquered their mind's stains, has done whatever it must be done, has relieved themselves from burden, has broken the bondage of birth, achieved freedom, freed due to achieved knowledge, then he is the best among others based on Truth (Dhamma).

The Buddha quoted, "Dhamma is the best thing for people In this life and the next as well."

Further, Buddha proves that Dhamma is indeed the best thing of all things in life. He took an example of King Pasenadi of Kosala Kingdom, who has now conquered the Sakyans. The Sakyans rever, praise, and serve him with respect.

But, towards the Buddha, who came from Sakyan people, King Pasenadi reveres, praises, and serves the Buddha with utmost respect. Even the monarch thinks like this: "The Samana Gautama had perfect birth, while I am not perfect.

The Samana Gautama is mighty, while I am weak. The Samana Gautama inspired awe and respect, while I do not. The Samana Gautama is vastly influential and charming, while I only possess small influence." As even the King respects Dhamma, revers Dhamma, obeys Dhamma, therefore he bows and praises the [Tathagatha].

The Buddha then advises Vasettha that whoever has strong, deep rooted, and established belief in the Tathagatha, he can declare that he is the child of Bhagava, born from the mouth of Dhamma, created from Dhamma, and the heir of Dhamma. Because the titles of the Tathagatha are: The Body of Dhamma, The Body of Brahma, the Manifestation of Dhamma, and the Manifestation of Brahma.

The Beginning of Life on Earth

In the second part of the Sutta, Buddha tells the story of how the human beings came to dwell on Earth. The Buddha told that sooner of later, after a very long time, there would be a time when the world shrink. As the universe shrinks, many of its inhabitants would die. Of these deceased creatures, some were born again (due to good karma) in the Heavenly realm of Abbhasara (Lucid Light). There, they floated for a very-very long time, as a bodiless, radiating extreme light. They don't eat or drink, as they nourish themselves from pure spiritual joy.

Then, after some very long time, when the World began to expand again, many of this Abbhasara creatures were born to these newly formed Earth. They floated above and around the Earth. At this time, there were not yet seen the Moon and the Sun, there were not yet Night and Day, there were not yet names and identity or female or male. The creatures were only known for creatures.

At that period, Vasettha, there was just one mass of water, and all was darkness, blinding darkness.... And sooner or later, after a very long period of time, savory earth spread itself over the waters where those beings were. It looked just like the skin that forms itself over hot milk as it cools. It was endowed with colour, smell, and taste. It was the colour of fine ghee or butter and it was very sweet, like pure wild honey.

Some of the creatures of light (the Abbhasaras) who had curiosity and greedy nature began to dive and tasted the savory Earth's substance. At that moment, the creature found out that it tasted so delicious. Thus, greed started to seep in and it ate the substance voraciously, greedily, thus calling also its comrades (who were flying above and on earth) to join in the feast. Not long afterwards, the creatures began to eat so greedily and due to the huge amount of the mud substance, they could feed on it for a very long time.

As they ate and ate, their luminous body began to be coated by the mud substance, formed a coarser body, then suddenly, the sun and moon were seen, so did the stars, and also Night and Day began on Earth. The logical explanation of this was that the creatures were the self-luminating, so blinding and luminating that they didn't notice the Sun. The Earth was covered in their light. So, when the materialization took place, the light faded inside their newly conceived 'body' of mud and thus the night and day became apparent to them. Then, as the night and day became apparent, season and years also appeared.

Their body was still coarse and roughly shaped. Thus, after a very long time, the mud-like substance began to exhaust. Then, mushroom-like plants began to grow so fast that it replaced the mud-like ocean. The creatures began to devour them as well, and they found it also so delicious as sweet honey and milk. Their body hardened more and details began to turn finer.

After another very long time, the mushrooms also began to exhaust, replaced by cassava or turnip-class plants. They also began to devour it night and day, and thus they began to notice differences amongst them. As the changes of their body varies one another, concept of difference arised. The beautiful and the ugly concept was born. The beautiful scorns the ugly and they became arrogant of their appearance.

Then, after the turnips, the earth were grown with rice-plants. The first rice plants were without husk and kernels. The sweet and honey-like rice flourished seeds abundantly. The people consumed them for a very long time. But there are people who became greedy and lazy. They took more rice than they needed for one day's meals. They began to take two, four, eight, and sixteen days' of rice reserves as they were too lazy to take rice everyday. Owing to this, many other creatures began to store and hoard the rice. The generation time rice plants became slower and slower. Usually, it took only one night for the plant to grow and ready to be consumed, but by the karmic power, the plant began to grow slower and slower. Also the rice grew in kernel and husks, scattered, of which the creatures must work, nurse, maintain, harvest, and cook them to obtain the white rice.

By this time, the body of the creatures had been finely evolved. There were already distinction of male and female. The man became preoccupied with women and vice versa. Then, as they were deeply attracted to one another, passion and desire aroused, and they enganged in sexual relationship. The people who saw a couple doing sexual activity scold them, and usually the couple were forbidden of entering the village for a certain period of time. Owing to this, the indulgent couple built closed dwellings where they indulged in sexual activity.

The Birth of Social Order and Castes

In the third part, the Buddha explained about the origin of Castes, their titles, and their order in the society system which were still rigidly effective in Buddha's time.

The Khattiya Caste (Rulers)

The rice plants, as mentioned earlier, began to grow in separate plot and people began to divide lands and tend each other's cluster of rice fief. They became preoccupied in tending their own field. Then, as the evil and greed aroused, there were people who begin stealing others' crops. At first, the others only warn the culprit and the culprit promise that he will never repeat it again. But when it does repeat several times, the people begin punishing him with fist, stones, and then sticks. That is the origin of punishment forms. Then, people begin to think that they are too busy to heed every crime and abuse happen in their society. They grieved on the rising of evil amongst their people. But most of their time had already been invested in tending their fief. So, they appointed someone to rectify what is right and what is wrong, give warnings to those who need it, give punishment to those who deserve it, and in return, they will give him share of their rice. So, they went to the fairest, ablest, most likeable, and most intelligent person and appointed him to do the judging and passing out sentences on the reward of a share of rice. The appointed person thus agreed and the people bestowed upon him the title : 'Maha-Sammata' meaning: The People's Choice. Then, they bestowed also the second title: 'Khattiya' meaning the 'Lord of the Rice

Field', and finally the third title: 'Raja' which means 'Who gladdens people with Dhamma (or Truth)'. This order was created by the people's wish and need, based on the Dhamma and not from others. The Buddha stated again that Dhamma is indeed the best of all things.

The Brahmin Caste

Then, amongst the people, some of them begin to think like this: "Evil deeds have risen amongst us, like :theft, lies, murders, sexual abuses, punishment, and banishment. Now let us set aside evil, unuseful, and impolite things." The word Brahmins came, as it meant: "They who put aside Evil and unwholesome things" (1). They set up retreats and huts in the forests and meditated there. They come to the city at morning and evening only to gather food and after finished gathering food, they return to their huts and meditations. People notice this and 'Those who meditated' were called 'Jhayanti' or 'Jhayaka'.

There are other people, who can't meditate or dwell in huts in the forest. So, they settled in the cities, not meditate, but compile books. The people called them 'Ajjhayaka' which meant 'They who don't meditate'. At first the Ajjhayaka is viewed lower than Jhayaka but in the Buddha's time, the Ajjhayaka has been viewed higher in status than the Jhayakas.

The Vessa (Traders) and the Suddha (Hunters)

Among the people who had settled and had family, some began to adopt various trade. From the word 'Various' comes the 'Vessa' or the merchant caste. The remainder of these people preferred the work of hunting. The Sudda caste come from the word 'Sudda' which means: 'They Are Base Who Live By The Chase'. All of the castes, from Brahmin, Khattiya, Vessa, and Suddha were originated from these people, and not from others; in accordance to the Dhamma and not by others.

The Ascetics

But from the four clans, there were people who were not satisfied with their living, left their home and became celibate ascetics. These are the origin of the fifth caste formed from all the four castes' people who left their lay life and became an ascetic.

Buddha's Conclusion

The Buddha then concluded his discourse to Vasettha and Bharadvaja: (Due to the governance of Dhamma which became the root of all castes and people,) Anyone, from any the caste, did demerit and wrong doings, live a bad life of speech, thoughts, views, and wrong doings, they would end up after the death, in the realm of sufferings, hell, loss, and torture.

But anyone, from any caste, did merit and good deeds, live a good life of speech, thoughts, and deeds; have the right view, after their death, they would end in realm of happiness and heaven.

Anyone, from any caste, did both merit and demerit, live a good and bad life of speech, thoughts, and deeds; have either right or bad view, after their death, they could end in the realm of suffering or the realm of joy.

Anyone, from any caste, who lived a life of disciplined deeds, speeches, thoughts, who had trained and developed himself in the seven factors of Enlightenment, then he would attain the eradication from the of mind in this current life.

Anyone, from four castes, who became a bhikku (Monk), arahant, People who had eradicated stains of Mind, had done what must be done, had relieved himself from burden, who had attained freedom, who had broken the bondage of birth, who had been freed due to knowledge; then they would be declared as the best from all of them, in accordance to the Truth (Dhamma) and not from the basis of not Truth (adhamma).

The Buddha quoted, "Dhamma is the best thing for people In this life and the next as well."

The Buddha quoted the verses of Brahma Sandakumara: *"The Khattiya is the best among those who maintain their lineage;* He with knowledge and conduct is best of gods and men." then, the Buddha asserted that the verse is indeed true, according to the Dhamma, profitable, and true. *The Khattiya's best among those who value clan;* He with knowledge and conduct is best of gods and men." Thus the discourse ended with Vasettha and Bharadvaja rejoiced in hearing the words of Buddha.

Digging Deeper on the Sutta

While the story of the world's beginning is considered a myth, on the other hand, the Buddhist doctrine requires a constant sceptical approach, where one must see and prove it before one believes it (ehipassiko). However, the profound insight of the Buddha in two major fields: science (cosmology) and social structure's origin indeed was revolutionary on his era.

On the science part, Buddha implied the theory of the Evolution of Universe, where it is said to shrink and then expand in repeated cycles.

While on the social science part, the Buddha's words implied on the equality of origin in human race, whether by their sex, appearance, or by another categories which founded later based on physiological differences. Buddha also emphasized that the social structure is formed voluntarily, based on righteousness and necessity, not based on Divine Forces as some theories stated.

The Monarchy is also formed voluntarily, and the people elect the most righteous and capable person, which implied the Democracy concept. The Monarch accept 'share of rice' as his reward to rectify the social order, which is the origin of voluntary reward which evolves into taxation concept. However, the Buddha states that the Monarch is regarded worthy not of his divine right but due to his righteousness in deeds. The Buddha's message was clear, however, that the best thing in the world is Truth (Dhamma) and everything is created, measured, and valued based on Truth and not from other.

MAUDGALYAYANA

Maudgalyayana also known as Mahamaudgalyayana or Mahamoggallana, was one of the Buddha Shakyamuni's closest disciples. A contemporary of famous arhats such as Subhuti, Sariputra, and Mahakasyapa, he is considered the second of the two foremost disciples of the Buddha, together with Sariputta.

Moggallana was most accomplished of all the Buddha's disciples in the various supernatural powers. These abilities included being able to use mind-reading for such things as detecting lies from truths, transporting himself from his body into the various realms of existence, speaking with ghosts and gods. He was also able to do things like walking through walls, walking on water, flying through the air, and moving with a speed comparable to the speed of light.

Varying accounts in the Pali Canon show Maudgalyayana speaking with the deceased in order to explain to them their horrific conditions and give them an understanding of their own suffering, so that they may be released from it or come to terms with it. Moggallana was able to use his powers of mind-reading in order to give good and fitting advice to his students, so they could attain results quickly.

Death: The Arhat's Karma

Maudgalyayana's demise came when he was travelling in Magadha. Some accounts put forth that religious cultists stoned him to death, others say it was robbers. The general consensus is that he was killed in a brutal fashion. When asked why Maudgalyayana had not protected himself, and why a great arhat would suffer such a death, the Buddha said that because Maugalyayana had contracted such karma in a previous life (he had murdered his innocent parents in a previous life), he had resigned himself to accept his fate and expedite such a death, that it would be done with as soon as possible. Further, the Buddha stated that even supernatural powers will be of little or no use to oneself in avoiding their karma, especially when it is so heavy.

Maha Moggallana Thera

The second of the Chief Disciples of the Buddha. He was born in Kolitagama near Rajagaha, on the same day as Sariputta (they were both older than the Buddha), and was called Kolita after his village. His mother was a brahminee called Moggali (Moggallani), and his father was the chief, householder of the village. Moggallana's and Sariputta's families had maintained an unbroken friendship for seven generations, and so the children were friends from their childhood. Sariputta had five hundred golden palanquins and Moggallana five hundred carriages drawn by thoroughbreds. One day the two friends went together to see a mime play (giraggasamajja), and there, realizing the impermanence of things, decided to renounce the world. They first lived as disciples of Sanjaya, and then wandered all over Jambudipa, discussing with all learned men, but finding no satisfaction. Then they separated, after agreeing that whoever first succeeded in finding what they sought should inform the other.

Sariputta and Mahamoggallana

After some time, Sariputta, wandering about in Rajagaha, met Assaji, was converted by him to the faith of the Buddha, and became a sotapanna. He found Moggallana and repeated the stanza he had heard from Assaji (ye dhamma hetuppabhava, etc.), and Moggallana also became a sotapanna. The two then resolved to visit the Buddha at Veluvana, after an unsuccessful attempt to persuade Sanjaya to accompany them. Sanjaya's disciples, however, five hundred in number, agreed to go, and they all arrived at Veluvana. The Buddha preached to them, and ordained them by the "ehi bhikkhu pabbajja." All became arahants except Sariputta and Moggallana. Moggallana went to the hamlet of Kallavala in Magadha, and there, on the seventh day after his ordination, drowsiness overcame him as he sat meditating. The Buddha knew this, and appearing before him, exhorted him to be zealous. That very day he attained arahantship.

On the day that Sariputta and Moggallana were ordained, the Buddha announced in the assembly of monks that he had assigned to them the place of Chief Disciples and then recited the Patimokkha. The monks were offended that newcomers should be shown such great honour. But the Buddha told them how these two had for a whole asankheyya and one hundred thousand years strenuously exerted themselves to win this great eminence under him. They had made the first resolve in the time of Anomadassi Buddha. Moggallana had been a householder, named Sirivaddha, and Sariputta a householder, called Sarada. Sarada gave away his immense wealth and became an ascetic. The Buddha visited him in his hermitage, where Sarada and his seventy four thousand pupils showed him great honour. Anomadassi's chief disciple, Nisabha, gave thanks, and Sarada made a vow that he would become the chief disciple of some future Buddha. Anomadassi saw that his wish would be fulfilled and told him so.

After the Buddha's departure, Sarada went to Sirivaddka, and, announcing the Buddha's prophecy, advised Sirivaddha to wish for the place of second disciple. Acting on this advice, Sirivaddha made elaborate preparations and entertained the Buddha and his monks for seven days. At the end of that time, he announced his wish to the Buddha, who declared that it would be fulfilled. From that time, the two friends, in that and subsequent births, engaged in good deeds.

Sariputta and Moggallana are declared to be the ideal disciples, whose example others should try to follow. In the Saccavibhanga Sutta the Buddha thus distinguishes these "twin brethren" from the others: "Sariputta is as she who brings forth and Moggallana is as the nurse of what is brought forth; Sariputta trains in the fruits of conversion, Moggallana trains in the highest good. Sariputta is able to teach and make plain the four Noble Truths; Moggallana, on the other hand, teaches by his iddhi-patihariya." Moggallana's pre eminence lay in his possession of iddhi power. He could create a living shape innumerable times and could transfer himself into any shape at will. Thag.vs.1183; he is recorded as saying that he could crush Sineru like a kidney bean, and, rolling the earth like a mat between his fingers, could make it rotate like a potter's wheel, or could place the earth on Sineru like an umbrella on its stand. When the Buddha and his monks failed to get alms in Veranja, Moggallana offered to turn the earth upside down, so that the essence of the earth, which lay on the under surface, might serve as food. He also offered to open a way from Nalerupu-cimanda to Uttarakuru, that the monks might easily go there for alms; but this offer was refused by the Buddha.

Several instances are given of this special display of iddhi. Once, at the Buddha's request, with his great toe he shook the Migaramatupasada, and made it rattle in order to terrify some monks who sat in the ground floor of the building, talking loosely and frivolously, regardless even of the fact that the Buddha was in the upper storey.

On another occasion, when Moggallana visited Sakka to find out if he had profited by the Buddha's teaching, he found him far too proud and obsessed by the thought of his own splendour. He thereupon shook Sakka's palace, Vejayanta, till Sakka's hair stood on end with fright and his pride was humbled. Again, Moggallana is mentioned as visiting the Brahma world in order to help the Buddha in quelling the arrogance of Baka Brahma. He himself questioned Baka in solemn conclave in the Sudhamma-Hall in the Brahma world and made him confess his conviction that his earlier views were erroneous. Thag.vs.1198; Thaga.ii.185; S. i.144f. ; other visits of his to the Brahma world are also recorded when he held converse with Tissa Brahma.

In the Maratajjaniya Sutta we are told how Mara worried Moggallana by entering into his belly, but Moggallana ordered him out and told him how he himself had once been a Mara named Dusi whose sister Kali was the mother of the present Mara. Dusi incited the householders against Kakusandha Buddha and was, as a result, born in purgatory.

But, according to the Commentaries, Moggallana's greatest exhibition of iddhi power was the subjugation of the Naga Nandopananda. No other monk could have survived the ordeal because no other was able to enter so rapidly into the fourth jhana; which was the reason why the Buddha would give permission to no other monk but Moggallana to quell the Naga's pride. Similar, in many ways, was his subjection of the Naga who lived near the hermitage of Aggidatta. Moggallana could see, without entering into any special state of mind, petas and other spirits invisible to the ordinary mortal eye. He would visit various worlds and bring back to the Buddha reports of their inhabitants, which the Buddha used in illustration of his sermons. The Vimanavatthu contains a collection of stories of such visits, and we are told that Moggallana's visits to the deva worlds-e.g., that to Tavatimsa were very welcome to the devas.

Though Moggallana's pre eminence was in iddhi power, yet in wisdom, too, he was second only to Sariputta. These two could answer questions within the range of no other disciple of the Buddha. The Buddha paid a compliment to Moggallana's powers of preaching, when, having preached himself to the Sakyans in their new Mote Hall at Kapilavatthu, he asked Moggallana, after their departure, to talk to the monks, as he himself was weary. And Moggallana spoke to them of lusts and of the means of getting rid of them. At the end of the sermon the Buddha praised him warmly. Mention is made elsewhere of eloquent sermons preached by him on the jhanas, on qualities which lead to true emancipation, and of visits paid to him by Sakka in company with numerous other gods in order to hear him preach. Other devas also went to hear him-e.g., Candana, Suyama, Santusita, Sunimitta and Vasavatti. He was also consulted by those, such as Vacchagotta, and Vappa, eager to learn from him the teachings of the Buddha. When the Buddha went to preach the Abhidhamma in Tavatimsa, it was to Moggallana that he entrusted the task of preaching to the people who were waiting for his return. Moggallana, therefore, provided for these people spiritually, while Anathapindika looked after their bodily needs. When the time drew near for the Buddha's return, Moggallana, at the request of the people, went to Tavatimsa, diving into the earth and climbing Sineru, in full view of them all, in order to find out what the Buddha intended doing, so that the people might be kept informed. No task, which he might be told by the Buddha to perform, seemed to Moggallana too insignificant. Thus we find him employed by the Buddha as messenger to the arahant Uggasena, telling him that the Buddha wished to see him. He was also sent to

Sakkhara, to Macchariya Kosiya, to check his miserliness and bring him to Jetavana; and to Silava, whom Ajatasattu was plotting to kill. When Visakha was building the Migaramatupasada and the Buddha was away on one of his journeys, Moggallana, because of his iddhi power, and five hundred monks were left to supervise the work, which was carried through without difficulty. The Buddha placed great faith in his two chief disciples and looked to them to keep the Order pure. There is one instance recorded of Moggallana seizing a wicked monk, thrusting outside and bolting the door. Once, when a monk charged Sariputta with having offended him as he was about to start on a journey, Moggallana and Ananda went from lodging to lodging to summon the monks that they might hear Sariputta vindicate himself.

Their fame had reached even to the Brahma world, for we find Tudu Brahma singing their praises, much to the annoyance of the Kokalika monk. When Devadatta created a schism among the monks and took five hundred of them to Gayasisa, the Buddha sent Sariputta and Moggallana to bring them back. They were successful in this mission. Kakudha Koliyaputta, once servant of Moggallana and later born in a huge manomayakaya, had warned Moggallana of Devadatta's intrigues against the Buddha, but the Buddha ignored this information carried to him by Moggallana. When Rahula, the Buddha's son, was ordained, Sariputta was his preceptor and Moggallana his teacher. Moggallana seems to have carried out diligently the charge laid on him by the Buddha of looking after the monks' welfare. Among the verses, attributed to him in the Theragatha, are several containing exhortations to his colleagues; some of the colleagues are mentioned by name-e.g., Tissa, Vaddhamana and Potthila. Elsewhere mention is made of his living at Kalasila, with a company of five hundred monks, watching over them and discovering that all were arahants. Vangisa witnessed this and praised Moggallana in verse before the Buddha.

The love existing between Moggallana and Sariputta was mutual, as was the admiration. Sariputta's verses in praise of

Moggallana are even more eloquent than those of Moggallana in praise of Sariputta. Their strongest bond was the love of each for the Buddha; when away from him, they would relate to each other how they had been conversing with him by means of the divine ear and the divine eye. E.g., S.ii.275ff.; Moggallana elsewhere also tells the monks of a conversation he held with the Buddha by means of these divine powers. For another discussion between Sariputta and Moggallana.

In the Mahagosinga Sutta we find them staying in the Gosingasalavana in the company of Maha Kassapa, Ananda, Revata and Anuruddha, engaged in friendly discussion, referring their conclusions to the Buddha for his opinion. Sariputta, Moggallana, and Anuruddha are again mentioned as staying in the Ketakivana in Saketa. Among discussions between Anuruddha and Moggallana is recorded one in which Anuruddha speaks of the value of cultivating the four satipatthanas. It seems to have been usual for Sariputta and Moggallana, in their journeys, to travel together at the head of the monks, and lay disciples, who gave alms to the monks, were anxious to include them in their invitations. Velukandaki in Dakkhinagiri; and Cittagahapati in Macchikasanda.

Moggallana died before the Buddha, Sariputta dying before either. The Theragatha contains several verses attributed to Moggallana regarding Sariputta's death. Sariputta died on the full moon day of Kattika and Moggallana two weeks later, on the new moon day.

According to the Commentaries his death resulted from a plot of the Niganthas. Moggallana used to visit various worlds and return with his report that he had discovered that those who followed the Buddha's teaching reached happy worlds, while the followers of the heretics were reborn in woeful conditions. These statements diminished the number of the heretics and they bribed brigands to kill Moggallana. They surrounded the Elder's cell in Kalasila, but he, aware of their intentions, escaped through the keyhole. On six successive days this happened; on the seventh, they caught him and beat him, crushing his bones and leaving him for dead. Having recovered consciousness, with a great effort of will, he dragged himself to the Buddha in order to take his leave, and there he died, to the sorrow of the deva worlds. This sad death is said to have been the result of a sin committed by him in a previous birth. Acting on the instigation of his wife, he had taken his blind parents into a forest, where, pretending that they were attacked by thieves, he had beaten them to death. For this deed he suffered in hell for innumerable years, and in his last birth lost his life by violence.

Moggallana in the Mahayana Sutras

The *Ullambana Sutra* is the main Mahayana Sutra in which Maudgalyayana is mentioned. The sutra covers the topic of filial piety, and was a discourse given to Maudgalyayana by the Sakyamuni Buddha. Of particular popularity in Japan, Ullambana is the foundation for Obon, which has striking similarities to Confucian and Neo-Confucian ideals in that it deals with ancestor worship. It is for this reason that Ullambana is often subject to criticism, and has often been called inauthentic because its Confucian leanings are often at odds with other Buddhist teachings.

5

Buddhist Temples in Japan

PROVINCIAL TEMPLE

Emperor Shomu of Japan established provincial temples in each province of Japan. Todaiji, the provincial temple of Yamato Province, served as the head of all these kokubunji and Hokkeji held that duty for the kokubun niji.

The words "kokubunji" and "kokubun niji" gave rise to many place names that continue to today, including:

- Kokubunji, Kagawa
- Kokubunji, Tokyo
- Kokubunji, Tochigi.

SENSO-JI

Senso-ji is an ancient Buddhist temple located in Asakusa, Taito, Tokyo. It is Tokyo's oldest temple, and one of its most significant. Formerly associated with the Tendai sect, it became independent after World War II. Adjacent to the temple is a Shinto shrine, the Asakusa Jinja.

Senso-ji is the focus of Tokyo's largest and most popular *matsuri* (Shinto festival). This takes place over 3–4 days in late spring, and sees the surrounding streets closed to traffic from dawn until late evening.

Dominating the entrance to the temple is the *kaminari-mon* or "Thunder Gate". This imposing Buddhist structure features a massive paper lantern dramatically painted in vivid red-and-black tones to suggest thunderclouds and lightning. Within the precincts stand a stately five-story pagoda and the main hall, devoted to Kannon Bosatsu.

Many tourists, both Japanese and from abroad, visit Senso-ji every year. Catering to the visiting crowds, the surrounding area has many traditional shops and eating places that feature traditional dishes (hand-made noodles, sushi, tempura, etc.). Nakamise-dori, the street leading from the Thunder Gate to the temple itself, is lined with small shops selling souvenirs ranging from fans, *ukiyo-e* (woodblock prints), kimono and other robes, Buddhist scrolls, traditional sweets, to Godzilla toys, t-shirts, and cell-phone trinkets.

These shops themselves are part of a living tradition of selling to pilgrims who walked to Senso-ji. Within the temple is a quiet contemplative garden kept in the distinctive Japanese style.

History

The temple is dedicated to the bodhisattva Kannon. According to legend, a statue of the Kannon was found in the Sumida River in 628 by two fishermen, the brothers Hinokuma Hamanari and Hinokuma Takenari. The chief of their village, Hajino Nakamoto, recognized the sanctity of the statue and inshrined the statue by remaking his own house into a small temple in Asakusa so that the villagers could worship the Kannon.

The blessings of the Kannon gradually received a high reputation throughout Japan, and people near and far flocked to Asakusa to venerate the statue.

SHITENNO-JI

Shitenno-ji is a Buddhist temple in Osaka, Japan.

The prince Shotoku constructed this temple in 593, using the construction firm Kongo Gumi. It is the oldest officially administered temple in Japan, although the temple buildings have been rebuilt over the centuries. It is also home to a major flea market on the 21st of each month.

Access to Shitennoji is via a 10 minute walk from Tennoji station, on the JR, Midosuji and Tannimachi train lines.

SOJI-JI

Soji-ji is one of two main temples of the Soto sect of Zen Buddhism. The temple was originally founded in 740 in Noto, but was totally destroyed by fire in 1898. It was rebuilt over a period of several years and reopened in its present location at Tsurumi, Yokohama in 1911.

Zenshuji Soto Mission is a direct branch of Soji-ji, located in North America.

TAISEKI-JI

Taiseki-ji is the head temple of the Nichiren Shoshu school of the Nichiren branch of Japanese Buddhism. It is located on the lower slopes of Mt. Fuji in Fujinomiya, Shizuoka Prefecture, Japan.

Taiseki-ji was founded in 1290 CE by Nikko, one of Nichiren's immediate disciples. In addition to being Nichiren Shoshu's head temple, Taiseki-ji is the school's administrative Centre, and its chief abbot is simultaneously the high priest of Nichiren Shoshu. The temple is visited by several hundred thousand pilgrims a year, and its compound is known for several historically significant buildings, its gardens, and the old weeping cherry trees that line its *tatchu* (main path lined with lodging temples).

Taiseki-ji today

In addition to being Nichiren Shoshu's head temple, Taiseki-ji is also its administrative Centre, and the high priest of Nichiren Shoshu doubles as the temple's chief abbot. The temple's and school's current head is High Priest Nichinyo Hayase (1935–).

High Priest Nichinyo assumed the position on December 16, 2005, and is the 68th in a lineage Nichiren Shoshu traces back to Nichiren (1222–1282). He is commonly styled 68th High Priest Nichinyo Shonin in English.

Because it is the head temple of Nichiren Shoshu and therefore home of the Dai-Gohonzon, Nichiren Shoshu's ultimate object of veneration, Taiseki-ji is visited by believers from all around the world who come on personal pilgrimages, to participate in regular ceremonies, or to take part in large events such as temple-group pilgrimages, workshop-like study programs, and large rally-like meetings.

Regular ceremonies and Events

- First gongyo of the year (from 2:30AM on January 1)
- New Year's pilgrimage (January 1–4)
- Koshi-e (Memorial services for and commemoration of 2nd High Priest Nikko, February 6–7)
- Nichiren's birthday (February 16)
- Spring *Higan-e* (March 20 or 21)
- Airing of the Treasures ceremony (April 6–7)
- Summer study workshops (June–July)
- *Urabon-e* (August 15)
- Gonan-e (Commemoration of the Tatsunokuchi Persecution, September 12)
- Kanshi-e (Memorial services for and commemoration of 26th High Priest Nichikan, September 18–19)
- Autumn *Higan-e* (September 23)
- Ushi-e (Memorial services for and commemoration of 9th High Priest Nichiu, September 29)
- Mokushi-e (Memorial services for and commemoration of 3rd High Priest Nichimoku, November 14–15)
- Nichiren Daishonin Gotai-e (often called *Oeshiki*; memorial services for and commemoration of the life and teachings of Nichiren Daishonin, November 20–21).

Events in bold are positioned as the two most important ceremonies of the year.

History

Founding and Early Period

According to Nichiren Shoshu tradition, Taiseki-ji was founded in 1290 by Nichiren's disciple Nikko on a tract of land called Oishi-ga-hara donated by the district steward, Nanjo Tokimitsu (1259–1332).

The name derives from an alternate reading of the kanji for Oishi, which means temple. Tokimitsu was one of Nichiren's lay followers and he looked up to Nikko as his personal teacher. It started with one small temple building but grew gradually as Nikko's disciples built sub-temples. It went through further growth phases during the mid-Edo period and in the post-World War II period.

Edo Period

Meiji and Showa Periods to WWII

Prominent High Priests

- Ninth High Priest Nichiu
- Twenty-sixth High Priest Nichikan
- Fifty-ninth High Priest Nichiko (the last high priest to support celibacy for Buddhist monks)
- Sixty-sixth High Priest Nittatsu
- Sixty-seventh High Priest Nikken.

Buildings

Sanmon Gate

The Sanmon gate is Taiseki-ji's "front door" and has been designated as a prefectural cultural asset. It was built in 1717 with donations from Tenneiin, the wife of sixth Shogun Tokugawa Ienobu.

Mutsubo

The first Mutsubo was erected in 1290, making this historically Taiseki-ji's first building. Has has been rebuilt many times since. The current structure, which uses much keyaki heartwood, was completed in 1988.

Reception Hall

The *Daikyakuden* was first built in 1465. The current structure, a wood-clad steel-framed structure, was completed in 1998 and replaced previous steel reinforced concrete building built in 1964.. A pre-war building, which had been requisitioned by the military, burnt down in a June 1945 fire that claimed the life of 62nd High Priest Nikkyo.

The Grand Reception Hall is the site of *ushitora Gongyo*, a prayer service performed daily at the transition from the "hour of the ox (*ushi*)" to the "hour of the tiger (*tora*)". The service begins at about 2:30AM and ends about an hour later. This is believed to mark the transition from "darkness" to "light" as well as the hour at which all Buddhas attain enlightenment. The service is customarily officiated by the high priest or his proxy. During the service, the officiating priest sits at the front of the room, to the left of and facing the congregation of priests and laity gathered in front of the altar. This signifies that he is "guiding" the congregation to the Gohonzon so they can achieve enlightenment. The purpose of the service is, among other things, to pray for the spread of Nichiren Shoshu throughout the world and thereby bring about peace and prosperity for all humankind.

Mieido

The original Mieido was built in 1522. The Mieido houses an image of Nichiren (hence its name) dating from 1388. The current, classical structure was built in 1632 and has had several subsequent renovations, the most recent major one in 1971. It was designated a cultural asset by Shizuoka Prefecture in 1971.

Hoando

The Hoando houses the Dai-Gohonzon, the supreme object of veneration in Nichiren Shoshu.

The Hoando is built in the style of a traditional Japanese storehouse to signify that *kosen rufu* has yet to be achieved. Loosely defined, kosen rufu means that the Nichiren Shoshu faith has taken hold as the primary religion of the world's people, a situation believed to have be achieved when about one-third of a population believes in Nichiren Shoshu, another third knows of it but is not hostile, and the remaining third is ignorant of it to some degree or another. This is significant to the Nichiren Shoshu faithful because they believe that, according to Nichiren's will, the Dai-Gohonzon is not to be made publicly accessible, but rather "stored away" and only viewed by those who have asked for and been granted an audience by the high priest, until kosen rufu has been achieved. A further symbol of this is that, different from all other Nichiren Shoshu altars, the one in the Hoando is not decorated with an offering of evergreens, and non-believers are permitted in the building only on special occasions. The Hoando replaced the Shohondo, the Dai-Gohonzon's previous home. Before the Shohondo was completed in 1972, the Dai-Gohonzon had been kept locked away in a storehouse called the Treasure House or enshrined in the Hoanden, another storehouse-like structure built behind the Treasure House.

Treasure House

Pagoda

Completed in 1749, Taiseki-ji's pagoda faces west rather than the usual south to signify that Nichiren Buddhism would spread from the east (Japan) to the west (back to the land of Sakyamuni Buddha and beyond). It is the largest five-storied pagoda along the Tokaido Highway. The structure was designated a national cultural treasure in 1966. It is opened every February 16 for ceremonies to celebrate Nichiren's birthday.

TODAI-JI

Todai-ji, the Eastern Great Temple, is a Buddhist temple in Nara, Japan. Reputedly the largest wooden building in the world, it houses a giant statue of the Buddha Vairocana (Jp. *Dainichi*; it means 'Buddha that shines throughout the world like the sun'), known in Japanese simply as the Daibutsu ('YIN, "great Buddha"). The temple also serves as the Japanese headquarters of the Kegon school of Buddhism. Sika Deer, themselves officially protected as National Treasures and regarded as messengers of the gods by Shinto, roam the grounds freely and are not afraid of humans.

History

During the Tempyo period, people suffered from disasters and epidemics. In 743, Emperor Shomu issued a law which stated that the people should make a Buddha to protect themselves. He believed Buddha's power could help the people. 420,000 people contributed and 2,180,000 people worked to build it. The Great Buddha itself was designed by Kuninaka-no-muraji Kimimaro whose grandfather was an immigrant from the Korean Baekje Kingdom. Under his direction the 53 foot high statue was cast in forty-odd stages, the head and neck being cast together as a separate shell 12 feet high. According to legend, nearly 2,600,000 in total helped construct the Buddha at that time; this number equates to nearly the half of the people in Japan at that time and is probably exaggerated. The temple was established in 745 and the Buddha was completed in 751, having consumed most of Japan's bronze production for several years and leaving the country almost bankrupt. The statue has been recast several times since for various reasons including earthquake damage, and the temple rebuilt twice after fire. The current hands of the statue were made in the Momoyama Period (1568-1615), and the head was made in the Edo Period (1615-1867). The current building finished in 1709 although immense is actually 30% smaller than its predecessor. The original complex also contained two 100 m pagodas, probably the tallest buildings in the world at the time behind the pyramids. These were destroyed by earthquake.

Todai-ji was the provincial temple of Yamato Province and the head of all the provincial temples. The Shosoin was its storehouse, and now contains many artifacts from the Tempyo period of Japanese history. On May 20, 1994, the international music festival *The Great Music Experience* was held at Todai-ji, supported by the UNESCO. Among other artists were the Tokyo New Philharmonic Orchestra, X Japan, INXS, Bon Jovi, Bob Dylan, Tomoyasu Hotei, Roger Taylor, classic Japanese drummers, and a Buddhist monk choir. The event was broadcast on May 22 and May 23, 1994, in 55 countries all over the world.

The size of the Buddha

- Height : 14.98 meters
- Face : 5.33 meters
- Eyes : 1.02 meters
- Nose : 0.5 meters
- Ears : 2.54 meters
- Weight : 500 metric tonnes.

Trivia

- One of the supporting posts in the Great Buddha Hall has a hole that has been bored through the base. Visitors try to pass through the hole which is said to be the same size as one of the Daibutsu's nostrils. Legend has it that those who pass through it will be blessed with enlightenment in their next life. Children usually have no trouble getting through but adults sometimes get stuck and need to be pulled out.

ZENKO-JI

Zenko-ji is a 7th century Buddhist temple in Nagano, Japan. The city, established in 1897, was once a town built around the temple. Zenko-ji is perhaps most famous for its involvement in the battles between Uesugi Kenshin and Takeda Shingen in the 16th century, when it served as one of Kenshin's bases of operations.

Zenko-ji belongs to both the Tendai and Jodo Shu schools of Buddhism, and is co-managed by 25 priests from the former School and 14 from the latter. It enshrines images of the Amida Buddha, the primary one of which is a*hibutsu*, a hidden Buddha, which is not normally shown to the public. This *hibutsu* is rumored to be the first Buddha statue to ever be brought to Japan. There is also a passage under the temple where worshippers, in complete darkness, try to touch a key hanging on the wall in order to gain enlightenment. The key represents the Key to the Western Paradise of the Amida Buddha. The hidden Buddha statue, or *hibutsu*, is shown once every six or seven years, and attracts many worshippers. The last time it was on display, in 2003, Zenko-ji joined with Motozenko-ji and the Zenko-ji of Kofu, Yamanashi Prefecture, in discussions. The *hibutsu* will be on display next in 2010.

History

Zenko-ji was originally built during the reign of Emperor Kimmei, in the 6th century, but was moved several times before coming to its present location. The current site, in what was then Motozen village, was originally called Motozenkoji. At the end of the Kamakura period (1185-1333), many temples copied Zenko-ji's famous Buddha statue, and many new temples were built around the country calling themselves 'Zenko-ji' or 'Shin-Zenko-ji' (New Zenko-ji). In the Sengoku period, when Zenko-ji became involved in the struggles between Uesugi Kenshin and Takeda Shingen, the chief abbot was afraid it would be burnt to the ground. He built a new Zenko-ji in what is now Kofu, Yamanashi Prefecture, which still stands. In 1598, Toyotomi Hideyoshi moved the *hibutsu* to Kyoto, and then to Shinano. The *hibutsu* and the Zenkoji temple itself have since been moved once more back to Nagano.

ZENPUKU-JI

Zenpuku-ji, also known as Azabu-san, is a Jodo Shinshu temple located in the Azabu district of Tokyo, Japan. Founded by Kukai in 824, Zenpuku-ji was originally a Shingon temple. Shinran visited the temple during the Kamakura period and brought the temple into the Jodo Shinshu sect.

Under the 1859 Treaty of Amity and Commerce, the first Tokyo legation of the United States of America was established at Zenpuku-ji under Consul-General Townsend Harris. Fukuzawa Yukichi, the founder of Keio University, is buried at the temple, and Keio staff visit the temple on February 3 of each year (the anniversary of his death).

RYOAN-JI

Ryoan-ji is a Zen temple located in northwest Kyoto, Japan. Belonging to the Myoshinji school of the Rinzai branch of Zen Buddhism, the temple is one of the *Historic Monuments of Ancient Kyoto*, a UNESCO World Heritage Site.

The site of the temple was originally a Fujiwara family estate.

To many, the temple's name is synonymous with the temple's famous *karesansui* (dry landscape) rock garden, thought to have been built in the late 1400s. The garden consists of raked gravel and fifteen moss-covered boulders, which are placed so that, when looking at the garden from any angle (other than from above) only fourteen of the boulders are visible at one time. It is traditionally said that only through attaining enlightenment would one be able to view the fifteenth boulder.

In an article published by the science journal Nature, Gert J. Van Tonder and Michael J. Lyons analyse the rock garden by generating a model of shape analysis (medial axis transformation) in early visual processing.

Using this model, they show that the empty space of the garden is implicitly structured, and is aligned with the temple's architecture. According to the researchers, one critical axis of symmetry passes close to the centre of the main hall, which is the traditionally preferred viewing point. In essence, viewing the placement of the stones from a sightline along this point brings a shape from nature (a dichotomously branched tree with a mean branch length decreasing monotonically from the trunk to the tertiary level) in relief.

The researchers propose that the implicit structure of the garden is designed to appeal to the viewers unconscious visual sensitivity to axial-symmetry skeletons of stimulus shapes. In support of their findings, they found that imposing a random perturbation of the locations of individual rock features destroyed the special characteristics.

SAIHO-JI

Saiho-ji is a Rinzai Zen Buddhist temple located in Matsuo, Nishikyo Ward, Kyoto, Japan. The temple, which is famed for its moss garden, is commonly referred to as "Koke-dera", meaning "moss temple", and is also known as "Koinzan Saiho-ji". The temple, primarily constructed to honour Amitabha, was first founded by Gyoki, and was later restored by Muso Soseki. In 1994, Saiho-ji was registered as a UNESCO World Heritage Site, as part of the "Historic Monuments of Ancient Kyoto".

History

According to temple legend, Saiho-ji was constructed during the Nara Period by Gyoki, on the location of one of Prince Shotoku's former retreats. The temple first operated as a Hosso temple dedicated to Amitabha, and was known as "Saiho-ji", a homophone of the current name. The name was selected because Amitabha is the primary Buddha of Western Paradise, known in Japanese as "Saiho Gokuraku Jodo". Legend states that such famous Japanese monks as Kukai and Honen later served as the chief priests of the temple. Although the veracity of these legends is questionable, it is believed that such a predecessor to the current temple did, in fact, exist.

Over time, the temple fell into disrepair, and in 1339, the chief priest of the nearby Matsunoo Shrine, Fujiwara Chikahide, summoned the famous Japanese gardener Muso Soseki to help him revive Saiho-ji as a Zen temple. At this time, Muso decided to change the temple's name, to reflect its new Zen orientation. The temple became "Saiho-ji", the name being selected not only because it was a homophone of the original name, but also because the kanji were used in phrases related to Bodhidharma: "the coming of Bodhidharma from the West" and "Bodhidharma's teachings shall spread and come to bear fruit like a five-petaled flower". Saiho-ji was destroyed by fire during the Onin War, and twice ravaged by floods during the Edo Period, but has since been rebuilt.

Ironically, the moss for which the temple is known was not part of Muso's original design. According to French historian François Berthier, the garden's "islands" were "carpeted with white sand" in the fourteenth century. The moss came much later, of its own accord during the Meiji era (1860-1912), when the monastery lacked sufficient funds for upkeep.

Layout

The famous moss garden of Saiho-ji, is situated in the eastern temple grounds. Located in a grove, the garden is arranged as a circular promenade, centred around Golden Pond. The pond is shaped like the Chinese character for "heart" or "mind" and contains three small islands: Asahi Island, Yuhi Island and Kiri Island. The area around the pond is said to be covered with more than 120 varieties of moss, believed to have started growing after the flooding of the temple grounds in the Edo Period.

The garden itself contains three tea houses: Shonan-tei, Shoan-do, and Tanhoku-tei, which were partially inspired by phrases from the Chan work *Biyan Lu*.

- Shonan-tei was originally built during the 14th century, but was subsequently destroyed. It was later restored by Sen no Shoan. Iwakura Tomomi was famously sheltered here towards the end of the Edo Period. Shonan-tei is registered as an important cultural property.
- Shoan-do was constructed in 1920, and contains a wooden image of Sen no Shoan, after whom the teahouse was named.
- Tanhoku-tei was donated to the temple in 1928 by potter Zoroku Mashimizu.

The eastern temple grounds also contains the main temple hall, the study, and a three-storied pagoda.

- The main hall of the temple, known as Sairai-do, was reconstructed in 1969, and it was in this year that the current image of Amitabha was enshrined. The paintings on the sliding doors are the work of Insho Domoto.

- The three-storied pagoda was erected in 1978, and is used to store copies of sutras, written by Rinzai adherents. The pagoda was constructed to honour Bhaisajyaguru.

The northern temple grounds contains a Zen rock garden, and a temple hall known as Shito-an. The arrangement of stones in the rock garden is said to be demonstrative of Muso's creative genius. The gardens of Saiho-ji are collectively considered to be both a historical landmark and a "special place of scenic beauty" in Japan.

Other significant items within the temple grounds include a stone monument engraved with a Kyoshi Takahama haiku, and another stone monument, engraved with some of the writings of Jiro Osaragi. A portrait of Muso Soseki is considered to be an important cultural property.

Tourism

Until 1977, the temple was open to admission by the general public, but currently, visitors are admitted only by prior application (by return postcard), and the fee to visit the temple (¥3,000) is the highest in Kyoto. Before being permitted access to the garden, visitors must engage in up to two hours of zazen and the hand-copying or chanting of sutras. It is said that these regulations were put into place in order to protect the delicate moss from the hordes of tourists that plagued the temple prior to 1977.

SANJUSANGEN-DO

Sanjusangendo is a Buddhist temple in Higashiyama District of Kyoto, Japan. Officially known as "*Rengeo-in*", Sanjusangendo belongs to and is run by the Myoho-in temple, a part of the Tendai school of Buddhism. The temple name literally means *Hall with thirty three spaces between columns,* describing the architecture of the long main hall of the temple.

History

Taira no Kiyomori completed the temple under order of Emperor Go-Shirakawa in 1164. The temple complex suffered a fire in 1249 and only the main hall was rebuilt in 1266. In January, the temple has an event known as the *Rite of the Willow*, where worshippers are touched on the head with a sacred willow branch to cure and prevent headaches. A popular archery tornumant known as Toshiya is also held here on the same since the Edo period.

Important Features

The main deity of the temple is *Sahasrabhuja-arya-avalokiteshvara* or the Thousand Armed Kannon, the statue of the main deity was created by the Kamakura sculptor Tankei and is a National Treasure of Japan.

On both right and left sides of the main statue stand in 10 rows and 50 columns, 1000 statues of the Thousand Armed Kannon, of these 124 statues from the original temple were rescued from the fire of 1249, while the remaining 876 were constructed in the 13th century.

The statues are made of Japanese cypress. Around these statues stand 28 statues of guardian deities. There are also two famous statues of Fujin and Raijin.

TENRYU-JI

Tenryu-ji —more formally known as Tenryu Shiseizen-ji— is the head temple of the Tenryu sect of Rinzai Zen Buddhism, located in Susukinobaba-cho, Ukyo Ward, Kyoto, Japan. The temple was founded by Ashikaga Takauji, primarily to venerate Gautama Buddha, and its first chief priest was Muso Soseki. As a temple related to both the Ashikaga family and Emperor Godaigo, the temple is held in high esteem, and is ranked as the most important (Rinzai) Zen temple in Kyoto. In 1994, it was registered as a UNESCO World Heritage Site, as part of the "Historic Monuments of Ancient Kyoto".

History

In the early Heian Period, Empress Tachibana no Kachiko, wife of Emperor Saga, founded a temple called Danrin-ji on the site of present-day Tenryu-ji. The temple fell into disrepair over the next four hundred years, before, in the mid-thirteenth century, Emperor Gosaga and his son Emperor Kameyama turned the area into an imperial villa they christened "Kameyama Detached Palace". The name "Kameyama", which literally means "turtle mountain", was selected due to the shape of Mt. Ogura, which lies to the west of Tenryu-ji—it is said to be similar to the shape of a turtle's shell. All Japanese temples constructed after the Nara period have a sango, a mountain name used as an honorary prefix. Tenryu-ji's sango, Reigizan, was also selected due to the shape of Mt. Ogura.

The palace was converted into a temple at the behest of Ashikaga Takauji, who wished to use the temple to hold a memorial service for Emperor Go-daigo. Ashikaga became the shogun in 1338, and Go-daigo died in Yoshino the following year. Ashikaga opposed the failed Kemmu Restoration, which was started by Emperor Go-daigo, and the emperor decreed that Ashikaga should be hunted down and executed.

When his former-friend-turned-enemy passed away, Ashikaga recommended that Zen monk Muso Soseki construct a temple for his memorial service. It is said that the temple was originally going to be named Ryakuo Shiseizen-ji, Ryakuo being the name of the reign of the emperor of the northern court at that time. However, Ashikaga Takauji's younger brother, Tadayoshi supposedly had a dream about a golden dragon flitting about the Oi River (also known as the Hozu River), which lies south of the temple, and the temple was instead named Tenryu Shiseizen-ji—the term "Tenryu" literally means "dragon of the sky". In order to raise the funds to build the temple, a trading vessel called "Tenryujisen" was constructed and set asail. A ceremony was held on the seventh anniversary of Emperor Go-Daigo's death in 1345, which functioned as both a celebration of the completion of the temple, and as Go-daigo's memorial.

The temple prospered as the most important Rinzai temple in Kyoto, and the temple grounds grew to roughly 330,000 square meters in size, extending all the way to present-day Katabira-no-Tsuji station on the Keifuku Railway. At one time, the massive grounds were said to contain some 150 sub-temples, however, the temple was plagued with numerous fires, and all of the original buildings have been destroyed. During the middle ages, the temple met with fire six times: in 1358, 1367, 1373, 1380, 1447 and 1467. The temple was destroyed again during the Onin War and subsequently rebuilt, but in 1815 it was lost to yet another fire. The temple was severely damaged during the Hamaguri Rebellion in 1864, and most of the buildings as we see them today are reconstructions from the latter half of the Meiji period. The garden to the west of the abbey, created by Muso Soseki, shows only traces of its original design.

The tombs of Emperors Gosaga and Kageyama lie within the temple grounds.

Layout

On the eastern boundary of the temple grounds lie two gates: Chokushi Gate and Middle Gate, from which the path to the temple itself leads west. Generally, Zen temple grounds are designed so that they face the south, with major buildings aligned along the north-south axis. Tenryu-ji's layout is an exception to this principle. Sub-temples line both sides of the path, which leads to the lecture hall. There are numerous buildings behind the lecture hall, such as large abbey, the small abbey the kitchen, the meditation hall, and Taho-den hall, however, each of these is modern reconstruction.

- Chokushi gate is a one-storey gate, constructed in yotsuashimon style. It is the oldest structure on the temple grounds and is representative of the style of the Momoyama Period.
- The teaching hall is located at the Centre of the temple grounds, which is unusual for a Zen temple. The extant version is a 1900 reconstruction. It contains an image of Gautama Buddha, flanked by two guardians. The

decorative painting of a dragon on the ceiling called Unryu-zu is the work of Suzuki Shonen.

- Ohojo was constructed in 1899.
- Kohojo constructed in 1924.
- Taho-den was constructed in 1934. Although it is a modern building, it was constructed in Kamakura Period style. It contains a wooden image of Emperor Go-Daigo.

Cultural Properties

The "important cultural properties" of Tenryu-ji include:

- Three portraits of Muso Soseki, and paintings of Avalokitesvara and Seiryo Hogen Zenji/Yunmen Daishi
- The wooden carving of Gautama Buddha.
- Various illustrations and writings in the document archive, such as Shanaingoryo-ezu, Okoshokyokanji-no-ezu, Oeikinmyo-ezu, Toryoeiyo-bakuseki, and various writings of Kitabatake Chikafusa
- The garden, created by Muso Soseki, features a circular promenade around Sogen Pond, and is registered as both a special place of scenic beauty and a historical landmark.

TEMPLES AND SHRINES IN KYOTO

Kyoto, Japan is world-renowned for its ancient and beautiful temples and shrines. It is arguably the cultural Centre of Japan, and its holiest city. Many of the most famous, most sacred, or most historically significant temples and shrines in Japan are in Kyoto. In addition, many of these temples and shrines are included in the UNESCO category of "Historic Monuments of Ancient Kyoto (Kyoto, Uji and Otsu Cities)" as World Heritage Sites.

FUSHIMI INARI-TAISHA

Fushimi Inari Taisha is a shinto jinja (shrine) dedicated to the spirit Inari, located in Fushimi-ku, Kyoto, Japan.

It is especially well known for the thousands of vermilion torii lining the paths on the hill on which the shrine is located. The torii gates are all donations from individuals, families or companies. The Inari spirit is considered to be the protector of grains, especially rice, and has thus historically been associated with wealth. Company officials often make offerings to Inari shrines in the form of barrels of rice wine (sake) or torii gates. Torii gates are wood and are replaced about every ten years.

At the bottom of the hill is the Go-Honden Shrine and the Sakura-mon gate. After following the torii-lined hiking paths, a visitor can stop at various food stalls that specialize in Kitsune udon, a popular noodle dish named after foxes (kitsune) which are regarded as the messengers of Inari, the shinto deity of harvest.

Statues of kitsune are often found depicted in Inari shrines with a key (for the rice granary) in their mouths. At the top of the hill is the main shrine. Unlike most Shinto shrines, Fushimi Inari Taisha – in keeping with typical Inari shrines – has an open view of the main idol object (a mirror).

In addition to the more famous torii-lined walking paths going from the "front" of the shrine area, walking paths from the rear do exist. They go through a bamboo forest that offers a far different experience than the main route. The paths start/emerge near the sports fields belonging to Ritsumeikan High School.

The easiest way to get to Fushimi Inari shrine is to take the train. Japan Railway Inari Station (about 5 min. from Kyoto Station on the Nara Line, cost ¥150) is directly across the street from the Sakura-mon gate. The next closest station is Keihan Fushimi-Inari station.

It is considered one of the most beautiful spots in Kyoto and one of the symbols of Japan. A drawing in Kiyoshi Nozaki's book *Kitsune: Japan's Fox of Mystery, Romance and Humour* depicts the shrine in 1786 and says that its two-story entry gate was built by warlord Toyotomi Hideyoshi (1536-1598). The shrine draws several million visitors over the New Year holiday.

HONGAN-JI

Hongan-ji is the name of a number of Buddhist temples across Japan's history. However, it refers primarily to a pair of temples, which were once one, in Kyoto.

History

The Hongan-ji was established as a temple in 1321, on the site of the Otani Mausoleum, where Shinran, the founder of the Jodo Shinshu (True Pure Land) sect was buried. Kakunyo became the first chief priest of the Hongan-ji, and dedicated it to the worship of Amida Buddha. The Hongan-ji first gained power and importance in the 15th century, when Rennyo became its eighth chief priest. However, the Tendai sect, based on Mount Hiei, saw this expansion as a threat and attacked the Hongan-ji three times with their army of warrior monks. Rennyo fled to Yoshizaki, where he founded the Ikko sect.

During the Sengoku period, fearing the power of the monks of the Hongan-ji, Oda Nobunaga tried to destroy it. For ten years, he laid siege to the Ishiyama Hongan-ji in Osaka, one of the two primary temple fortresses of the Ikko sect. In 1602, just after Tokugawa Ieyasu became Shogun, he declared that the Hongan-ji be split in two. Kyonyo, the 12th chief priest of Hongan-ji became the first of the Higashi Honganji (or, 'The Eastern Temple of the Original Vow'), while Junyo became chief priest of the Nishi Honganji (or, 'The Western Temple of the Original Vow').

During the Meiji Restoration in the 1860s, the government set down new guidelines for the management of religious organizations. An organization called Shinshu Otani was put in control of the Higashi Hongan-ji.

In 1987, the temple was renamed "Shinshu Honbyo", or New Buddhist Mausoleum, and its purpose was reverted back to that of a mausoleum. While the temple is therefore, officially, no longer "Higashi Hongan-ji," most still regard it as such. The buildings have not been changed or moved, and of course the historical cultural and religious significance of the place cannot be changed. In 1996, a new Higashi Hongan-ji was established in the Higashiyama (Eastern Mountain) area of Kyoto by Otani Kohrin, the 25th head priest.

Nishi Hongan-ji

The Nishi Hongan-ji, like the Higashi Hongan-ji, features a huge Goei-do0, founder's hall and a smaller Amida-do0, or Buddha hall, housing an image of the Amida Buddha. The Nishi Hongan-ji's *Kura*, or storehouse, houses many National Treasures, most of which are not on view for the public. The *shoin*, or study hall, is also quite famous; it is split into two sections, the *shiroshoin*, or white study hall, and the *kuroshoin*, or black study hall. The Kuroshoin is never opened to the public, but the Shiroshoin opens twice a month.

Nishi Hongan-ji also contains Hiunkaku, a large tea pavilion, and two noh stages, one of which claims to be the oldest in existence, and the Kokei no Niwa gardens.

Higashi Hongan-ji

The massive Goei-do (founders' hall) Gate of Higashi Hongan-ji is often one of the first things one sees walking north from JR Kyoto Station. Nearly identical to Nishi Hongan-ji in layout, it too features an Amida-do, and a larger Goei-do. The Goei-do at Higashi Hongan-ji dates from 1895 and vies with a number of other structures for the claim of largest wooden building in the world.

A few blocks from the main grounds of the Higashi Hongan-ji is the Shosei-en garden, owned by the temple. Poet-scholar Ishikawa Jozan and landscape architect Kobori Enshu are said to have contributed to its design in the 17th century.

Other Temples of the Name

- Tsukiji Hongan-ji, Tokyo
- Ishiyama Hongan-ji, destroyed 1580, now the site of Osaka Castle
- Yamashina Hongan-ji.

KITANO TENMAN-GU

Kitano Tenman-gu is a Shinto shrine in Kyoto, dedicated to Tenjin-san, the *kami* of scholarship. It was built in 942, to appease the angry spirit of scholar and poet Sugawara no Michizane, who had been exiled as a result of political maneuvers of his enemies in the Fujiwara clan. The shrine was dedicated to him, and in 986, he was deified and conferred the title of Tenjin (Heavenly Deity).

The grounds are filled with Sugawara's favourite tree, the *ume*, and during the blooming season of the plum blossoms the shrine is often very crowded. Kitano-tenmangu is popular with students praying for success in exams. On the 25th of every month, the shrine plays host to a flea market, similar to that of To-ji temple. A Kyoto proverb proclaims, "Fair weather at Toji market means rainy weather at Tenjin market," calling to mind Kyoto's fickle weather.

KIYOMIZU-DERA

Kiyomizu-dera refers to several Buddhist temples but most commonly to *Otowa-san Kiyomizu-dera* in Eastern Kyoto, and one of the best known sights of the city. The temple dates back to 798, but the present buildings were constructed in 1633. The temple takes its name from the waterfall within the complex, which runs off the nearby hills-*kiyoi mizu* literally means *pure water*.

The main hall of Kiyomizu-dera is notable for its vast veranda, supported by hundreds of pillars, which juts out over the hillside and offers impressive views of the city. The expression "to jump off the stage at Kiyomizu" is the Japanese equivalent of the English expression "to take the plunge". This refers to an Edo period tradition that held that, if one were to survive jumping from the stage, one's wish would be granted.

This appears plausible: the lush vegetation below the platform might cushion the fall of a lucky pilgrim, though the practice is now prohibited. 234 jumps were recorded in Edo period and of those, 85.4 percent survived. The fall is indeed only 13 metres, which remains impressive for a wooden construction. Beneath the main hall is the waterfall *Otowa-no-taki*, where three channels of water drop into a pond. Visitors to the temple collect the water, which is believed to have therapeutic properties, from the waterfall in metal cups. It is said that drinking the water of the three streams confers health, longevity, and success in studies.

The temple complex contains several other shrines, notably *Jishu-jinja*, decidated to *Okuninushino-Mikoto*, a god of love and "good matches". *Jishu-jinja* possesses a pair of "love stones" placed 18 metres apart, which lonely visitors attempt to walk between with their eyes closed. Success in reaching the other stone, eyes closed, is taken as a presage that the pilgrim will find love. One can be assisted in the crossing, but this is taken to mean that an intermediary will be needed. The person's romantic interest can assist them as well.

The complex also includes all the fixtures of a popular temple, being one of the most-visited attractions of the city: hawkers offering various talismans, incense, and*o-mikuji* (paper fortunes ranging from "great fortune" to "great ill") abound. Indeed the high popularity of the place means that tourists will find it difficult to take pictures on the main temple's platform.

KOZAN-JI

Kozan-ji is an Omuro Buddhist temple located in Ume-gahata Toganoo-cho, Ukyo Ward, Kyoto, Japan. The temple was founded by famous monk Myoe and is renowned for its numerous national treasures and important cultural properties, in particular a picture scroll called Chojujinbutsu-giga. The temple celebrates Biyakkoshin, Zenmyoshin and Kasuga Myoshin, as well as the temple's tutelary Shinto deity. In 1994, it was registered as part of the UNESCO World Heritage Site "Historic Monuments of Ancient Kyoto".

History

Togano, located deep in the mountains behind Jingo-ji temple, which are famous for their autumn foliage, is considered an ideal location for mountain asceticism, and there have long been many small temples in this location. In addition to Kozan-ji, there have been other temples in the area, such as Toganoo-ji and Toganoo-bo. According to legend, these were said to have been established by the imperial orders of Emperor Konin in 774, however, the accuracy of these claims is not clear.

In 1206, Myoe, a Kegon Buddhist priest who had been serving at nearby Jingo-ji, was granted the land to construct a temple by Emperor Go-Toba. He selected the name Hidesakishokozan-no-tera. The temple's name was taken from a line in the Avatamsaka sutra: "When the sun appears, it first casts its light upon the highest mountain."

The temple was destroyed numerous times by fire and war. The oldest extant building is Sekisui-in, which dates from the Kamakura Period.

Layout

Jingo-ji houses a diagram of Kozan-ji that was drawn in 1230, some 20 years after it was constructed. The diagram is registered as an important cultural property, because it shows the original layout of the temple. From the diagram, we know that Kozan-ji originally consisted of a large gate, a main hall, a three-storied pagoda, a hall dedicated to Amitabha, a hall dedicated to Lohan, a bell tower, a scripture hall, and a Shinto shrine dedicated to the tutelary deity of the area. However, all of these buildings have since been destroyed, save for the scripture hall, which is now known as Sekisui-in.

In addition to Sekisui-in, today's Kozan-ji also contains a main hall (originally part of Ninna-ji, relocated to Kozan-ji) and a hall dedicated to the founding of the temple, which houses an important carved wooden bust of Myoe. Both of these buildings, however, are modern reconstructions.

Cultural Properties

The temple possesses numerous national treasures and important cultural properties, however, the majority of them are currently on loan to national museums in Kyoto and Tokyo.

National Treasures

- Sekisui-in-Built in the Kamakura Period. Irimoyazukuri style, having a gabled, hipped, shingled roof.
- Chojujinbutsu-giga-a four-piece scroll, drawn entirely in India ink. Unlike most Japanese picture scrolls, there are no words written on the scroll; it consists solely of pictures. The first, most famous scroll contains images of anthropomorphized animals, such as rabbits, frogs and monkeys. This humorous scroll is said to show the roots of Japan's manga culture. The second scroll contains accurate portrayals of real-life animals. The third scroll consists of two parts: images of humans playing various games in the first part, and caricatures of animals in the second. The final scroll is a crudely-drawn caricature of man. The first and second scrolls have been dated to the late Heian-period, and the third and fourth scrolls have been dated to the Kamakura period. The original scroll is currently entrusted to the Tokyo National Museum. The copy on display at Kozan-ji is a reproduction.
- Kegon-shu Soshi Eden-created in the Kamakura period, this picture scroll portrays the lives of Korean Kegon founders Uisang and Wonhyo.
- Yupian-a Tang period copy of a Chinese dictionary created during the Liang Dynasty. This is the oldest Chinese character dictionary in Japan.
- Tenrei Bansho Meigi-valued as the only remaining copy of an old kanji dictionary compiled by Kukai. It was copied in 1114.
- Myoho-ki-A Tang period collection of Buddhist tales. Now disappeared from China, this is the only known copy in existence.

Important Cultural Properties

An incredible number of buildings, picture scrolls, carvings, furnishings and old writings have been registered as important cultural properties. The most significant among these include:

- A lacquered wooden statue of Bhaisajyaguru in seated posture created towards the end of the Nara period. Originally the Centre of a *sanzonzo* (a trio of Buddhist statues with the primary image in the Centre and flanked by two attendants), the attendant images were removed during the Meiji period. The image of Suryaprabha now rests in the Tokyo National Museum, and the image of the Chandraprabha in the university museum of the Tokyo National University of Fine Arts and Music.
- A wooden statue of Myoe in sitting posture created in the Kamakura Period and located in the hall dedicated to the founding of the temple.
- A pair of wooden deer statues created in the Kamakura period. These statues, of a buck and a doe, were uniquely constructed to look like *komainu*, the lion statues that guard the entrance to a Shinto shrine. Deer are messengers of Kasuga Myojin, the temple god, and as such, it is believed that these statues were placed in front of Kasuga Myojin's altar.
- A statue of Biyakkoshin in standing posture, constructed in the early Kamakura period. As the name indicates, the statue is painted white in its entirety—from its clothes to the pedestal. This is said to represent the snow of the Himalayas.
- The Kozan-ji document archive, which contains thousands of scriptures and records, some of which date back to the Heian Period.
- Koben Yume-no-Ki-a record of Myoe's dreams from 1196 to 1223. His dreams are said to have exerted a great deal of influence on his religious thinking.

TO-JI

"To-ji" is a Buddhist temple of the Shingon sect in Kyoto, Japan. Its name means East Temple, and it once had a partner, Saiji (West Temple). They stood alongside the Rashomon, the gate to the Heian capital. It is also known as, which indicates that it previously functioned as a temple providing protection for the nation. To-ji is located in Minami-ku near the intersection of Omiya Street and Kujo Street, southwest of Kyoto Station. Although often associated with the famous priest Kobo Daishi (Kukai), To-ji was established in 796 A.D., two years after the capital moved to Heian-kyo. Kukai was put in charge of To-ji in 823 A.D. by order of Emperor Saga. Its principal image is of Yakushi Nyorai, the healing Buddha.

The pagoda of To-ji stands 57 m high, and is the tallest wooden tower in Japan. It dates from the Edo period, when it was rebuilt by order of the third Tokugawa Shogun, Iemitsu. The pagoda has been, and continues to be, a symbol of Kyoto. Entrance into the pagoda itself is permitted only a few days a year.

The buildings at Toji temple house a variety of ancient Buddhist sculpture. The grounds feature a garden and pond, in which turtles and koi swim. The grounds also house an academically rigorous private school, Rakunan, from which many students are sent to elite universities.

Recognizing the historical and spiritual significance of To-ji, UNESCO designated it, along with several other treasures in Kyoto Prefecture, as part of the "Historic Monuments of Ancient Kyoto" World Heritage Site.

On the 21st of each month, a famous flea market is held on the To-ji temple grounds. This market is popularly called Kobo-san, in honour of Kobo Daishi, who died on March 21st. The flea market feautures a variety of antiques, art, clothes, pottery, some food, and typical second-hand flea market goods. By far the largest market is held on December 21st, as it is the last of the year.

A similar market is held on the 25th of every month at Kitano Tenmangu, also called Tenjin. A Kyoto proverb proclaims, "Fair weather at Toji market means rainy weather at Tenjin market," calling to mind Kyoto's fickle weather.

A smaller, less-crowded, antique-oriented market is held at the To-ji grounds on the first Sunday of each month.

TEMPLES AND SHRINES IN HIROSHIMA

Hiroshima Gokoku Jinja is a Japanese Shinto Shrine in Hiroshima, Japan.

Overview

The original shrine was founded in 1868, the first year of the Meiji period, in Futabanosato Hiroshima. The shrine was established to mourn the Hiroshima-Han victims of the Boshin War.

In 1934 it was dismantled and moved to where the Hiroshima Municipal Stadium now stands, and in 1939 its name was changed to the Hiroshima Gokoku Shrine.

In 1945 it was destroyed by the atomic bombing, and was rebuilt within the Hiroshima Castle in 1965 with the aid of donations from the citizens of Hiroshima.

The Hiroshima Gokoku Shrine is one of the most popular places for celebrating Hatsumode and Shichi-Go-San in Hiroshima.

MITAKI-DERA

Mitaki-dera is a historic Japanese temple in the city of Hiroshima, Japan.

Overview

Mitaki-dera was founded in the year 809 during the Daido era.

Mitaki-dera is familiar with the name of "Mitaki-Kannon".

There are three falls, and the water will be used as an offering of water to the victims of the atomic bomb during the Hiroshima Peace Memorial Ceremony.

The Taho-to was dismantled from Hiro-Hachiman-jinja in Hirogawa, Wakayama in 1951, to hold a memorial service for the victims of the atomic bomb.

There is the wooden seated statue of Amida Nyorai in the Taho-to.

Mitaki-dera is famous for sakura, autumn leaves and maples.

Mitaki-dera is the 13th of Chugoku 33 Kannon Pilgrimage.

ANTAI-JI

Antai-ji is a Buddhist temple that belongs to the Soto Zen school. It is located in northern Hyogo prefecture, Japan, where it sits on about 50 hectares of land in the mountains, close to a national park on the sea of Japan. It accepts visitors in the summer months, but is inaccessible during the winter.

Kyoto

Antai-ji was founded in 1923 by Oka Sotan as a monastery for scholars to study the Shobogenzo. At that time it was located in northern Kyoto, and many leading scholars studied there. Vacated during the second world war, in 1949 Sawaki Kodo (1880-1965) and Kosho Uchiyama (1912-1998) moved into Antaiji and made it a place for the pure and simple practice of sitting Zazen. During the late sixties, the name of this small temple became known both in Japan and abroad for its practice of Zazen and formal begging.

Northern Hyogo

The increase of visitors and the many new houses being built around the temple created much noise, which made it difficult for the practice of Zazen to continue at the Kyoto location.

Therefore the following abbot, Watanabe Koho (1942), decided to move Antaiji to its present location in northern Hyogo. Together with the quietude of the mountains, he was looking for a new life style that would bring Zen back to self sufficiency. The former abbot Miyaura Shinyu (1948-2002) protected this quiet life of Zazen while putting the ideal of a self sufficient monastery into practice, until his sudden death in the snow in February of 2002. His disciple, the German monk Muho Noelke (1968-), continues as the present abbot.

CHIONIN TEMPLE

Chionin Temple is the headquarters of the Jodo Shu (Pure Land Sect) founded by Honen (1133-1212), who proclaimed that sentient beings are reborn in Amida Buddha's Western Paradise (Pure Land) by reciting the nembutsu, Amida Buddha's name.

The vast compounds of Chion-in include the site where Honen settled to disseminate his teachings and the site where he died.

History

The original temple was built in 1234 by Honen's disciple, Genchi (1183-1238) in memory of his master and was named Chion-in. Numerous buildings in the complex were burnt down in 1633, but were entirely rebuilt by the third Tokugawa Shogun Iemitsu (1604-51) these are the palatial structures that stand today.

Architecture

The colossal main gate, San-mon Gate, was built in 1619 and is the largest surviving structure of its kind in Japan. Chion-in has a large and small guest houses in the Irimoya roof style called Ohojo and Kohojo that are designated Important Cultural Heritages. Both guest houses were built in 1641.

There are two interesting features to note about Chion-in. First, the roof beams are all carved with the family crest of the Tokugawa family: three hollyhock leaves.

Another feature is the umbrella found stashed in the rafters outside the main temple. One of the architects who helped rebuild the temple placed the umbrella in the rafters to help bring rain (and thereby ward off fire).

Lastly, an interesting feature inside the temple are the very squeaky boards. The wooden boards where built with metal ends that would rub against the metal joints they were attached too, created a piercing noise as people step on them. This was intentionally done so that when the Tokugawa family stayed at the temple, they could detect unwanted intruders at night.

DAITOKU-JI

Daitoku-ji is a Rinzai Buddhist temple located in Kyoto, Japan. The temple complex has the mountain-name *Ryuho-zan*, literally meaning "dragon treasure mountain." It was established in 1319 by *Shuhomyocho* who is also called *Daito Kokushi*. Daitoku-ji was frequented by Emperor Go-Daigo and was counted as one of the five sacred mountains (temples).

But after the Ashikaga shogunate was established, it was removed from the list and the shogunate chose to ignore it in favour of other temples that had not openly opposed them. It then decided to stay away from meddling in politics and to focus on Buddhist teachings through Zen practices. During the Onin War, some of its temples were burned down and it was subsequently rebuilt by rich merchants of Sakai. After the Ashikaga shogunate fell, many daimyo donated and supported Daitoku-ji. Many of Daitoku-ji's temples were constructed before and early Edo period. The *karamon* of Daitoku-ji is believed to be a remnant of Toyotomi Hideyoshi's richly decorated palace, Jurakudai and is a national treasure of Japan.

The first of three gates was constructed in 1526. The temple has such national treasures as *Kannon Enkaku-zu* and *Daito Kokushi Gazo*. There are also six temples constructed by various daimyo and patrons.

- *Obai-in*-Constructed by Kobayakawa Takakage
- *Shinj-uan*-Believed to be constructed by Ikkyu. The garden by Murata Tamamitsu and wall paintings by Soga Dasoku and Hasegawa Tohaku
- *Daisen-in*-The main temple is a national treasure. Also with a rock garden
- *Juko-in*-The wall painting by Kano Eitoku
- *Ryoko-in*-Constructed by Kuroda Nagamasa. The tea room *Mittan* is widely known

- *Koho-an*-Constructed by Kobori Enshu. The tea room *Bosen* is widely known.

Ikkyu and Sen no Rikyu are two of the many famous people who had been influenced by Daitoku-ji. A rumor has it that Sen no Rikyu completed two of Daitoku-ji's three gates in 1589 and this was his undoing. It is said that he chose to have a statue of himself in the chamber at the top of the second gate. Toyotomi Hideyoshi, who also frequented Daitoku-ji, realized that he and everyone else who pass through the gate to enter will be looked down on by the statue. He commanded that the offending statue be removed and ordered Sen no Rikyu to commit seppuku. While it is true that Sen no Rikyu did commit seppuku, the reason for it is not known.

EIHEI-JI

Eihei-ji is one of two main temples of the Soto sect of Zen Buddhism. Eiheiji is located about 10 km east of Fukui City in Fukui prefecture, Japan. Its founder was Eihei Dogen.

Eiheiji is the main training temple of Soto Zen. The standard training for a priest in Eiheiji is a two year period of practice.

Zenshuji Soto Mission is a direct branch of Eiheiji, located in North America.

In addition, the San Francisco Zen Centre, founded by Shunryu Suzuki Roshi, is officially associated with Eiheiji. Over the years, several of San Francisco Zen Center's students have spent time practicing at Eiheiji. In 2005, the son of Suzuki Roshi, Hoitsu Suzuki, became Abbot of Eiheiji. His frequently visits San Francisco Zen Centre, have further solidified relations. In addition, Sojun Mel Weitsman, abbot of San Francisco Zen Centre and Berkeley Zen Centre, received dharma transmission from Hoitsu Suzuki.

ENGAKU-JI

Engaku-ji is one of the most important Zen Buddhist temple complexes in Japan. It is situated in the city of Kamakura, in Kanagawa prefecture to the south of Tokyo. It is very close to the Kita-Kamakura railway station on the Tokyo to Yokosuka line, and indeed the railway tracks cut across the formal entrance to the temple compound, which (showing Chinese influence) is by a path beside a pond which is crossed by a small bridge.

The temple was founded in 1282 by a Chinese Zen monk at the request of the then rule of Japan, the regent Hojo Tokimune after he had repelled a Mongolian invasion in the period 1274 to 1281. Tokimune had a long-standing commitment to Zen and the temple was intended to honour those of both sides who died in the war, as well as serving as a centre from which the influence of Zen could be spread. According to the records of the time, when building work started a copy of the Engaku-kyo, the sutra on Perfect Enlightenment, was dug out of the hillside in a stone chest during the initial building works, giving its name to the temple.

The fortunes of the temple have waxed and waned over the centuries. Its present form is owed to the Zen priest Seisetsu, who reconstructed and consolidated it towards the end of the Edo era. In the Meiji era, Engaku-ji became the chief centre for Zen instruction in the Kanto region; Kosen Roshi and Soyen Shaku were successively abbots in this period, and Daisetz Teitaro Suzuki was a student under them. Zazen courses are still held in the temple.

Fire has damaged many of the buildings at different times, and the dates given below refer to the building of the structures currently seen. From the entrance, the buildings of the temple rise up a wooded hillside, with the major buildings in a straight line in the Chinese style; the austere buildings and the trees blending in a satisfying overall composition. There are altogether 18 temples on the site. Among the buildings and other monuments are:

- the two-storied main gate, San-mon (1783), with framed calligraphy by the Emperor Fushimi;
- a large modern Buddha Hall or Butsu-den (1964);
- Shari-den, built in the sixteenth century in the style of the Chinese Song dynasty, which houses what is claimed to be a tooth of the Buddha;

- the thatched Butsunichi-an which is the burial site of Hojo Tokimune;
- Obai-in, a small thatched temple containing a statue of Kannon;
- Ogune (1301), at 2.5 metres tall the largest of all the many temple bells of Kamakura.

Of these, Shari-den and Ogune have been designated as Japanese national treasures.

There is a small charge (as of 2005, 200 yen) for visitors to enter the temple complex, and additional similar charges to enter a few of the buildings. Booths selling tourist items are located near the entrance, below the San-mon, and there are refreshment facilities in the garden of the Shari-den and at the platform where the Ogune bell is located, from where there are extensive views across the valley to other temple complexes in the Kita-Kamakura neighbourhood, such as Jochi-ji and Tokei-ji.

ENGYO-JI

The Shoshazan Engyo-ji is a temple of the Tendai sect in Himeji, Hyogo, Japan. It was founded by Shoku Shonin in 966.

The complex of buildings is at the top of Mt Shosha and can be reached by cable car, and is often visited by pilgrims. Scenes from *The Last Samurai* were filmed here.

HORYU-JI

Horyu-ji is a Buddhist temple in Ikaruga, Nara Prefecture, Japan. Its full name is *Horyu Gakumonji*, or Learning Temple of the Flourishing Law, named as such because the site serves as a seminary as well as a monastery. The temple is widely acknowledged to have some of the oldest wooden buildings existing in the world. While there are older and more important temples, Horyu-ji is the most celebrated temple in Japan. In 1993, Horyu-ji was nominated as a UNESCO World Heritage Site and the Japanese government lists it as a National Treasure.

History

The temple was originally commissioned by Prince Shotoku, using the construction firm Kongo Gumi; at the time it was called "Ikaruga-dera". This first temple was completed in 607. Horyu-ji was dedicated to Yakushi, the Nyorai of healing and in honour of the prince's father. Excavations done at the present site of the temple confirmed that Prince Shotoku's palace occupied the eastern part of where temple sits today. Also discovered were the ruins of a temple complex which was south of the prince's palace and not within the modern temple complex. The temple was hit by lightning and burned to the ground in 670. From 670 to 700 the temple was reconstructed in its original style but reoriented in a northwest position. The temple has been repaired and reassembled in the early twelfth century, in 1374, and 1603. It is estimated that only fifteen to twenty percent of the Kondo contains materials from the original reconstruction.

The Soga clan defeated Shotoku's family in a power struggle and Shotoku's family was summarily exterminated. It is a testament of the respect of the prince that a rival family, the Soga, permitted the reconstruction of a temple for a rival and powerless family.

The temple later became a major religious Centre for Hosso Buddhism.

Fire controversy

Although, the majority consensus view is that the current temple is a reconstruction from the fire of 670, there is still a debate as to whether the fire actually occurred. Proponents of the theory that there was no fire point out the absence of proof of a fire based on soil samples of the temple complex, the fact that the temple measurements were based on the Goguryeo shaku instead of the Tang shaku, and the archaic style of the temple that is incongruent with architectural styles of the early eighth century.

Proponents of the fire theory point out that the Nihon Shoki states that there was a massive fire in 670 in which not a single building was left standing; the biography of Prince Shotoku states that there was a temple fire in 610. The excavations that uncovered the older temple site is accepted as conclusive proof that there was an original temple that burned down and that the current temple was a reconstruction.

Architecture

The current temple is classified into two areas, the western Sai-in area and the eastern To-in. The western part of the temple contains the kondo (Golden Hall) and the temple's five-story pagoda. The To-in area holds the octagonal Yumedono Hall (Hall of Dreams) and sits 122 meters east of the Sai-in area. The complex also contains monk's quarters, lecture halls, libraries, and dining halls.

While most early Japanese temples were arranged like their Korean and Chinese prototypes, the reconstructed Horyu-ji breaks from those patterns by arranging the kondo and pagoda side-by-side in the courtyard.. The statue of Yakushi of the original temple was saved during the fire of 670. While the temple was being rebuilt the Shaka Triad was commissioned or had been already cast. Because the temple builders wanted to honour both statues equally, the kondo and pagoda were set next to each other creating a unique arrangement.

Excavations at Yamadadera shows discrepancies between a temple dated to 643 and the Horyu-ji suggesting that the oldest buildings of the temple are not representative of the pure Asuka style.

The temple architecture was strongly influenced by the Korean kingdom of Baekje, with whom Wa (Japan) enjoyed close relations, and gives clues as to what Baekje architecture would look like. There is evidence that Baekje architects, craftsmen, and artisans provided the technical expertise to help the Japanese build the Horyu-ji, as the Japanese at the time were likely to have lacked skills to undertake such a massive structural enterprise. Baekje artisans helped build the first Japanese Buddhist temple, Hoko-ji (Asuka-dera) at the end of the sixth century. Additionally, the bracket work of a

Baekje gilt bronze pagoda matches the Horyu-ji bracket work exactly. In the book of Samguk Sagi concerning the affairs of Baekje, it is recorded that the Yakushi was created by a Baekje craftsmen by Prince Shotoku to assist the recovery of his father, who, as it turned out, passed away before the completion of the temple complex.

Pagoda

The five-story pagoda stands at 32.45 meters in height (122 feet) and is widely regarded as one of the two oldest wood buildings in the world. It is likely of Baekje Korean or Tang Chinese style and was probably completed in 700. The brackets and railings of the pagoda are almost identical to those of the kondo. Of note is the probable existence of a reliquary or sarira casket underneath the pagoda. The massive foundation stone, set three meters into the ground, contains a hollow for relics. Unfortunately, because of the weight of the pagoda itself, the treasures will probably never be retrieved. Visitors are not allowed to enter the pagoda and far from having a function is designed to inspire people.

Kondo

The kondo is widely regarded as the other oldest wood building extant in the world. The hall measures 18.5 meters by 15.2 meters. It is based on Chinese and Korean prototypes. The hall is double roofed with curved corners and the original Kondo roof had to be held up with extra posts because they extended more than four meters past the building. Repair work on the roof structure and upper part of the hall was stopped during the Second World War because of the damage being done to the famous wall murals in the interior of the temple. During this renovation, on January 26, 1949, a fire broke out in the temple because of a heating pad and severely damaged the remaining portion of the structure and the wall murals. Because the fire had singed the wood to a depth of three centimeters it was determined that the burnt areas would have to be rebuilt with new wood. The charred leftovers of the original reconstruction are now housed in a fire-proof warehouse where only a select few are allowed to study them and glean information about ancient building techniques. The hall also holds the famous Shaka Triad.

Yumedono

It is believed that Prince Shotoku resided in this hall to study the Buddhist scripture. The present incarnation of this hall was built in 739 and repaired in the ninth century. The hall also contains the famous Yumedono or Guze or Kuze Kannon; which is only displayed at certain times of the year.

Treasures

The treasures of the temple are considered to be a time capsule of Buddhist art from the sixth and seventh century. Much of the frescoes, statues, and other pieces of art within the temple, as well as the architecture of the temple's buildings themselves show the strong cultural influence from Korea, China, and India and demonstrated the international connection of the countries of East Asia.

Murals

The Korean monk Tamjing (Doncho in Japanese) from Goguryeo is credited as the painter of the famous murals on the walls of the Kondo.

Kudara Kannon

The Kudara Kannon is a statue of Kannon and made of gilded camphor wood. It is 210 centimeters in height and therefore very tall. The statue is very thin which also creates the illusion of height. The word Kudara is the Japanese for the Baekje Kingdom. The statue is unique in Japanese art. Some art critics believe it to be a Korean creation. Another source suggests that the statue was carved in Japan but does not describe its origins.

Yumedono (Guze) Kannon

This Kannon is a statue that supposedly is the representation of Prince Shotoku. It is approximate six feet and one inch and some sources believe that Shotoku was that height. It is 197 centimeters in height. The kannon is made of gilded wood. It is suggested that the statue was made to assuage the dead prince's spirit based on the fact that the halo was attached to the statue by a nail driven through the head. The statue bears a close resemblance to extant portraiture of the prince. The Kannon retains most of its' gilt. It is in superb condition because it was kept in the Dream Hall and wrapped in five hundred meters of cloth and never viewed in sunlight. The statue was held to be sacred and was never seen until it was unwrapped at the demand of Ernest Fenollosa, who was charged by the Japanese government to catalogue the art of the state and later became a curator at the Boston Museum. Fenellosa believed that the Kannon was Korean. Additionally, it is suggested that the Kannon is a Korean synthesis of Northern and Southern Chinese influences. However, other art historians suggest that this figure is based on the Tori style.

Shaka Triad

Tori Busshi is credited with the casting of this massive Buddhist statue. It is a triad and so the Centre Buddha is attended by two other figures. The figure is dated to 623 and the style originates in Northern Wei art. The style of the statue is also known as Tori style and is characterized by the two-dimensionality of the figure and the repetitive pattern-like depictions of the cloth the triad sits upon.

KOTOKU-IN

Kotoku-in is a Buddhist temple of the Pure Land sect in the city of Kamakura in Kanagawa Prefecture, Japan. The temple is renowned for the Great Buddha, a monumental outdoor bronze statue of Amida Buddha which is one of the most famous icons of Japan. The statue stands at 13.35 meters high and weighs approximately 93 tons, and is the second largest monumental Buddha in Japan after Todaiji in Nara. The statue probably dates from 1252, in the Kamakura period, when temple records report the construction of a bronze statue.

However, it is unclear whether that is the present statue. The statue was built inside a wooden temple but that building washed away in a tsunami sometime during the Muromachi period in the late fifteenth century. The statue remains. The statue is referred to as 'The Buddha at Kamakura' in several verses that preface the initial chapters of the novel Kim by Rudyard Kipling, 1901.

The Great Buddha

The Great Buddha of Kamakura is a monumental outdoor bronze statue of Amida Buddha in the Kotoku-in Temple in Kamakura, Kanagawa Prefecture, Japan. It is believed that the statue was originally cast in 1252, following an idea by the priest Joko, who also collected donations to build it. The sculptors were One-Goroemon and Tanji-Hisatomo.

The statue is approximately 13.35m tall and weighs approximately 93 tons. The statue is hollow, and visitors can view the interior for a mere 20 Yen a person.

The Great Buddha was originally housed in a temple, but this was washed away by a tsunami in 1495, since then the statue has stood in the open air. Repairs were carried out in 1960-1961, when the neck was strengthened and measures were taken to protect it from earthquakes.

Details

- Weight; 93 tons
- Height; 13.35m
- Length of Face; 2.35m
- Length of Eye; 1.0m
- Length of Mouth; 0.82m
- Length of Ear; 1.90m
- Length from knee to knee; 9.10m
- Circumference of thumb; 0.85m

KUONJI

Kuonji is the major temple in Yamanashi Prefecture, Japan. It is the head temple of the Buddhist sect, Nichren-shu. Locally it is referred to as the Minobu-san Temple, after the mountain upon which it is built.

It is famous for its 287 steps of stone stairs known locally as the steps of enlightenment which are climbed by chanting pilgrims regularly each year. The golden dragon painted on the black ceiling of the main temple is a notable feature usually pointed out by monks at the temple as the dragon has five toes, making it a Japanese dragon.

The blossoming of thousands of cherry trees, including the hundred-year-old weeping cherry tree in the garden, also makes this temple a popular tourist destination.

Over 1.5 million people visit the temple annually. It is reached by bus or car and then climbing the 287 steps, or alternatively scaling the sloping road which curves around the back of the temple.

Behind the temple proper is a cable car which takes tourists and pilgrims up to the top of the mountain and further temple buildings.

MII-DERA

Mii-dera, formally called Onjo-ji, is a Buddhist temple located at the foot of Mount Hiei, in the city of Otsu, in Shiga Prefecture. It is only a short distance from both Kyoto, and Lake Biwa, Japan's largest lake. The head temple of the Tendai Jimon sect, it is something of a sister temple to Enryakuji, at the top of the mountain, and is one of the four largest temples in Japan. Altogether, there are 40 named buildings in the Mii-dera temple complex.

History

Founding, and Feuds

In the year 672, Onjo-ji was founded, following a dispute

over Imperial succession. Emperor Tenji had died, and his son was killed by Tenchi's brother, who was then enthroned as Emperor Temmu. Temmu founded Onjouji in honour and memory of his brother. The name "Mii-dera," literally 'Temple of Three Wells,' came about nearly two centuries later. It was given this name by Enchin, one of the earliest abbots of the Tendai Sect. The name comes from the springs at the temple which were used for the ritual bathing of newborns, and in honour of Emperors Emperor Tenji and Emperor Temmu, and Empress Jito, who contributed to the founding of the temple. Today, the Kondo, or Main Hall, houses a spring of sacred water. Under Enchin's guidance, from 859 to his death in 891, Mii-dera gained power and importance, eventually becoming (along with Todaiji, Kofuku-ji, and Enryakuji) one of the four chief temples charged with the spiritual guidance and protection of the capital.

It was during this time also that Enryakuji & Mii-dera split away from one another, developing two branches of the Tendai sect, called Jimon and Sammon. For the most part, this was more a geographic rivalry than an ideological schism, but it was an intense one nonetheless, and only grew more severe after Enchin's death. The rivalry turned violent in the second half of the 10th century, over a series of official appointments to other temples, and similar slights.

The zasu of Enryakuji in 970 formed the first permanent standing army to be recruited by a religious body. Mii-dera can be assumed to have established one very soon afterwards. In 989, a former abbot of Mii-dera by the name of Yokei was to become abbot of Enryakuji; but none of the monks of Enryakuji would perform services under his direction. He soon resigned. But in 993, the monks of Mii-dera took revenge, destroying a temple where Ennin, founder of Enryakuji's Sammon sect, had once lived. The monks from Enryakuji retaliated, destroying more than 40 places associated with Enchin. In the end, over 1,000 monks of Enchin's Jimon sect fled permanently to Mii-dera, cementing the split between the two Sects. Over the course of the 10th, 11th and 12th centuries, there continued to be similar incidents, over the appointment of abbots (*zasu*), involving many *sohei*, or warrior monks. Mii-dera was burned to the ground by the *sohei* of Enryakuji four times in the 11th century alone. There were, however, times that the two united against a common enemy, including an attack on the Kofukuji in Nara in 1081 (avenging the burning of the Mii-dera by Kofukuji monks that same year), and a united attack on Nara once more in 1117.

The Genpei Wars

At the end of the 12th century, the attentions of the monks of Mount Hiei were turned towards a greater conflict: the Genpei War. The Taira and Minamoto families supported different claimants to the Chrysanthemum Throne, and in June of 1180, the Minamoto brought their claimant, Prince Mochihito, to the Mii-dera, fleeing from Taira samurai. Mii-dera asked for aid from Enryakuji, but was denied. The monks of the Mii-dera joined the Minamoto army, and fled to the Byodoin, a Fujiwara clan villa, which had been converted to a monastery by Mii-dera monks. Angered at the Mii-dera/Minamoto alliance, Taira no Kiyomori ordered the destruction of Mii-dera, and of many of the temples of Nara. The monks of Mii-dera figured once more in the Genpei War, fighting alongside Taira sympathisers against Minamoto no Yoshinaka, who invaded Kyoto in 1184, setting fire to the Hojujidono Palace and kidnapping the Emperor Go-Shirakawa.

Following the Genpei War, there was a long period of relative peace, as the temples of Kyoto and Nara, including the Mii-dera, were rebuilt. As the temples regained strength, rivalries reappeared, though little to no violence actually erupted between Mii-dera and Enryakuji. In 1367, when a novice from Mii-dera was killed at a toll barrier established by the temple of Nanzenji, warrior monks from Mii-dera set out to attack Nanzenji; when the Shogun's forces were sent to quell the rebellion, they discovered Mii-dera's monks to be supported by *sohei* from Enryakuji and Kofukuji as well. A year later, another battle erupted, over comments made by the abbot of Nanzenji; the monks of Mii-dera, along with their allies, defeated the Shogun's forces once again.

Sengoku Period and Beyond

In the late 16th century, Mii-dera, along with many of the other nearby temples, sought alliances, for military (defensive) strength, as well as military power. The territories of the Asai and Asakura families were closest to Mount Hiei, but these families, as well as others the temples had allied with, were rivals of Oda Nobunaga. These two families suffered heavy defeats at the hands of Nobunaga and his chief general Hideyoshi Toyotomi, so in 1571 they sought a stronger alliance with the temples. That same year, Nobunaga set to destroying everything on Mount Hiei, starting with the town of Sakamoto at the foot of the mountain, and setting his sights on Enryakuji at the summit. Much of Mii-dera was destroyed, as the warrior monks failed against Nobunaga's large and highly trained samurai army.

Following these attacks, the monks of Mount Hiei were finally granted a reprieve, and rebuilt their temples once more. Mii-dera has never been attacked or destroyed since then.

Halls & Treasures

Within the Kondo and Hondo (the Main Hall and Buddha Hall) of Mii-dera, there are at least six statues of the Buddha, sacred personal possessions of various Emperors, including Emperor Tenji, which are hidden away and shown only on rare, special occasions, as well as one large statue of the Miroku, or Maitreya, Buddha in the Centre of the Hall. The Kondo was built in 1599, and is a replacement for the original, built in 672 and destroyed by the Taiko Hideyoshi Toyotomi. Mii-dera also has a Kannon-do, built in 1072, a hall dedicated to Kannon, Bodhisattva of Compassion. Mii-dera is the fourteenth temple in a Pilgrimage of 33 Temples devoted to Kannon in the Kansai area.

NANZEN-JI

Zuiryusan Nanzen-ji is a Zen Buddhist temple in Kyoto, Japan. Emperor Kameyama established it in 1291 on the site of his previous detached palace. Nanzenji is one of the Five Great Zen Temples of Kyoto. It is also the headquarters of the Nanzenji branch of Rinzai Zen.

NARITA-SAN

Narita-san is a Buddhist temple located in central Narita city, Chiba prefecture, Japan.

This temple is one of the most well known in the Kanto region of Japan and is only surpassed in visitors during the O-shogatsu period (lit: New year period) by the Meiji Shrine in Tokyo. The temple grounds are comprised of a main gate, a steep stairwell and the main buildings (including a couple five-story pagodas), and a garden area with large pond. A very small zoo is also within the temple grounds.

The mail hall is a Buddhist worship area. The interior is based on Indian Buddhist design but has a distinct Japanese impression. Throughout the day visitors come to sit and to pray aloud.

Tourism

Travellers leaving Japan via Narita International Airport commonly stop by to visit. The temple is within 10 minutes walking from either the JR Narita Station or the Keisei Narita Station and both paths offer many small shops selling Japanese snacks and other foodstuffs and also Japanese good-luck charms such as Daruma dolls.

Special Events

At the beginning of the year locals flock to Narita-san for the O-shogatsu holidays to pray.

In spring the Taiko festival occurs at Narita-san. One can observe taiko drum play and dancing at this time.

OFUNA KAN'NON

The Ofuna Kan'non or Muga sozan Ofuna Kan'nonji is a Buddhist temple in Kamakura, Kanagawa, Japan. The outstanding feature of the temple is a 25 meter tall 1,900 ton reinforced concrete statue of Kan'non which is dedicated to the bodhisattva Kan'non or Kuan Yin.

Construction of the Temple began in 1929 by the Soto(Zen) Buddhist sect. The outline of the statue was complete by 1934 but work was suspended at the outbreak of the Pacific War. The Ofuna Kan'non Society continued construction work in 1954 and the Temple was finally completed in 1960.

The Kan'non incorporates stones from ground zero of Hiroshima and Nagasaki to commemorate those who died in the explosions of the atomic bombs. A fire originating from the atomic fires of Hiroshima burns in a mushroom-formed statue.

6

East Asian Buddhism

East Asian Buddhism is a collective term for the schools of Buddhism that developed in the East Asian region, most of which are part of the Mahayana transmission. These include Chinese Buddhism, Korean Buddhism, Japanese Buddhism, and Vietnamese Buddhism. The schools of Buddhism most prominent in Sri Lanka and the Southeast Asian countries is Theravada Buddhism. Mahayana thought had originated in Indian Buddhist philosophers, whose teachings would filter into East Asian Mahayan.

BUDDHISM IN KASHMIR

Kashmir has been one of the most important centres for the spread and development of Buddhism. Buddhism was an important part of the classical Kashmiri culture, as is reflected in the Nilamata Purana and the Kalhana's Rajatarangini. Buddhism is generally believed to have become dominant in Kashmir in the time of Emperor Ashoka, although it was widespread there long before his time. It enjoyed the patronage not only of the Buddhist rulers but of Hindu and early Muslim rulers too. From Kashmir, it spread to the neighbouring Laddakh.

Surrendra

The first known ruler of Kashmir, Gonanda (mentioned by Kalhana in his Rajatarangini), was related to Jarasandha, who ruled Magadha during the time of the Kurukshetra war.

Surrendra is perhaps the fist Buddhist ruler of Kashmir. He erected the first viharas in Kashmir. One of these, known as Narendrabhavana, was in the city of Sauraka (Suru, beyond the Zoji La.) The other vihara was at Saurasa, corresponding to the village Sowur on the shore of Anchar Lanke to the north of Srinagar.

Mauryan Period

Ashoka

Kalhana claims that though it was situated far from the Mauryan capital (Pataliputra), Kashmir enjoyed all the benefits of Ashoka's benign rule. The provincial capital Shrinagari (Srinagar) was 'resplendent with prosperity and wealth.' According to some Buddhist writers including Taranatha, the Buddhist preacher Madhyantika introduced saffron cultivation into Kashmir. Buddhism and Shaivism flourished side by side in Kashmir during Ashoka's time and received the Emperor's patronage in equal measure. Kalhana notes that Ashoka built two Shiva temples at Vijayeshvara (Bijbihara), and ordered several others renovated. In Vitastatra (Vethavutur) and at Shuskaletra (Hukhalitar) he built a number of viharas and stupas. He deputed Madhyantika for the propagation of Buddhism in Kashmir and Gandhara.

Ashoka's Successors

Buddhism suffered a temporary eclipse during the reign of Ashoka's successors Jalauka and Damodara. Kalhana describes how a large number of Buddhist scholars were vanquished in debates with Jalauka's guru Avadhuta, and hence traditional observances were slowly revived. Later, however, Jalauka created a big vihara, the Krityashramavihara, in the vicinity of Varahamula (Baramulla), which was still existed as late as the 11th century. The history of Kashmir after Damodara is not certain until the time of the Kushanas.

Kushana Period

The Kushana period saw a great resurgence of Buddhism

in Kashmir, especially during the reign of Kanishka. The fourth Buddhist Council was held in Kashmir, under the presidency of Katyayaniputra, in Kanishka's time. The south Indian Buddhist philosopher Nagarjuna lived in Kashmir during the Kushana period.

Post-Kushana Reaction

During the reign of Abhimanyu, which in Kalhana's chronicle follows that of Kanishka, Buddhist scholars under the guidance of Nagarjuna defeated the Shaivite clergy in debates, encouraging people to choose Buddhism. However, during the time of Chandradeva, revival of knowledge of the works of Patanjali, like the Mahabhashya which had become rare, led to a resurgence of Shaivism. By the time of Gonanda, the old philosophy was completely revived. Nothing is known about the religious affiliations of Pratapaditya, a scion of the Gupta dynasty and his successors, except that they are stated to have ruled well, and fullest liberty of faith was accorded. Buddhism is stated by Kalhana and Hiuen Tsang to have suffered severe setbacks under the Huns, especially under Mihirakula, whom Hiuen Tsang describes as a great persecutor of the Buddhists.

Meghavahana

Upon Mihirakula's death, Kashmir was ruled by Meghavahana, who belonged to the old ruling dynasty of Kashmir. Meghavahana was a staunch Buddhist, who issued a proclamation against killing of all animals at the very time of his coronation, and built numerous stupas.

Buddhist Influence in Kashmir

In Kalhana's time, and before, there was no apparently no distinction between "Hindus" and Buddhists in Kashmir. Kalhana himself used Buddhist terms and expressions as a Buddhist would.

Nilamata Purana was the text of the worshippers of Nila Naga, the Naga worship was common in Kashmir. It mentions the prevalence of Buddhist worship as a common practice in

Kashmir. Here are some quotes from Nilamat Purana from Kashmir (trans. by Dr. Ved Kumari). It correctly represents the religious spirit of ancient India.

709-710a : O Brahman, the god Visnu, the lord of the world, shall be (born as) the preceptor of the world, Buddha by name, at the time when the Pusya is joined with the moon, in the month of Vaisaksha, in twenty eighth Kali Age.

710b-12 : Listen from as to how his worship should be performed in the bright-half, from that period onwards, in uture. The image of Buddha should be bathed (with water rendered holy) with all medicinal herbs, all jewels and all scents, in accordance with the sayings of the Sakyas. The dwellings of the Sakyas (i.e. Viharas) should be whitewashed with care.

713 : Here and there, the Caityas-the abodes of the god-should be provided with paintings. The festival, swarming with the actors and the dancers, should be celebrated.

714 : The Sakyas should be honoured with Civara (the dress of a Buddhist mendicant), food and books. All this should be done till the advent of Magha.

715 : *O twice-born, eatable offerings should be made for three days. Worship with flowers, clothes etc. and charity for the poor (should continue for three days).*

Kalhana's Rajatarangini mentions that a monumental metallic image of Buddha once stood in Srinagar, which was eventually destroyed by Sikandar Butshikan. A significant number of beautifully crafted Buddhist bronzes have survived. In Kashmir valley, a Buddhist Bhikshu was present in Baramula in 13th century. The Kashmiri Pandits still worship the triratna symbol.

BUDDHISM IN BANGLADESH

About 0.5% of Bangladesh population adheres to the Theravada school of Buddhism. Most of the practitioners are from the south-eastern district of Chittagong and Chittagong Hill Tracts.

Demographic Overview

Most of the followers of Buddhism in Bangladesh live in the south-eastern region, especially in the Chittagong district. Also, there are people of Arakanese descent living in the sub-tropical Chittagong Hill Tracts. Most of these people belong to the Chakma, Chak, Marma, Tenchungya and the Khyang, who since time immemorial have practiced Buddhism. Other tribals, notably those who practice Animism, have come under some Buddhist influence, and this is true in the case of the Khumi and the Mru, and to a lesser extent on the other tribals.

History

Bangladesh (historical Bengal) has a unique place in the history of Buddhism, mainly for two reasons. Firstly, Bengal was the last stronghold of Indian Buddhism where it could survive as a socio-cultural force until the 12th century, despite its disappearance from other parts of the Indian subcontinent. Secondly, it is generally claimed that Bengal was the home of a form of Buddhism, namely, the Tantric Buddhism. Tantric Buddhism is a later development in Bengal and therefore it remains to be seen what specific factors are responsible for turning the pure form of Buddhism into tantricism and whether the mystic and esoteric practices in the Buddhism of Bangladesh are of distinctively Bengali origin.

Early Origins

In the early days of Buddhism, many kings and rulers like Bimbisara, Ashoka, Kanishka patronized the spread of Buddha's teaching. This continued until the Palas and Chandras of Bengal in the 12th century. Of course, Buddhism faced hostility from some of the rulers, but throughout the first millennium and beyond, Buddhism thrived in Bengal.

It is possible that Buddhism entered Bengal before Asoka's time. After attaining enlightenment, the Buddha is said to have delivered his first sermon at Saranath and then moved to Magadha, Kosala, Vaishali and other places within what was known as Majjhimadesha or Madhyadesha. In the Divyavadana, the eastern boundary of the Majjhimadesha is said to have extended as far as pundravardhana (North Bengal). Furthermore, the Buddha is said to have received considerable support from King Bimbisara of Magadha who not only dedicated Venuvana as a residence for monks, but also remained his close friend and a great patron of his Dhamma throughout his life. Since Bengal was adjacent to Magadha, it is possible that the Buddha had visited parts of Bangladesh as suggested by Hiuen Tsang, who notes that Asoka had erected stupas at various places in Bengal and Orissa to commemorate these visits.

Asoka's Reign and the Post-Maurya Period Epigraphic and other sources reveal that Buddhism had established a powerful footing in Bengal during Asoka's reign. The discovery of a Mauryan inscription in Brahmi characters at Mahasthangarh in the district of Bogra bearing the name Pudanagala (Pundranagara) and the recovery of many Mauryan coins and other artifacts dating from the fourth and third centuries BC suggest that the Gangetic delta was under the control of the Mauryan empire. The Chinese traveller, I-tsing, is said to have noticed Asoka's stupas near tamralipti (Tamluk) and Karnasuvarna (modern Burdwan and Murshidabad districts) in current West Bengal, in Pundravardhana (North Bengal) and in Samatata (Bangladesh). The port of Tamralipti to the west of the Bhagirathi-Hooghli river, in particular, played an important role during Asoka's rule. It was from here, according to Mahavangsa, that the Buddhist mission from Asoka's capital city, Pataliputra, sailed for Sri Lanka to spread the message of the Buddha.

Post-Mauryan Period

With the decline of the Maurya Empire, Buddhism lost the royal patronage which it once enjoyed. Pusyamitra, after killing his master, Brhadratha, declared himself the emperor and ascended the throne of Magadha. He founded the Sunga dynasty in the 2nd century BC. With the resurgence of the Sungas, Buddhism met with its first major setback. Buddhism, once a thriving religion, declined in the absence of the royal patronage, as also because of the unfavourable attitude of the Sunga kings towards Buddhism and the Sangha.

Contrary to this position, some Indian scholars are of the view that the orthodox Sunga kings were not intolerant towards Buddhism, and that Buddhism continued to prosper even during the time of the Sunga kings. During the Sunga period, Buddhism was in existence in Bengal, and this can also be inferred from a terracotta tablet that was found at a place called Tamralipti. This terracotta tablet is currently on exhibit at the Asutosh Museum, University of Calcutta.

The Kushana period (around 1st century) gave further impetus to Buddhism when Kanishka raised Buddhism to the status of the state religion, erected stupas and chaityas, built monasteries and, like Asoka, sent missions abroad. The discovery of Buddha images, copper and gold coins and inscriptions, belonging to this period, indicate the flourishing status of Buddhism during the reign of Kaniska.

Gupta Dynasty

Kings of the Gupta dynasty were devout adherents of a Brahminical faith, sometimes called as *Parama Bhagavatas*, and they patronized and revived Brahminism, but they also possessed a tolerant outlook which allowed Buddhism to flourish. In the meantime, rise of the two powerful Hindu cults of Saivism and Vaisnavism, brought Buddhism closer to Hinduism. In its spiritual nihilism, Buddhism was approximated to the Bhakti movements so much so that, by the middle of the 6th century, the Buddha was accepted as an avatar of Vishnu.

According to Chinese sources, Maharaja Gupta, also known as Shri Gupta, the first ruler of the Gupta dynasty, built a Buddhist temple and offered it to Buddhist monks from China along with a gift of twenty four villages. This temple is believed to have remained a sacred place till the 7th century.

Samudra Gupta, although a devout worshipper of Vishnu, also proved to be a great patron of Buddhism. It was during his reign that cultural relations between India and Ceylon were established. His teacher and guide, the celebrated Buddhist scholar Vasubandhu, was appointed minister, and, with the permission of the Ceylonese King Meghavanna, a monastery was built at Bodh Gaya for the monks and pilgrims of Ceylon. Chandra Gupta II who, like his father Samudra Gupta, was a devout Vaisnava by faith, gave full freedom to the practice of other faiths in his empire.

Fa-hien's Account

During his visit to Bengal, Fa-hien is said to have travelled eastward along the course of the Ganges river, and during his journey, he came across Buddhist stupas and monks at several places. In a place named Tamralipti, Fa-hien is said to have spent two years, and visited twenty-two monasteries, inhabited by monks who lived in accordance with the Buddhist Vinaya.

Archaeological evidences also support Fa-hien's account about the thriving state of Buddhism in the Gupta period. An inscription found at Gunaigarh near Comilla, bearing the year 188 of the Gupta era (corresponding to 506 or 507 of the Christian era), records a gift of land by Maharaja Vainya Gupta in favour of the Buddhist Avaivarttika Sangha of the Mahayana sect.

The Sangha, founded by the Acharya Shantideva and housed in a monastery called *Ashrama Vihara*, was dedicated to Avalokiteshvara. The inscription also refers to other Buddhist monasteries, one of which was known as *Raja Vihara*, which literally translates into *Royal Vihara*. Two Buddhist sculptures, a standing image of the Buddha found at Biharail in Rajshahi district and a gold-plated bronze image of Manjushri discovered at Balai Dhap mound at Mahasthana in Bogra, also bear testimony to the flourishing state of Buddhism during the rule of the Gupta kings.

Both the Hinayana and Mahayana sects of Buddhism flourished during the Gupta period. A number of Buddhist inscriptions, seals, images and manuscripts in Gupta characters, discovered at various archaeological excavations sites, testify to the thriving state of the early Hinayana schools, namely, the Sarvastivadins, the Sammatiyas (or the Vatsiputriyas) and

Sthavirvadins. Gradually, Hinayana lost its hold, and Mahayana took ascendancy over Hinayana. Mahayana, with its ultra-altruistic principles, its scope for devotion and worship, and its opening of the state of Bodhisattvahood began to capture the imagination of common people, and acquired the status of an important religious movement. As Mahayana grew popular, Bodhisattvas such as Manjusri, Avalokitesvara and the goddess Prajnaparamita rose to occupy important positions.

The *Adi Buddha* and Amitabha Buddha also received special attention. Worship of Bodhisattva images along with the image of the Buddha turned into a common practice. The Mahayanists are said to have revered the Prajna texts just as the Hinayanists revered their Vinaya and Abhidharma books. The Mahayanists are also said to have practised spells (dharanis) for religious purposes.

Hiuen Tsang visited India in the 7th century and visited almost all the major places associated with Buddhism in Bangladesh. According to him, there were six or seven Buddhist monasteries at Kajangala near Rajmahal, housing over three hundred monks.

In the northern part of the country, he also claimed to have seen a belvedere built of stone and brick, with a broad and high base, artistic ornamentation and distinct carved images of the Buddha and the devas. At Pundravardhana he is said to have found twenty Buddhist monasteries with more than 3,000 monks who practised both Hinayana and Mahayana. The magnificent Po-shi-po, with spacious halls and storeyed chambers, occupied by over 700 monks, was located in the vicinity of the capital of Pundravardhana. There is also mention of a temple with an image of Avalokitesvara not far from this establishment, which attracted visitors from far and near.

Fa-hien visited India in the 5th century, and found that some of the old Buddhist centres like Kapilavastu and Saraswati were in a neglected and ruinous state, while Pataliputra, Mathura, Bodh Gaya, Sarnath and Nalanda were flourishing as active centres of Buddhism.

The great monastery of Nalanda, which was founded by Kumara Gupta Mahendraditya, rose to prominence in the Gupta period and in course of time turned into a university and became the greatest centre of Buddhist learning in Asia. From an early date, the Buddhists of Bengal were closely linked with this great institution, although it was situated in Magadha.

Prior to Hiuen Tsang's visit to Nalanda, Acharya Dharmapala had been the high priest of its monastery. He was succeeded by his disciple Acharya shilabhadra, a scion of a Brahmana king of Samatata. It was under Silabhadra's guidance that Hiuen Tsang studied Buddhist philosophy, including the vedas and Sangkhya Shastras, for five years. Not only scholars from Bengal but also its kings, the Guptas, the Palas etc., contributed to the development of the great institutions at Nalanda.

Post-Gupta Period

During the post-Gupta period, Harsavardhana gave Buddhism a new impetus. But, in the 6th century, Shashanka came to the throne, who was hostile to Buddhism. According to Hiuen Tsang's account, Shashanka ordered the extermination of the Buddhist monks in and around Kushinagar; he cut down the holy Bodhi tree of Bodh Gaya and threw into the Ganges a sacred stone bearing the footprints of the Buddha. He is also said to have removed a Buddha image from a temple close to the Bodhi tree and replaced it with an image of Hindu god Lord Shiva.

Contrary to this, the reign of Emperor Harsavardhana (606-647) was one of resurgence and renewed progress and development. Despite being a worshipper of Shiva and Surya, Harsavardhana had great leanings towards Buddhism, and his elder brother, Rajyavardhana, and sister Rajyashri both were being devout Buddhists. Harsa was at first a follower of the Hinayana sect, but, in later life, became an ardent follower of Mahayana.

Some of his notable contributions to the cause of Buddhism include erecting stupas on the banks of the Ganges, building monasteries at places sacred to Buddhism, and forbidding the slaying of animals. Another of his important contributions to Buddhism was his convening regularly the quinquennial convocation in which he gave away in religious alms everything he possessed. Harsa used to summon Buddhist monks once a year for religious discussions. Harsa was specially attached to Nalanda and extended help liberally.

After Harsavardhana, the Khadga dynasty is said to be the first Buddhist dynasty to rule an independent Bengal between the 7th and 8th centuries AD. The discovery of two copperplates, one at Ashrafpur, 30 miles north-east of Dhaka and another at Deulbari, 14 miles south of Comilla, gives valuable information about this royal dynasty.

These copperplates mention the names of three kings, Khadgodyama, Jatakhadga and Devakhadga, and include the names of the queen and the son of Devakhadga, Prabhavati and Rajaraja or Rajarajabhata. I-tsing's account notes that as many as fifty-six Buddhist priests from China visited India and its neighbouring areas in the latter half of the 7th century AD. One of these monks, Sheng-chi, who visited Samatata, mentions Rajabhata as its king and describes him as an ardent worshipper of the three gems (*Triratna*), that is, the Buddha, Dhamma and Sangha. There were 30 monasteries with more that 4,000 monks in Samatata alone during the pilgrim's visit.

Pala Dynasty

The Pala Dynasty ruled Bengal from 8th to 12th century, and this period is regarded as the golden age of Buddhism in Bengal. The Pala rulers were devout Buddhists (*Parama-saugata*), and were also equally sympathetic to other religious faiths. Palas invoked the Buddha at the beginning of their official records and proceedings. Under the royal patronage of the Pala kings, Buddhism and all institutions associated with Buddhism continuously flourished and thrived in Bengal for four centuries under the patronage of the Pala kings. During the same period, Buddhism was almost wiped out in other parts of the Indian subcontinent, and at the same time, it also became a dominant force in neighbouring regions, extending its influence to Tibet in the north and the Malaya peninsula in the south.

Archaeological and epigraphic discoveries indicate the generous support of the Pala rulers towards Buddhism, and instances of the Palas' patronage of Buddhism are numerous. According to Tibetan Buddhist tradition, King Gopala (750-770) built a monastery at Nalanda and established many schools for dissemination of Buddhist principles. According to Taranatha, many distinguished Buddhist teachers flourished during the reign of King Gopala, prominent among them were Danashila, Vishesamitra, Sura and Prajavarman. The Odantapuri Vihara was an example of rare architectural beauty. The famous Sam-ye monastery of Tibet is believed to have been built on the model of this great Vihara.

King Dharmapala (770-781) continued the religious policy of his father, and he also extended liberal support to Buddhist establishments. He founded the famous Vikramshila Vihara on a hill top on the bank of the Ganges river in Magadha. This Vihara soon rose to prominence as an international centre of learning and emerged as a university, second only to Nalanda. Vikramshila University maintained contact with Tibet and several Tibetan scholars participated in the affairs of the university throughout the rule of the Pala dynasty. Several of Vikramashila scholars, who once numbered 3000 in the 12th century, composed numerous books in Sanskrit, and also translated them into Tibetan. The curricula of the university included logic, metaphysics, grammar, tantras, and rituals. Importantly, the reigning monarch of the land awarded degrees to the students.

A monastery, built by King Dharmapala at Somapura Rajshahi district, and now better known as the Somapura Mahavihara (Naogaon) and which became a model for many such monasteries in South-east Asia, stands as a magnificent testament to the Pala patronage of Buddhism. King Dharmapala is also said to have established at least fifty religious schools designed to teach Buddhist philosophy, and to study

Prajnaparamita in particular. He was a great patron of the Buddhist writer, Haribhadra, and, during his reign, as in his father's, many distinguished Buddhist teachers, such as Purnavardhana, Prabhakara, Kalyanagupta, Sagaramegha, Bhuddhajapada, flourished.

Under King Devapala (810-850), the Pala empire reached the zenith of its glory, and Bengal became a paramount power. King Devapala is said to have granted an endowment of five villages for the upkeep of a monastery founded by King Balaputradeva of Java, Sumatra and Malaya. Not only did he complete the Somapura establishment, he also showed keen interest in the well-being of the Vikramshila Vihara.

Mahipala I, the ninth king of the Pala dynasty and rightly called the founder of the second Pala empire, is responsible for the revival of the past glory of the Buddhist establishments. He repaired the Buddhist monuments at Nalanda and constructed two new temples at Bodh Gaya. Many famous monasteries were built during the Pala period of which mention may be made of Jagaddala, Traikutaka, Pandita, Devikota, Pattikeraka, Sannagara, Phullahari and Vikramapuri.

Chandra Dynasty

Buddhism flourished during the reign of the Chandra dynasty in Harikela (eastern and southern parts of Bengal). The discovery of a large Buddha stupa, Salbana Vihara and other inscriptions at the Mainamati hills, four miles to the west of Comilla, still bears testimony to the condition of Buddhism during the Chandra kings. According to Tibetan sources, Buddhist tantricism flourished under the Chandra rule. The famous Buddhist scholar of Vikramapura, Atish Dipankar Srigyan, is believed to be related to the Chandra dynasty.

The Pala Kingdom was not only the last stronghold of dying Buddhism in India, it was also responsible for the rise of Tantric Buddhism. This new phase of Mahayana Buddhism has been variously designated by Charles Eliot and others as 'late', 'degenerate', and 'corrupt'. Such allegations are based on the assumption that when Buddhism entered Bengal, it gradually came under the powerful influence of tantric beliefs and practices, including what are known as sexo-yogic practices, which made it fall away from the purity of its early form and eventually develop into what came to be known as esoteric or magical Buddhism.

Professor Trevor Ling opines that in Bengal from the time of Asoka to the Pala period, both the Hinayana and Mahayana, not the tantric, forms of Buddhism were practised.

He describes the classical pattern of Buddhism as a three-cornered relationship between Sanga, king and people and emphasizes that the Buddhism of the Pala period was a true representative example of this classical pattern. Trevor Ling and many others believe that the Pala rule in Bengal heralded an era of progress in culture, religion, education, literature, art and sculpture. Amongst other achievements of the Palas, Ling has particularly mentioned their active patronage of Bangla language and literature. It was in a popular new language, a proto-Bangla form, that the Buddhist poets composed what are known to be the first poems of Bangla literature, the famous charyapada, a Tantric work of twenty-three Buddhist Tantrikists known as Siddhas.

Decline and Revival

The Sena Dynasty gained prominence after the decline of the Palas. The Senas were orthodox followers of Saivaism or Vaisnavism. Under them, the royal support for Buddhism ended. As a consequence, Buddhism soon began to decline and disintegrate. Another contributing factor was the coming of Islam through the subsequent defeat of the Sena dynasty at the hands of Muhammad bin Bakhtyar Khalji. After that, many of the surviving Buddhist monks fled to Nepal, Tibet or Bhutan. The Buddhist laity were either converted to Islam or were integrated into the fold of Brahmanism. Buddhism, as a separate entity, was almost extinct, surviving in many debased forms of popular practices such as dharma thakur puja or the puja of jagannath. The decline of Buddhism, however, did not result in its total disappearance from the land of its birth, and it continued to survive in various forms of popular worship, rites and rituals until its resurgence in modern India. With its rediscovery in its parent country, the traditions of Buddhism were significantly recognized so that the Asokan pillar, the sacred Wheel of Law (Dharmachakra) and the Singhanada sculpture from Saranatha are now a part of Indian national life and heritage. The renewal of Buddhism in India today is attributed to Dr. BR Ambedkar, the architect of the Indian Constitution, who led the mass conversion of millions of untouchables or 'Scheduled Castes' to Buddhism in 1956. In Bengal, however, the revival of Buddhism seems to have taken place centuries before Dr. BR Ambedkar's introduction of the neo-Buddhist movement in Maharastra and other places. In the districts of Chittagong and the Chittagong Hill Tracts, the south-eastern parts of Bangladesh, a Buddhist minority had been practising Theravada long before the Moghuls and the British arrived in Bengal. In course of time, these Buddhists reformed their Sangha and in 1887 founded the Chittagong Buddhist Association, believed to be the first Buddhist society to be formed in the South Asian sub-continent.

SRI LANKAN BUDDHISM

Sri Lankan Buddhism belongs to the Theravada tradition. About 69% of the country adheres to Buddhism. Sri Lanka is the country with longest continuous history of Buddhism. Theravada has been the major religion in the island since soon after its introduction in the 2nd century BC by Venerable Mahinda, the son of the Emperor Ashoka of India during the reign of Sri Lanka's King Devanampiyatissa. During this time, a sapling of the Bodhi Tree was also brought Sri Lanka and became known as Sri Maha Bodhi. The Pali Canon was put into writing in Sri Lanka around 30 BC.

The different orders of the Therevada are referred to as nikayas, and in Sri Lanka there are three:

- Siam Nikaya, founded in the 18th century by a Thai monk who perceived corruption in the sangha and wished to purify its practices

- Amarapura Nikaya, founded in 1800 after ordination within Burma by lower-caste Buddhists who objected to the previously dominant practice of selective ordination from the higher-castes
- Ramanna Nikaya, founded in 1864 by Ambagahawatte Saranankara.

BUDDHISM IN NEPAL

About 11% of Nepal's population practices Buddhism, consisting mainly of groups of Tibeto-Burman origin.

Overview

Buddhist influences are evident in the culture of Nepal, including that of many Hindu and Animist castes. Due to Nepal's close proximity to Tibet, Tibetan Buddhism is the most widely practised form.

The Newar practice Vajrayana Buddhism, which is another name for Tibetan Buddhism. Many Buddhist groups are also influenced by Hinduism.

Buddhism is the dominant religion of the thinly-populated northern areas, which are inhabited by Tibetan-related peoples, namely the Sherpa, Lopa, Manangi, Thakali, Lhomi, Dolpa and Nyimba. They constitute a small minority of the country's population.

Ethnic groups that live in central Nepal, such as Gurung, Lepcha, Tamang, Magar, Newar, Yakkha, Thami and Chepang, are also followers of Buddhism. These ethnic groups have larger populations compared to their northern neighbours. They came under the influence of Hinduism due to their close contacts with the Hindu castes. In turn, many of them eventually adopted Hinduism and have been largely integrated into the caste system.

The Kirant tribes, especially the Limbu and the Rai, have also adopted Tibetan Buddhist practises from their Buddhist neighbours. The Jirel, which is considered a Kirata tribe, have also adopted Tibetan Buddhism.

History

Buddhism During the Kirata Period (?-300)

According to archaeological and historical records, Gautama Buddha, the founder of Buddhism, was born in Lumbini, Nepal in 563 BCE. After enlightenment at the age of 35 he return back to the place. His and his disciples' preaching soon spread Buddhism in the surrounding areas. It was believed that Gautama Buddha visited Nepal several times. According to Mulasarvastivadin Vinaya says thathis disciple, Ananda, came to the Kathmandu Valley during the rule of the seventh of the 28 Kirati rulers and stayed for a while in Patan, Nepal.

Buddhism During the Mauryan Period (300-400)

Emperor Ashoka from India put up a pillar at Lumbini, the birthplace of the Buddha in the 2nd century BC. It is also believed that Ashoka went to Patan and had four stupas built there. It is believed that his daughter Charumati established the village of Chabahil, which is located between Kathmandu and Bodhnath. There is a stupa and monastery in Chabahil that are said to date back to her time.

It is said that upon the expansion of the Mauryan dynasty into the Terai plains in Nepal, Buddhism was adopted by the ancestors of the Tharu and flourished until the resurgent Licchavi repelled its adherents in AD 200. But, in fact, the Tharu are the remainants of ancient Sakya, Koliya, Mourya and many other ancient tribes. Thus, obviously, Buddhism in Nepal has been flourishing since Buddha's time if we consider ancient Kapilvastu and Devdah in Nepal.

Buddhism During the Licchavi Period (400-750)

The Licchavi period saw the flourishing of both Hinduism and Buddhism in Nepal. Excellent examples of Buddhist art of the period are the half-sunken Buddha in Pashupatinath, the sleeping Vishnu in Budhanilkantha, and the statue of Buddha and the various representations of Vishnu in Changu Narayan.

Ancient Buddhist texts claim that Mulasarvasti Vadavinaya (better known as the Shakyas of Kapilvastu, Bhikshu Ananda, and the Baniyas of Sravasti) came to Nepal, then known as Newal, from Tibet.

Another Buddhist text, the Manjushrimula Kalpa, mentioned Manadeva as the King of Nepal Mandala. Researchers believe the Mulasarvastivadavinaya was written in the 2nd century CE, and that the Manjushriulakalpa was written during Manadeva's reign. The Swayambhu Purana, the ancient Buddhist Purana text, and a Licchavi inscription all mentioned Nepal Mandala.

Buddhist inscriptions and chronicles and Tibetan sources also record a few tantric Buddhist deities, namely Aksyobhya, Amitabha, Vajrayogini, Vajrabhairava, Usnisavijaya and Samantabhadra. Strong influence from Animist cults resulted in belief in Buddhist deities such as the Pancaraksas.

Religious tolerance and syncretism were stressed during the Licchavi period. King Manadeva paid homage at both Hindu and Buddhist sites. His family subsequently found expression for their beliefs in various different religions.

The worship of the Caitya and the Rath Jatra cart festival of Avalokitesvara were introduced around this period. Many ancient sites in the Kathmandu Valley were identified with major Buddhist Caityas, such as Swayambhunath, Bodnath, Kathmandu and the four "Ashoka" stupas of Patan, and another two hundred stone caityas dating from the Licchavi Period, were testified to the widespread antiquity of caitya worship.

It is possible that this practice, in its earliest incarnation, was related to the worship of stones, which may have originated in the early, rival Kirata inhabitants of the Valley, prior to the Licchavis. According to one of the earliest Licchavi inscriptions, Caitya worship ordinarily consisted of ritual circumambulation of the caitya and offering standard items such as incense, coloured powder, oil lamps and ablutions. At times, the inscriptions indicate, it could even involve resurfacing an existing Caitya and covering the new surface with many elaborate paintings.

Chaitya worship was an important factor in bringing more of the proto-Newar tribal inhabitants into the Buddhist fold, as it was a devotional practice designed for the general public. Thus, the masses probably began practicing the cart festival of Avalokitesvara/Matsyendranath (Bungakya) during the latter half of the seventh century A.D.

This festival was celebrated by hundreds or even thousands of people, who helped to construct and transport a huge, wheeled cart that bore the image of Avalokitesvara for several days or weeks along a specific route. The introduction of this festival must have been an instant success among the majority of the Kathmandu Valley population. This strengthened Buddhism's standing in relation to the other Hindu and Animist faiths of the Valley at the time.

Forty stone inscriptions made some mention of Buddhism throughout the Licchavi period. Most of the references are concerned with monasticism. However, almost nothing is known about the day-to-day life in the Vihara monasteries or how they functioned administratively.

The names of the fifteen Buddhist monasteries are known, and it is clear from the context in which some of these are named that they are among the most important religious sites of that time. It is not known for certain what schools of Buddhism were most prominent at the time. But the strongest early influences (aside from an even earlier probable substratum of Pali Buddhism) probably came from the Mahasanghika, Sammitiya and the Sarvastivada schools. The Makhyamaka and Yogacara schools were thought to be more influential in the later period with the emergence and growth of the Vajrayana school.

Inscriptional evidence also proves that there was a string of traditional methods of making religious gifts. These offerings were used for earning blessing and making merit, and the women of the Buddhist seem to have taken the lead in offering these gifts. Strikingly, parallel points within the Buddhist cave contain inscriptions of Maharastra, which predated the Licchvi Nepal. The references in the Licchavi inscriptions to the

Mahayana and Vajrayana will be mentioned below in connection with Buddhist art and notable Buddhist figures of the Licchavi period.

Buddhism During the Thakuri Period (600-1200)

The first Thaukri king, Amsuvarma, married his daughter Bhrikuti to the ruler of Tibet, King Songtsen Gampo. According to legend, she received the begging bowl of the Buddha as part of her wedding dowry. It is believed that she introduced Buddhism into Tibet. she is also believed as a reincarnation of the Green Tara of Tibetan Buddhism, who is seen in many Buddhist Thangkas. Thakuri period is known as the golden time for Buddhism.

Buddhism During the Malla Dynasty (1200-1769)

The Malla dynasty saw to the golden period of the syncretism of Hindu and Buddhist art forms by the Newar. The Paubha, the Newari counterpart of the Tibetan Buddhist Thangka, flourished in this period.

Buddhism During the Shah Dynasty (1769-1846)

The Shah dynasty saw the decline of Buddhism in Nepal where it eventually merged with Hinduism as the Hindu Gurkha rose to prominence. In the north, the Mustang kingdom ruled by the Buddhist Lopa and the Thakali saw to the flourishing of Vajrayana (Tibetan Buddhism) in the North.

Buddhism During the Rana Dynasty (1846-1951)

Modern Newar Buddhist practises in Nepal have largely been absorbed into mainstream Hinduism, although certain distinct practises, artforms and castes do remain. In the north, people of Tibetan origin continued to be the much-unchanged practises of Tibetan Buddhism, especially in the case of the Nyimba of Northwest Nepal.

On the other hand, the Thakali, who had traditionally played an important role in the Nepali society but yet retained Tibetan Buddhism, have begun to embrace Hinduism as well in the recent years.

Shah Dyansty (1951-Present)

After the overthrown of Rana dynasty, Buddhism gradually developed in the country. Theravadins played a great role for the revival campaign. Presently, there are three main Buddhist schools; Tibetan Buddhism, Newar Buddhism and Theravada Buddhism. Tourism is another important factor for promoting Nepali Buddhism to the world. Every year, Kathmandu can receive more than 10,000 travellers from all over the world just to visit the Boudha Chetiya and the Swayambhunath stupas.

BUDDHISM IN NEPAL AND NEPAL MANDALA

The historians of Nepal have given different views about the origin of Nepal. Some historians have argued that the country was named Nepal as a sage called 'Ne' had protected it. Some argued on the basis of *Swayambhu Purana* that the country was called Nepal Mandala because it was ruled judiciously by Dharmakar, the first king of Nepal. Nepal grammarians of Nepal Bhasha are of the view that Nepal is also called *Nepa.*

According to ancient Buddhist text, *Mulasarvasti vadavinaya,* Shakyas of Kabilvastu (Kapilvastu) and Baniyas of Sravasti, came to *Newal* (Nepal) from the north. Sometime later, Bhikshu Ananda also entered Newal. The word *Kabilvastu* refers to Kapilvastu and *Newal* refers to Nepal. It is to be recalled that the indigenous people of Nepal call themselves *Nepami* or *Newami.* Other people call them Newar.

Another Buddhist text *Manjushrimula Kalpa* has mentioned Manadeva as king of Nepal Mandala. Researchers have guessed that the time of the composition of *Mulasarvastivadavinaya* is 2 century A.D. And the time of the composition of Manjushriulakalpa is not beyond the reign of Manadeva (464–506A.D). *Swayambhu Purana,* the Buddhist Purana text, has mentioned Nepal Mandala. The word Nepal Mandala has also been carved in a Licchavi inscription.

Vajracharyas often use the word Nepal Mandala. In each and every Buddhist worship activity, first of all Nepal Mandala is uttered and only after this, Kantipur, Latitpur and Bhaktapur are mentioned. It is thus evident that the use of Nepal Mandala is prevalent since the pauranic time to the present day. Contextwise Nepal Mandala may mean different things. An attempt is made here to explain about Nepal Mandala.

The Buddhism of Nepal was greatly influenced by the Tibetan Buddhist tradition. The Buddhism of the Kathmandu Valley was influenced by Theravada Buddhism imported from Myanramar (Burma), Sri Lanka, Thailand, etc. since the last five decades. After from these two traditions, Buddhism prevailing in Nepal since the ancient times to the present day with its own typical tradition, culture, rituals, art is the original Buddhism of Nepal.

Nepal lipi (script of Nepal), Nepal Samvat, Nepal Bhasha have helped preserve the originality and identity of Nepal. Buddhism obtaining in Nepal and the traditional culture has also done the same. The terms like Nepal Mandala, Nepal Samvat, Nepal Bhasha, the religion, art and culture of Nepal are all connected with the Buddhism of Nepal and its tradition.

According to the Buddhist tradition of Nepal, Vajracharya Gurus, Shakya used to practise Samadhiyoga in 24 important religious sites of the Kingdom of Nepal. This is called *purva–seva* or *pitha–seva*. This tradition is alive to the present time. These pithas are the following:

1	Chandralakhu	-Pritha inside Narayanhitti Royal Palace
2	Pasikwo	-East of Tindhara Pathshala and behind Royal Nepal Academy
3	Kamaladi	-Kamaladi Ganeshsthan pitha
4	Lumadhi	-Bhadrakalipitha near Tundikhel
5	Phiwo	-Pitha near Army Headquarters
6	Pachali Naiajima	-Pachalibhairav Pitha

7	Kanga	-Kangesvaripitha. The way from Maruhiti and Dhoka Tole
8	Luti	-Indrayanipitha, near Shovabhagavati
9	Tanaju	-Phaikha, Harisidhi behind, Swayambhu
10	Mhasapi	-Mhepi, Nayabazar
11	Todana	-Nara, Tunaldevi
12	Kati	-Danchhi, below Changu hill
13	Misido	-Mahankali of Bhaktapur
14	Soruthi	-Shankhamol, Patan
15	Jallandhar	-Panga, Charkhala, charghar
16	Balkhu	-Way to Machhenarayan
17	Gwakhu	-Bhinduga, Chhetrapati, on the bank of river, on the border between Kathmandu and Dhading
18	Gadebheru	-Devighat, Trisuli
19	Tupya	-Navalinga (Bhadrakali), left of the way to Buddhanilkantha
20	Sadukuna	-Sadukola, Sankhu
21	Sameda	-Dolalghat
22	Otirtha	-Koshi area, Dumjaghat
23	Tyanga	-Bade Tyanga, Tikabhairab
24	Jhanga	-Jhangu, Koduwal

The above 24 places have been classified into three chakras (circles). The first eight pithas(1–8) have been included into the first circle. The second eight (9-16) pithas have been included into the second circle. The final eight (17-24) pithas have been included into the third circle. Kantewar Chhetrapala at Indrachowk is considered to be the centre of all the three circles. The first circle is called *chitta* (consciousness) chakra.

The second one is called *vaka*(speech) chakra. And the third one is called kaya (action) *chakra*. All the three chakras are also called chitaamandala, Vakamandala and Kayamandala respectively.

If we look at all the 24 pithas or Chinttachakra, Vakachakra and Kayachakra as an organised unit, we have the picture of great mandala. This is the main reason why Nepal is called Mandala. The final circle represents the climax of Nepal Mandala. The final circle is also the boundary of Vajrayana Buddhism in Nepal. Now let me discuss how Nepal was conceived as a mandala and kayachakra.

Vajrayana is an important branch of Buddhism. It is not necessary to tell about the popularity of Vajrayana and its influence and spread. Mandala occupies an important place in Vajrayana. The teaching of Vajrayana is not complete without Mandala. Without it the teaching of Vajrayana is not authentic. It is difficult to mention the number of Mandalas required in Vajrayana education. This is to say that there are innumerable Mandalas in Vajrayana.

According to Chakrasamvara mandala, 24 cells in Chittacakra, Vakchakra and Kayachakra mandalas are known by the following names :

Chittachakra :

1. Pullilamalaya
2. Jallandhar
3. Odiyana
4. Aburda
5. Godavari
6. Rameshwari
7. Devikot
8. Malawa.

Vakachakra :

9. Kamarupa
10. Odra
11. Trisakuni

12. Koshala
13. Kalinga
14. Lanpaka
15. Kanchhi
16. Himalaya.

Kayachakra :

17. Pretapuri
18. Guhyadevata
19. Saurastra
20. Suvarnadevata
21. Nagara
22. Sindhu
23. Malu
24. Kulata.

The above metioned 24 pithas are again classified into 10 special places. They are:

- Pullilamalaya, Jallandhar, Odiyana and Aburda fall under pitha.
- Godavari, Rameswari, Devikot and Malawa fall under sub-pitha.
- Kamarupa and Odra fall under Trisakuni and Koshala sub-area.
- Kalinga and Lanpak fall under *chhandoha* and Kanchhi and Himalaya fall under sub-*chhandoha*.
- Pretapuri and Guhyadevata fall under *Melapaka*. And Saurastra and Suvarnadwipa fall under sub-*Melapaka*.
- Nagara and Sindhu fall under *Samshan* and Malu and Kulata fall under sub-*Sanshan*.

There are other possible reasons:

a. Chakrasamvara is the principal deity of Vajrayana.
b. Compulsory chakrasamvara initiation of Vajracharyas, Shakyas, Urayas in Nepal.
c. Mention in Tibetan history of the handover of Chakrasamvara initiation tradition to Tibetan disciples by the Vajracharya Gurus of Nepal.

d. Continuation of *Purva Seva* in accordance with Chakrasamvara tradition.
e. Only those who are initiated into Chakrasamvara are entitled to *Purva Seva.*
f. Deity in Agam houses in most of the vihars of Nepal is chakrasamvara.
g. Availability of tantras related to chakrasamvara in adequate number in Nepal.
h. *Tri samadhi* (three kinds of samadhi) *Kriya* (activities) are compulsory in Buddhist worship activities in Nepal.

Chakrasamvara mandala is not the only basis of Nepal Mandala. But, it is only one of the factors connected with Vajrayana.

Just as there is the practice of *Purva Seva* on the basis of Chakrasamvara Mandala by conceiving Nepal Mandala, simplarly, there is the tradition of *purva seva* on the basis of *Swayambhu* Purana by coceiving Nepal as a different mandala. It is to be recalled here that when Manjudevacharya cut Kanpotalaparvat, water began to flow out of the valley. Even then the water did not dry up. Water was coming out from the root of lotus flower. In order to stop this Manjudevacharya did *Jalastambhanyoga.* On completion of this yoga, water began to come out from the root of the lotus. At that time Manjudevacharya had a *darshan* (glimpse) of the origin as well as sight of *Sri Nairatmadevi* (Hevajranairatma) and other vajrayana deities in the water that flowed out. Here, Sri Nairatmadevi and other deities must mean Sri Hevajranairatma and Sri Hevajranairatma Mandala.

According to the account of Swayambhu Purana, the establishments of Hevajranairatma by Manjudevacharya and Shantipur by Shantikaracharya is known. It is a traditional belief that the presiding deity of Shantipur is Mahasamvara. It is but natural that Mahasamvara should be connected with Mahasamvara Mandala. It is very much likely that Nepal Mandala was conceived in the tradition of Mahasamvara Mandala.

As mentioned in Swayambhu Purana, Manjudevacharya initiated Dharmashri Mitra, the Acharya of Vikramshila Mahavihar by writing the mandala of Dharmadhatu Vagisvara. He also gave instructions of*Dwadasachchyar*. Then Swayambhu chaitya became famous by the name of*Dharmadhatu Vagisvara*. Dharmadhatu Mandala is the foundation of Dharmadhatu Vagisvara Chaitya.

Within the Nepal Mandala itself, Lalitpur Mandala, Bhaktapur Mandal and Madhyapur Mandala have been conceived. Vajracharya and Shakyas are used to visiting the separate eight pithas of Lalitpur. There is also Kirtipur Chakramandala.

Vajracharyas who are involved in Bodhisattva charya activities create at least one chakra wherever they settle and consstruct the vihar there for propagation of Buddhism. Eight pithas in Lalitpur Mandala, Bhaktapur Mandal, and Madhyapur Mandala1 are as follows :

Lalitpur Mandala :

1. Nakhupitha
2. Balkumari
3. Yeppa
4. One on the way to Chovar
5. Dhantil
6. One on the way to Jawalakhel
7. Sikubi
8. Mahalakshmi.

Bhaktapur Mandal;

1. Centre at Bhairab-Tamadhitol
2. Brahmayani
3. Maheswari
4. Kaumari
5. Vaishnavi
6. Indrayani
7. Chamundra
8. Mahalakshmi.

Madhyapur Mandal – Thimi;

1. Brahmayani
2. Maheswari
3. Kaumari
4. Vaisnavi
5. Indrayani
6. Barahi
7. Chamundra
8. Mahalakshmi.

Now, an attempt is made to present Nepal Mandala from the angle of Prithvimandala.

According to the Buddhist tradition, there are four continents and four sub-continents. The names of four continents are :

1. Purva videhadwipa -in the east
2. Jambudwipa - in the south
3. Apar godavari -in the west
4. Uttara kuru -in the north.

The names of four sub-continents are :

1. Yaudwipa - in the Agnaya side.
2. Randwipa-in the Nairitya side.
3. Laudwipa-in the Vayuvya side.
4. Waudwipa- in the Ishan side.

Among the above four continents, Jambudwipa is a very important one. According to the Buddhist tradition Jambudwipa is divided into ten pithas. If study is done on the initiation of Vajracharyas, the role of Nepal Mandala in the Buddhism of Nepal becomes clear.

BUDDHISM IN INDIA

Buddhism arose in India and flourished for a long time. It eventually declined and disappeared from most regions of India around 13th century, but not without leaving a significant impact. In Himalayan areas like Ladakh, Arunachal Pradesh and Sikkim, Buddhist practice was continued. It has reemerged as a major faith in India in the past century.

Characteristics

Nikaya

- Theravada is the single remaining representative of the eighteen (or twenty) Nikaya schools of Indian Buddhism, which are sometimes referred to by the controversial term Hinayana. Theravada is now practiced mainly in Sri Lanka, Myanmar, Thailand, Cambodia, and Laos.
- Another prominent Nikaya school was the Sarvastivada, much of the doctrine of which was incorporated into Tibetan Buddhism. It included one of the main branches of Indian Abhidharma that was instrumental in the creation of Yogacara doctrine. Its system of monastic rules Vinaya is still used in Tibetan Buddhism and is also somewhat influential in monastic Chinese Buddhism.

Mahayana

For a full discussion of Mahayana Buddhism:

- Madhyamaka (Middle Way), of which the most significant thinker is Nagarjuna
- Yogacara founded by Asanga and Vasubandhu. Also known as Cittamatra, Vijnanavada (Mind Only, Consciousness-Mind Only).
- Tathagatagarbha A tenet of Indian and East Asian Buddhist thought based on the third turning of the wheel of dharma and central to Yogacara.

Vajrayana

A form of Indian Buddhism that emerged in roughly the 7th century AD and later became widespread in Tibet, and also found in Japan.

History

For a full account of the spread of Buddhism in India and

beyond, see the History of Buddhism and the Decline of Buddhism in India.

Modern Revival

At the beginning of the 20th century, Buddhism was almost non-existent in India (Buddhists represented under 5% of the total population of India at the time), the land of its origin. Certain tribal groups in Bengal continued to follow Buddhism, as did peoples in Ladakh and Sikkim where Tibetan culture was influential, but these groups were on the margins of Indian society.

Anagarika Dharmapala and his Followers

The original objective of the Maha Bodhi Society was to restore the glory of the Mahabodhi Temple at Bodh Gaya. But later, the scope of the its activities expanded to involve the promotion of Buddhism in India. In June 1892, a meeting of Buddhists was organized at Darjeeling. Dharmapala spoke to the Tibetian Buddhists and presented a relic of the Buddha to be sent to the Dalai Lama.

After decline of Buddhism in India, the Mahabodhi Temple was under the control of a Hindu *mahant* (abbott). Dharmapala started a campaign to return control of the temple to Buddhists.

A long legal battle ensued, which Dharmapala lost in 1906. Dharmapala built many viharas and temples in India, including the one at Sarnath, the place of Buddha's first sermon. He died in 1933, the same year he was ordained a bhikkhu. After India gained independence, the control passed from the Hindu*mahant* to the Bihar State Government of Bihar, which established a temple management committee. The first monk under the management committee was Anagarika Munindra, a member of the Maha Bodhi Society.

Dharmapala considered Buddhism an Aryan religion and stated that the next Buddha will be born in the Brahmin caste, in the city of Benares, which will then be called *Ketumati*. He also said that the Vedic Brahmanism, Zorastrianism, Muhammedanism, Judaism, Christianity, Confucianism and

Saiva Vedantism were "destructive religions". He considered *Buddhagama* (Buddhism), Jainism and Vaishnavism as the only non-destructive religions. He considered Buddhism as the oldest religion and the "only religion that stands by itself":

"Christianity and Islam are alien to the people in spirit; Brahmanism is only for the high castes; and the only religion that can help the teeming millions of India is the religion of Compassion of the Buddha, the Aryan prince of the solar line of Ikshvaku."

The Maha Bodhi Society mainly attracted upper-caste people.

Dalit Buddhist Movement

A Buddhist revivalist movement among Dalit Indians was initiated in 1890s by Dalit leaders such as Iyothee Thass, Brahmananda Reddy, and Dharmananda Kosambi. Sri Lankan Buddhist monks played big role for Dalit Buddhist movement in India.. In, 1956 B. R. Ambedkar converted to Buddhism along with followers, giving a major impetus to the Dalit Buddhist movement in India.

Others

Dharmananda Damodar Kosambi, a Goan, was another important Buddhist thinker of India.

S. N. Goenka, a meditation teacher trained in Burma is an active Buddhist leader in India. Goenka plans to build a stupa. The most significant part of this structure is that it will be more than twice as large as the presently largest dome structure in the world, namely the Gol Gumbaz at Bijapur in India. The stones are to be placed to form a load bearing dome structure without supporting pillars inside the hall.

British Involvement

British Buddhists have played a role in revival of Buddhism in India through the work of the Karuna Trust, a London-based Buddhist charity set up by members of the Western Buddhist Order and part of the FWBO. The Karuna Trust's work is inspired by Dr. Ambedkar and seeks to work towards his vision of liberty, equality, fraternity and justice. Karuna's work is also inspired by Sangharakshita, the founder of the Western Buddhist Order, who met Dr. Ambedkar in India. Sangharakshita deeply moved by the situation facing Dalit people, and addressed followers of Dr. Ambedkar at mass public meetings after the latter's death. The Karuna Trust was set up in 1980 by some of Sangharakshita's disciples to address the great material suffering and poverty experienced by millions of Dalit people across India. Through educational and training projects in India and Bangladesh, Karuna supports and enable of some of the world's most disadvantaged people, who are marginalised. Friends of the Western Buddhist Order (FWBO) is a Buddhist movement that was founded in the UK by Sangharakshita (formerly Dennis Lingwood) in 1967, followed by the Western Buddhist Order in 1968. In 1978 Indian wing of the FWBO founded, known as the Trailokya Bauddha Mahasangha Sahayaka Gana.

Japanese Involvement

A Japanese organization called the Ogawa Trust maintains Nagarjuna Hospital at Mansar, an English language school for poor students, an orphanage, cooperative home industries for women, and various other kinds of aid. The Ogawa Trust has also helped in the building of an ornate Buddhist temple at Kampti, a town near Nagpur.

An emerging religious organization called Soka Gakkai International has a chapter in India called Bharat Soka Gakkai. The group was first recognized by the Indian Government in 1986. However, the world-wide organization has been often been called a cult by it's critics; It's current leader, Daisaku Ikeda, has also been called a cult figure.

Taiwanese Involvement

Taiwanese Buddhists have contributed to the growth of Buddhism in India in multiple ways, one of which is in the ordination of Theravadin nuns. Taiwan, with one of the most active groups of nuns in the world, has begun to facilitate the ordination of women in India. In February 1998 a full ordination ceremony was held at Bodh Gaya by Taiwan's Fo Guang Shan Monastery. 132 applicants arrived to receive ordination as nuns and undertook a nine day period of training and questioning. Of these candidates 66 were from South Asia, and of these at least twenty-eight were from Maharashtra.

DECLINE OF BUDDHISM IN INDIA

The Decline of Buddhism in India, in the land of its birth occurred for a variety of reasons, and happened even as it continued to flourish beyond the frontiers of India. Buddhism was established in the area of ancient Magadha and Kosala by Gautama Buddha in the 6th century BCE, in what is now modern Uttar Pradesh and Bihar. Buddhism, over the next Over 1500 years became the region's dominant belief system, spreading across Indian sub-continent. After the death of Gautama Buddha, Buddhism saw rapid expanzion in its first century, especially in northern and central India.

The Mauryan Emperor Ashoka (304-232 BCE) and later monarchs encouraged the expansion of Buddhism into Asia through religious ambassadors. Chinese scholars traveling through the region between the 5th and 8th centuries CE, such as Faxian, Xuanzang, I-ching, Hui-sheng, and Sung-Yun, began to speak of a decline of the Buddhist *sangha*, especially in the wake of the White Hun invasion. A continuing decline occured after the fall of the Pala dynasty in the 12th century CE, continuiung with the later destruction of monasteries by Muslim conquerors. Buddhism was virtually extinct by the end of the 19th century. In recent times, Buddhism has seen a revival in India due to the influence of Anagarika Dharmapala, Dr. B. R. Ambedkar and Tenzin Gyatso.

Buddhism under Various Governments

The Sungas

Following the Mauryans, Pusyamitra Sunga is linked in legend with the persecution of Buddhists and a resurgence of a Hinduism that forced Buddhism outwards to Kashmir, Gandhara and Bactria.. There is some doubt as to whether he did or did not persecute Buddhists actively.

A Buddhist tradition holds him as having taken taking steps to check the spread of Buddhism as "the number one enemy of the sons of the Sakya's and a most cruel persecutor of the religion". The *Divyavadana* ascribes to him the razing of *stupas* and *viharas* built by Ashoka, the placing of a bounty of 100 dinaras upon the heads of Buddhist monks (*Shramanas*) and describes him as one who wanted to undo the work of Ashoka. This account has however been described as "exaggerated".

Historian Romila Thapar writes that the Asokavadana legend is, in all probability, a "Buddhist version of Pusyamitra's attack of the Mauryas", and reflects the fact that, with the declining influence of Buddhism in the Imperial court, Buddhist monuments and institutions would receive less attention.

Some historians have rejected the accuracy of the Buddhist texts that record Pushyamitra's persecution of Buddhists. The first accounts appear two centuries after Pushyamitra's reign in *Asokavadana* and the *Divyavadana*. Koenraad Elst posits that historical facts confirm that Pushyamitra allowed and patronized the construction of monasteries and Buddhist universities in his domains, as well as the still-existent stupa of Sanchi.

While Sir John Marshall states that it is possible that the original brick stupa built by Ashoka was destroyed by Pusyamitra and then restored by his successor Agnimitra. Arhaelogical evidence is scarce and uncertain.Following Ashoka's sponsorship of Buddhism, it is possible that Buddhist institutions fell on harder times under the Sungas but no evidence of active persecution has been noted. Etienne Lamotte observes: *"To judge from the documents, Pushyamitra must be acquitted through lack of proof."*

The Sungas were patrons of Hinduism and their lack of royal patronage was also a setback to Buddhism, resulting in the splintering of Buddhism into many forces. Some of them were: the *Saravastivadins*, *Mahasargikas*, *Sthaviravadha*, and *Yogacara*. This resulted in a diversity of opinions and interpretations that led to a conflict between warring schools shortly after the fall of the Mauryans. Later Sunga kings were seen as more amenable to Buddhism and as having contributed to the building of the stupa at Bharhut.

Hinduism traditionally does not evangelize. Hinduism competed in spirtual and political realm with Buddhism. Buddhism also flourished in the realms of the Bactrian kings.

Guptas

Buddhism and saw a brief revival under the Guptas. By the 4th to 5th century Buddhism was already in decline in northern India, even as it was achieving multiple successes in Central Asia and along the Silk Road as far as China. It continued to prosper in Gandhara under the Shahi kingdom.

White Huns

Central Asian and North Western Indian Buddhism weakened in the 6th century following the White Hun invasion who followed their own religions such as Tengri, Nestorian Christianity, and Manichean. Their King Mihirakula who ruled from 515 BC suppressed Buddhism destroying monasteries as far as modern-day Allahabad before his son reversed the policy.

Harsha

In the North and west the collapse of Harshavardana's kingdom gave rise to many small kingdoms. This led to the rise of the martial Rajputs clans across the gangetic plains and marked the end of Buddhist ruling clans along with a sharp decline in royal patronage until a revival under the Pala Empire in the Bengal region. Subsequently the replacement of Buddhist royal lines with Hindu royals and the rise of martial Rajput dynasties further pressured Buddhism.

Muhammad Bin Qasim

In AD 711, Muhammad bin Quasim attacked the southern shores of Sindh. Muhammad Bin Quasim is linked with Islamic persecution of Buddhists. Quasim destroyed a Buddhist holy site and built a mosque in it's place.

It was claimed that the Buddhists helped bin Qasim in conquering parts of India. Al-Baladhuri recorded that two "Samanis" went to Qasim to negiotiate for peace, however he also recorded that it was the inhabitants of Nirum who sent the priests to Qasim.

Muhammad bin Qasim also demolished temples and monasteries, e.g. he built at Nirun a mosque on the site of the temple of Budh.

Mahmud of Ghazni

By the 10th century Mahmud of Ghazni defeated the Hindu-Shahis effectively removing Hindu influence and ending Buddhist self-governance across Central Asia and the Punjab region. He demolished both stupas and temples during his numerous campaigns across north-western India but left those within his domains and Afghanistan alone even as al-Biruni recorded Buddha as the prophet "Burxan".

Mahmud of Ghazni is said to have been an iconoclast. Hindu and Buddhist statues, shrines and temples were looted and destroyed and many Buddhists had to take refuge in Tibet.

Pala's

In the east under the Palas in Bengal, Mahayana Buddhism flourished and spread to Bhutan and Sikkim. The Palas created many temples and a distinctive school of Buddhist art. Mahayana Buddhism flourished under the Palas, between the 8th and the 12th century before it collapsed at the hands of the attacking Sena dynasty.

Muhammad of Ghor

Muhammad attacked the north-western regions of the Indian subcontinent many times. Gujarat later fell to Muhammad of Ghor's armies in 1197. Muhammad of Ghor's armies destroyed many Buddhist structures, including the great Buddhist university of Nalanda.

In 1200 Muhammad Khilji, one of Qutb-ud-Din's generals destroyed monasteries fortified by the Sena armies, such as the one at Vikramshila.

Many monuments of ancient Indian civilization were destroyed by the invading armies, including Buddhist sanctuaries near Benares. Buddhist monks who escaped the massacre fled to Nepal, Tibet and South India.

The Mongols

In 1215 Genghis Khan conquered Afghanistan and devastated the Muslim world. In 1227 after his death his conquest was divided and Chagatai established the Chagatai Khanate where his son Arghun made Buddhism the state religion during which time he came down harshly on Islam and demolished mosques to build many stupas.

He was succeeded by his brother, and then his son Ghazan who converted to Islam and in 1295 who changed the state religion and after his reign and the splitting of the Chagatai Khanate little mention of Buddhism or the stupas built by the Mongols can be found in Afghanistan and Central Asia can be found in Afghanistan and central Asia.

Timur (Tamarlane)

Timur was a 14th-century warlord of Turco-Mongol descent, conqueror of much of Western and central Asia, and founder of the Timurid Empire.

Timur destroyed Buddhist establishments and raided areas in which Buddhism had flourished.

Mughals

Mughal rule also contributed to the decline of Buddhism. They are reported to have destroyed many Hindu temples and Buddhist shrines alike or converted many sacred Hindu places into Muslim shrines and mosques. Mughal rulers like Aurangzeb destroyed Buddhist temples and monasteries and replaced them with Islamic mosques.

IDEOLOGICAL AND FINANCIAL CAUSES

Financial Reasons

Buddhist monasteries were well-funded and life within was relatively easy. To avoid unwanted members, many monasteries became selective about whom they admitted, in some cases based on social class. This further cut off the sangha from Indian society.

Xuanzang's Report

Xuanzang reports in his travels across India during the 7th century that Buddhism was popular in Andhra, Dhanyakataka, and Dravida which today roughly correspond to the modern day Indian states of Andhra Pradesh and Tamil Nadu. He also reports numerous ruined and deserted stupas in the conquered Buddhist regions such as by the regions around modern day Nepal, as well as the persecution of Buddhists by Ssanka in the Kingdom of Gouda.

Xuanzang compliments the patronage of Harshavardana during this same period while noting in his travels that in various regions Buddhism was giving way to Jainism and Hinduism.

Philosophical Divergence with Adi Shankara

In 9th century A.D. the Buddhist philosophers started to lose ground with the Hindu Saint Adi Shankara. Shankaracharya debated with Buddhist monks and raised issues with Buddhist philosophy.

The rejection of the notion of Atman and yet the endorsement of rebirth, could not be explained by the Buddhists. The resurgence of Hinduism with the ideas of Shankaracharya led to reduction of royal patronage of the Buddhist monks. As political patronage failed it came under increasing pressure by Hinduism and the revival movements of Adi Shankara. Shakyamuni Buddha eventually came to be venerated as a manifestation of the Hindu god Vishnu.

Sufis and the Bhakti Movement

When Islam arrived in India, it sought conversion from, not assimilation to or integration with, the already present religions. Under Sufi influence, the pressures of caste and with no political support structure left in place to resist social mores many converted to Islam in the Bengal region.

After the Mongol invasions of Islamic lands across Central Asia, many Sufis also found themselves fleeing towards India and around the environs of Bengal. Here their influence, caste attitudes towards Buddhists, previous familiarity with converting Buddhists, a lack of Buddhist political power, Hinduism's resurgence through movements such as the Advaita and the bhakti movement, all contributed to a significant realignment of beliefs relegating Buddhism in India to the peripheries.

Islam

Hinduism traditionally does not evangelize. Hinduism does not allow conversion of non believers to the faith; it then tolerates the existence of other beliefs. When conquered, Islamic rulers have been known to force coversion or flee the land under Islamic rule; otherwise punishable by enslavement or even execution.

Buddhism suffered immensely during the Muslim conquest in the Indian subcontinent with muslim rulers such as Muhammad bin Qasim, Muhammad of Ghor, Qutb-ud-Din and Aurangzeb destroying temples and shrines and seeking conversion of Buddhists to Islam.

According to Dr. B. R. Ambedkar, "there can be no doubt that the fall of Buddhism was due to the invasions of the Muslims." He wrote: "Thus the origin of the word ["but", Persian for "idol"] indicates that in the Muslim mind idol worship had come to be identified with the religion of Buddha. To the Muslims they were one and the same thing.

The mission to break idols thus became the mission to destroy Buddhism. Islam destroyed Buddhism not only in India but wherever it went. Bactria, Parthia, Afghanistan, Gandhara and Chinese Turkestan (...) in all these countries Islam destroyed Buddhism."

The Arabic invaders described Indian Pagans as But-parast, and idol-breakers as but-shikan. The word "but" is derived from Buddhism, but the Arabs used it for "Indian paganism" in general. Therefore in Arabic chronicles it is not always evident if Buddhists, Hindus or other Indian religions are meant.

Survival of Buddhism in India

At the beginning of the modern era, Buddhism was very nearly extinct in mainstream Indian society. Some tribal peoples living in the territory of modern India did continue to practice Buddhism. In Bengal, the Bauls still practice a syncretic form of Hinduism that was strongly influenced by Buddhism. There is also evidence of small communities of Indian Theravada Buddhists existing continuously in Bengal in the area of Chittagong up to the present.

Buddhist institutions flourished in eastern India right until the Islamic invasion. Buddhism still survives among the Barua, a community of Bengali/Magadh descent that migrated to Chittagong region. Indian Buddhism also survives among Newars of Nepal.

In Orissa, Mahima Dharma, a derivative of Buddhism, survived until 18th century.

The Hindu Kayasthas, a community of scribes in North India, had been a supporter of Buddhism since the early period. They continued to support Buddhism until about 12th-13th century in some regions.

Buddhism survived in Kashmir valley until 13-14th century, perhaps slightly longer in the nearby Swat Valley. In Ladakh region, adjacent to Kashmir valley, Tibetan Buddhism survives. Tibetan Buddhism must have been popular in Kashmir at one time, as we learn from Rajatarangini of Kalhana.

In Tamilnadu and Kerala, Buddhism survived until 15-16th century. At Nagapattinam, in Tamil Nadu, Buddhist idols were cast and inscribed until this time, and the ruins of the Chudamani Vihara stood until they were destroyed by the Jesuits in 1867. In south in some pockets, it may have survived even longer.

BUDDHISM IN MONGOLIA

Buddhism in Mongolia has been influenced by Tibetan Buddhism. Traditional Mongols worshipped heaven (the "clear blue sky") and their ancestors, and they followed ancient northern Asian practices of shamanism, in which human intermediaries went into trance and spoke to and for some of the numberless infinities of spirits responsible for human luck or misfortune. In 1578 Altan Khan, a Mongol military leader with ambitions to unite the Mongols and to emulate the career of Chinggis, invited the head of the rising Yellow Sect of Tibetan Buddhism to a summit.

They formed an alliance that gave Altan Khan legitimacy and religious sanction for his imperial pretensions and that provided the Buddhist school with protection and patronage. Altan khan gave the Tibetan leader the title of Dalai Lama (Ocean Lama), which his successors still hold.

Altan Khan died soon after, but in the next century the Yellow Sect spread throughout Mongolia, aided in part by the efforts of contending Mongol aristocrats to win religious sanction and mass support for their ultimately unsuccessful efforts to unite all Mongols in a single state.

Monasteries (momg.*datsa*n) were built across Mongolia, often sited at the juncture of trade and migration routes or at summer pastures, where large numbers of herders would congregate for shamanistic rituals and sacrifices. Buddhist monks carried out a protracted struggle with the indigenous shamans and succeeded, to some extent, in taking over their functions and fees as healers and diviners, and in pushing the shamans to the religious and cultural fringes of Mongolian culture.

Tibetan Buddhism, which combines elements of the Mahayana and the Tantric schools of Buddhism with traditional

Tibetan rituals of curing and exorcism, shares the common Buddhist goal of individual release from suffering and the cycles of rebirth.

The religion holds that salvation, in the sense of release from the cycle of rebirth, can be achieved through the intercession of compassionate Buddhas (enlightened ones) who have delayed their own entry to the state of selfless bliss (nirvana) to save others. Such Buddhas, who are many, are in practice treated more as deities than as enlightened humans and occupy the centre of a richly polytheistic universe of subordinate deities, opposing demons, converted and reformed demons, wandering ghosts, and saintly humans that reflects the folk religions of the regions into which Buddhism expanded.

Tantrism contributed esoteric techniques of meditation and a repertoire of sacred icons, phrases, and gestures that easily lent themselves to pragmatic (rather than transcendental) and magical interpretation. The religion posits progressive stages of enlightenment and comprehension of the reality underlying the illusions that hamper the understanding and perceptions of those not trained in meditation or Buddhist doctrine, with sacred symbols interpreted in increasingly abstract terms. Thus, a ritual that appears to a common yak herder as a straightforward exorcism of disease demons will be interpreted by a senior monk as a representation of conflicting tendencies in the mind of a meditating ascetic.

In Tibet Buddhism thus became an amalgam, combining colourful popular ceremonies and curing rituals for the masses with the study of esoteric doctrine for the monastic elite.

The Yellow Sect, in contrast to competing sects, stressed monastic discipline and the use of logic and formal debates as aids to enlightenment. The basic Buddhist tenet of reincarnation was combined with the Tantric idea that buddhahood could be achieved within a person's lifetime to produce a category of leaders who were considered to have achieved buddhahood and to be the reincarnations of previous leaders. These leaders, referred to as incarnate or living Buddhas, held secular power and supervised a body of ordinary monks, or lamas (from a

Tibetan title bla-ma, meaning "the revered one)". The monks were supported by the laity, who thereby gained merit and who received from the monks instructions in the rudiments of the faith and monastic services in healing, divination, and funerals.

Buddhism and the Buddhist monkhood always have played significant political roles in Central and Southeast Asia, and the Buddhist church in Mongolia was no exception. Church and state supported each other, and the doctrine of reincarnation made it possible for the reincarnations of living Buddhas to be discovered conveniently in the families of powerful Mongol nobles.

Tibetan Buddhism is monastic. By the beginning of the twentieth century, Outer Mongolia had 583 monasteries and temple complexes, which controlled an estimated 20 percent of the country's wealth. Almost all Mongolian cities have grown up on the sites of monasteries.

Yihe Huree, as Ulaanbaatar was then known, was the seat of the preeminent living buddha of Mongolia (the Jebtsundamba Khutuktu, also known as the Bogdo Gegen and later as Bogdo Khan), who ranked third in the ecclesiastical hierarchy, after the Dalai Lama and the Panchen Lama. Two monasteries there contained approximately 13,000 and 7,000 monks, and the prerevolutionary Mongol name of the settlement known to outsiders as Urga, Yihe Huree, means big monastery. Over the centuries, the monasteries acquired riches and secular dependents; they gradually increased their wealth and power as those of the Mongol nobility declined.

Some nobles donated a portion of their dependent families—people, rather than land, were the foundation of wealth and power in old Mongolia—to the monasteries; some herders dedicated themselves and their families to serve the monasteries either from piety or from the desire to escape the arbitrary exactions of the nobility. In some areas, the monasteries and their living Buddhas (of whom there were a total of 140 in 1924) also were the secular authorities.

In the 1920s, there were about 110,000 monks, including children, who made up about one-third of the male population, although many of these lived outside the monasteries and did not observe their vows.

About 250,000 people, more than a third of the total population, either lived in territories administered by monasteries and living Buddhas or were hereditary dependents of the monasteries. With the end of Chinese rule in 1911, the Buddhist church and its clergy provided the only political structure available, and the autonomous state thus took the form of a weakly centralized theocracy, headed by the Jebtsundamba khutuktu in Yihe Huree.

By the twentieth century, Buddhism had penetrated deeply into Mongolian culture, and the populace willingly supported the lamas and the monasteries. Foreign observers had a uniformly negative opinion of Mongolian monks, condemning them as lazy, ignorant, corrupt, and debauched, but the Mongolian people did not concur. Ordinary Mongolians apparently combined a cynical and realistic anticlericalism, sensitive to the faults and the human fallibility of individual monks or groups of monks, with a deep and unwavering concern for the transcendent values of the church.

The Suppression of Buddhism

When the revolutionaries—determined to modernize their country and to reform its society—took power, they confronted a massive ecclesiastical structure that enrolled a larger part of the population, monopolized education and medical services, administered justice in a large part of the country, and controlled a great deal of the national wealth. The Buddhist church, moreover, had no interest in reforming itself or in modernizing the country.

The result was a protracted political struggle that absorbed the energies and attention of the party and its Soviet advisers for nearly twenty years. As late as 1934, the party counted 843 major Buddhist centers, about 3,000 temples of various sizes, and nearly 6,000 associated buildings, which usually were the only fixed structures in a world of felt tents. The annual income of the church was 31 million tugriks, while that of the state was 37.5 million tugriks. A party source claimed that, in 1935, monks constituted 48 percent of the adult male population. In a campaign marked by shifts of tactics, alternating between conciliation and persecution, and armed uprisings led by monks and abbots, the Buddhist church was removed progressively from public administration, was subjected to confiscatory taxes, was forbidden to teach children, and was prohibited from recruiting new monks or replacing living Buddhas.

The campaign's timing matched the phases of Josef Stalin's persecution of the Russian Orthodox Church. In 1938—amid official fears that the church and monasteries were likely to cooperate with the Japanese, who were promoting a pan-Mongol puppet state—the remaining monasteries were dissolved, their property was seized, and their monks were secularized.

The monastic buildings were taken over to serve as local government offices or schools. Only then was the ruling party, which since 1921 gradually had built a cadre of politically reliable and secularly educated administrators, able to destroy the church and to mobilize the country's wealth and population for its program of modernization and social change.

Uses of Buddhism

Since at least the early 1970s, one monastery, the Gandan Monastery, with a community of 100 monks, was open in Ulaanbaatar. It was the country's sole functioning monastery.

A few of the old monasteries survived as museums, and the Gandan Monastery served as a living museum and a tourist attraction. Its monks included a few young men who had undergone a five-year training period, but whose motives and mode of selection were unknown to Western observers.

The party apparently thought that Buddhism no longer posed a challenge to its dominance and that— because Buddhism had played so large a part in the country's history, traditional arts, and culture, total extirpation of knowledge about the religion and its practices would cut modern Mongols off from much of their past, to the detriment of their national identity. A few aged former monks were employed to translate Tibetan-language handbooks on herbs and traditional medicine. Government spokesmen described the monks of the Gandan Monastery as doing useful work. Today the monastery has been reinvigorated as the Gandantegchinlen Khiid Monastery by the post-Communist governments of the country.

Buddhism, furthermore played a role in Mongolia's foreign policy by linking Mongolia with the communist and the noncommunist states of East and Southeast Asia. Ulaanbaatar was the headquarters of the Asian Buddhist Conference for Peace, which has held conferences for Buddhists from such countries as Japan, Vietnam, Cambodia, Sri Lanka, and Bhutan; published a journal for international circulation; and maintained contacts with such groups as the Christian Peace Conference, the Afro-Asian People's Solidarity Organization, and the Russian Orthodox Church. It sponsored the visits of the Dalai Lama to Mongolia in 1979 and 1982. The organization, headed by the abbot of then-Gandan Monastery, advanced the foreign policy goals of the Mongolian government, which were in accord with those of the Soviet Union.

BUDDHISM IN MALAYSIA

Malaysia is a multiconfessional society, with slightly more than half of its people being Muslims. The internal conflicts the nation has faced have generally been precipitated by ethnicity rather than religion.

The country is officially a Muslim state, and the Government actively promotes the spread of Islam in the country and its friendship with other Muslim countries. Nevertheless, other religions are tolerated and the individual's right to the freedom of worship is listed in the country's constitution. The government also gives grants to religious bodies of other religions for building projects and other programs. All the major religious festival days of the Muslims, Buddhists, Hindus, and Christians have been declared national public holidays.

According the Malaysian constitution, the majority ethnic group, the Malays, are legally defined as Muslim. They constitute 58% of the population, with the remainder consisting mostly of Indians, who are generally Hindus, and Chinese, who are generally Buddhists or Christians. There are also a small number of other indigenous and immigrants; among the latter are Malaysians of Sinhalese, Thai, and Eurasian origin. Many of these immigrant peoples also profess the Christian faith, but there are also Buddhists among the Sinhalese and Thai. Nearly all of the Buddhists in Malaysia live in urban areas, since they are mostly engaged in business or employed in various professions.

The general climate of religious freedom in Malaysia indicates that Buddhism may have the opportunity to expand in the future. However, Buddhism has often been described as a gentle religion which does not carry out an active program to seek converts.

Recently, a number of Malaysian Buddhist leaders have responded to the decline in religious participation by the children of Buddhist families, have attempted to reformulate their message to address modern life more directly. Groups involved in these education efforts include such as the Buddhist Missionary Society. Missionary Society leaders have argued that, while many educated youths seek an intellectual approach to Buddhism, an equally large number of people prefer to approach the religion through the tradition of ceremony and symbolism. In response to these needs, religious practices are carried out, but in a way that is simple and dignified, removing what can be seen as superstition. Efforts are made to explain why sutras are chanted, lamps lit, flowers offered, and so on.

As a religion without a supreme head to direct its development, Buddhism is practised in various forms, which, although rarely in open conflict, can sometimes lead to confusion among Buddhists. In Malaysia, some ecumenical moves have been made to coordinate the activities of different types of Buddhists. One example is the formation of the Joint Wesak Celebrations Committee of the temples in Kuala Lumpur and Selangor, which coordinates the celebration of Wesak, a holiday commemorating the birth of the Buddha.

An initiative has also begun to form a Malaysian Buddhist Council, representing the various sects of Buddhism in the country to extend the work of the development of Buddhism, especially in giving contemporary relevance to the practise of the religion, as well as to promote solidarity among Buddhists in general.

MALAYSIAN THERAVADA

Theravada Buddhism had existed in Malaysia for centuries among the Thai ethnic community that lived along the peninsula's northern border with Thailand. A vigorous community, the Thai bhikkhu sangha had a benevolent influence on the other races especially the ethnic Chinese in the northern states. However, due to language and cultural differences, few Chinese ordained into the Thai bhikkhu sangha. Theravada Buddhism only began to have a significant impact on the Chinese Malaysian community early this century as a result of a curious combination of causes.

The Sri Lankans

The first Theravada society in Malaysia was the Sasana Abhiwurdhi Wardhana Society ("SAWS") which was registered at the end of the nineteenth century. Although serving the immigrant Sri Lankans, it was to play a remarkable role about fifty years later. Up till this time, the Sri Lankan bhikkhus it hosted, like the numerous Thai temples then existing, ministered to their particular ethnic community.

However, this was to change when a remarkable 32 year old bhikkhu by the name of Ven. K Sri Dhammananda, upon the invitation of the SAWS, stepped onto the shores of Malaysia in the last days of December 1951. Ordained as a samanera at age 12, and a bhikkhu at age 21, he had excelled as a scholar. In 1945, he entered the Benares Hindu University in India for further tertiary education. Among his contemporaries in the university were Ven. Saddhatissa and Ven Amritananda who later were to play important dhammaduta roles in England and Nepal respectively. In the year following his arrival in

Malaysia, Ven Dhammananda met the highest authority of the British colonial government, Sir Gerald Templar. At that meeting, he convinced Sir Templar that an effective means to counter the ongoing communist insurgency was to allow him to preach to the ethnic Chinese in the villages who were the main supporters of the insurgents.

In 1962, to further enhance his missionary efforts, he formed the Buddhist Missionary Society ("BMS"). This society printed the Ven.'s numerous booklets on the Dhamma and freely distributed them by the hundreds of thousands throughout the country.

These books were the first introduction to Buddhism for many. The Ven. also started a vigorous program of regular sermons at the Buddhist Maha Vihara, Brickfields in the capital city of Kuala Lumpur and at various societies scattered throughout the country. As a result, Theravada Buddhism captured the hearts of a large section of the English-speaking public. The Ven. was also ably assisted by several other Sri Lankan monks. Among the more notable were:

- Ven. Gunaratana who after 10 years (1958-1968) in Malaysia, left for USA where he established the Bhavana Society in West Virginia.
- Ven. Wimalajothi (1976-1987) who after returning to Sri Lanka set up the Buddhist Cultural Centre emulating the techniques he had learnt.
- Ven. Dhammaratana who excelled in social work and set up the Tiratana Orphanage and Tiratana Community Centre in Kuala Lumpur.

In December 1976, Ven. Dhammananda initiated a program enabling Buddhists interested in experiencing the life of a monk to ordain as samaneras for a short period of time. Since then, this novitiate program has been an annual affair and has resulted in several young men taking up the robe as a life commitment. Some of these bhikkhu disciples are pursuing studies in Sri Lanka or residing at the Brickfields Vihara.

Elsewhere, other temples set up by Sri Lankan monks also gained popularity. One such was the Mahindarama Vihara on the island of Penang under Ven. Pemaratana who resided there since 1957 till his death in 1997. Others are the Sri Lanka Buddhist Temple in the northern part of Kuala Lumpur under the abbot Ven. Saranankara and the Seck Kia Eenh temple in Melaka which although set up by locals have maintained a tradition of inviting Sri Lankan monks as residents.

The Odd American

The early years of dhammaduta work in Malaysia also came in the most unlikely person of Ven. Sumangalo. He was born in Alabama, USA as Robert Clifton, the eldest son to a Christian family that for 300 years had a tradition of giving its first son to be a Christian minister.

However in his teens he decided to become a Buddhist and for a brief period led a Buddhist group in California.

Coming to Malaysia in 1957 he was instrumental in setting up numerous youth groups in the major towns and centers of learning. Though few, if any, of these groups remain in their original form, their members became the pioneers of the lay Buddhist movement.

The Burmese

In Penang, the Burmese temple and some of the Thai temples had a significant effect on the Malaysians. The Burmese Dhammikarama temple in particular was very popular after Ven. Pannavamsa arrived to take up residency in 1961. His Dhamma classes were very popular and introduced many to the Dhamma. In 1979 he left for Los Angeles, USA to assist Ven.Silananda.

The Thais

One of the several Thai temples in Penang, Wat Ping Ban Onn set up the Malaysian Buddhist Meditation Centre with a resident Thai bhikkhu to teach the technique of meditation popularized by the Burmese monk Mahasi Sayadaw. This centre is closely associated with many Chinese Malaysian monks particularly those that pursue the path of meditative practice.

And the Malaysians Themselves

One of the earliest of such monks is the Ven. Sujivo. He ordained as a samanera shortly after his graduation from the prestigious University of Malaya in 1975. During his monastic training he practised under several masters including Sayadaw U Pandita in Sasana Yeiktha in Yangon, Myanmar. Ven. Sujivo, more than any other person, is responsible for developing a keen interest in vipassana meditation among a large section of the Theravada community through his teachings, retreats and books.

He set up Santisukharama, a meditation centre in a rubber tree plantation in Kota Tinggi on the southern tip of peninsular Malaysia. Since then he has inspired numerous meditation centers to be set up by various groups throughout the country and has also extended his teaching tours to East Malaysia and Australia.

Others include the Ven. Suvanno who ordained late in life after retiring from his job as a hospital attendant. The Ven. Suvanno is a charismatic speaker who is fluent in English as well as the vernacular Hokkien dialect. His talks draw large crowds and he is equally at ease speaking on the deeper suttas to the intellectuals or teaching the basic tenets to those new to the religion. He established the Buddhist Hermitage in the northern village of Lunas, one of the first monasteries to be set up by Malaysian bhikkhus. Another popular teacher was the Ven. Visuddhacara an ex-journalist with a major newspaper. At one time, he lived in the forest and authored books from time to time, but now he has reverted back to lay life although still active in Dhamma work.

The Ven. Aggacitta is lesser known but among the bhikkhus is respected for his knowledge of Vinaya and the Buddhist scriptures. In Myanmar he trained in both the scholarly and meditative practices.

Ven. Aggacitta is the translator of U Pandita's book "In This Very Life" published by the Buddhist Publication Society, Sri Lanka. In early 2000, he initiated a promising and ambitious project. Called the Sasanarakkha Buddhist Sanctuary, it comprises the establishment of a forest monastery specially for the proper training of Malaysian bhikkhus. It's primary objective is to train monks in learning, morals and meditative wisdom and to evolve a Malaysian Theravada identity guided by the scriptural tradition

Another Chinese Malaysian bhikkhu is the Ven. Mahinda. While a layman, he was pursuing his tertiary studies in New Zealand when he met an itinerant Buddhist lay-preacher. He decided to quit his final year university studies to follow the preacher on his world tours.

He later returned to Malaysia and was ordained under the Ven. K Sri Dhammananda. Although he is presently based in Aloka Meditation Centre near Sydney, Australia, he makes annual trips to Malaysia to conduct the novitiate program at the Buddhist Maha Vihara, Brickfields. The Ven. Katapunna who established Solitude Grove, a small forest hermitage in Penang is also a popular teacher. Before returning to Malaysia he spent several years in Sri Lanka, India and Bangladesh.

At present, it is estimated that there are as many as 80 Malaysian bhikkhus, excluding those of ethnic Thai descent. An encouraging observation is that many of the recent ordinations were of young men, several of whom have had tertiary education.

However, as the country has no facilities whatsoever for the training of bhikkhus, many of them travel to Thailand or Myanmar to ordain and practise under various teachers. A smaller number who pursue scholarly study are training in the bhikkhu schools of Sri Lanka while the rest reside in various small temples and hermitages mostly in and around Penang island.

Till today, there has been no strong initiative to organise themselves or unite into an indigenous bhikkhu sangha. Thus, with the passing of the era of the Sri Lankan dhammaduta monks, the future of the Malaysian bhikkhu sangha may very well rest on the success of the Sasanarakkha Buddhist Sanctuary project..

BUDDHISM IN MYANMAR

Buddhism in Myanmar is predominantly of the Theravada tradition or the southern school. About 90% of Myanmar practises Buddhism. Adherents are most likely found among the dominant ethnic Bamar (or Burmans), Shan, Rakhine (Arakanese), Mon, Karen, and Chinese who are well integrated into Burmese society. Among ethnic Bamar, Theravada Buddhism is practised often in conjunction with nat worship. Monks, collectively known as the Sangha are venerated members of Burmese society.

Myanmar's history of Buddhism is portrayed by a landscape filled with pagodas which is why the country is often called "the land of pagodas." The Shwedagon Pagoda in Yangon is surrounded by myths, and represents the people's faith who have worshipped there for generations. Every village in Myanmar has a pagoda, which is the place for worship and education.

The culture of Myanmar is deemed synonymous with its Buddhism. There are many Burmese festivals all through the year, with most of them related to Buddhism. The Burmese New Year, *Thingyan*, also known as the water festival, has its origins in Hindu tradition but it is also a time when many Burmese boys celebrate *shinbyu*, a time when a Buddhist boy enters the monastery for a short time as a novice monk. It is the most important duty of all Burmese parents to make sure their sons are admitted to the Buddhist Sangha by *shinbyu*.

History

The history of Buddhism in Myanmar extends nearly a millennia. The *Sasana Vamsa*, written by Pinyasami in the 1800s, summarises much of the history of Buddhism in Myanmar.

During the reign of King Anawrahta Theravada Buddhism became prevalent among the Burmese. Prior to his rule existed a form of Mahayana Buddhism, known as Ari Buddhism. It included the worship of Bodhisatta and nagas, and corrupt monks. Anawrahta was converted by Shin Arahan, a monk from Thaton to Theravada Buddhism.

In 1057, Anawrahta sent an army to conquer the Mon city of Thaton in order to obtain the *Tipitaka* Buddhist canon. Mon culture, from that point, came to be largely assimilated into Bamar culture in Bagan. Despite attempts at reform, certain features of Ari Buddhism and traditional nat worship continued. Following kings of Bagan built such a large large number of monuments, temples, and pagodas in order to honour Buddhist beliefs and tenets that Bagan soon became major archaeological site. Burmese rule at Bagan continued until the invasion of the Mongols in 1287.

The Shan, in the meanwhile, established themselves as rulers throughout the region now known as Myanmar. Thihathu, a Shan king, established rule in Bagan, by patronising and building many monasteries and pagodas. Bhikkus continued to be influential, particularly in Burmese literature and politics.

The Mon kingdoms, often ruled by Shan chieftains, fostered Theravada Buddhism in the 1300s. Wareru, who became king of Mottama (a Mon city kingdom), patronised Buddhism, and established a code of law (*Dhammathat*) compiled by Buddhist monks. King Dhammazedi, formerly a Mon monk, established rule in the late 1400s at Innwa and unified the Sangha in Mon territories. He also standardised ordination of monks set out in the Kalyani Inscriptions. Dhammazedi moved the capital back to Hanthawaddy (Bago). His mother-in-law Queen Shin Sawbu of Pegu was also a great patron of Buddhism. She is credited for expanding and gilding the Shwedagon Pagoda giving her own weight in gold.

The Bamar, who had fled to Taungoo before the invading Shan, established a kingdom there under the reigns of Tabinshwehti and Bayinnaung who conquered and unified most of modern Myanmar. These monarchs also embraced Mon culture and patronised Theravada Buddhism.

In the reigns of succeeding kings, the Taungoo kingdom became increasingly volatile. In the mid-1700s, King Alaungpaya expanded the Bamar kingdoms and established the Konbaung dynasty. Under the rule of King Bodawpaya, a son of Alaungpaya, a unified sect of monks (Thudamma) was created within the kingdom. Bodawpaya restored ties with Sri Lanka started by Anawrahta, allowing for mutual influence in religious affairs.

In the reigns of the Konbaung kings that followed, both secular and religious literary works were created. King Mindon Min moved his capital to Mandalay. After Lower Burma had been conquered by the British, Christianity began to gain acceptance. Many monks from Lower Burma had resettled in Mandalay, but by decree of Mindon Min, they returned to serve the Buddhist laypeople. However, schisms arose among the Sangha, which were resolved during the Fifth Buddhist Synod, held in Mandalay. From 1868-1871 in the Kuthodaw Pagoda, the Tipitaka was engraved on 729 marble slabs. A new *hti* (the gold umbrella that crowns a stupa) encrusted with jewels from the crown was also donated by Mindon Min for the Shwedagon now in British Burma.

During the British administration of Lower and Upper Burma also known as Burma Proper, government policies were secular. Hence, monks were not protected by law. Likewise, Buddhism was not patronised by the colonial government.

This resulted in tensions between the colonised Buddhists and their European rulers. There was much opposition to efforts by Christian missionaries to convert Burmese people (Bamar, Shan, and hill tribes). Today, Christianity is most commonly practised by the Chin, Kachin, and the Kayin. Notwithstanding traditional avoidance of political activity, monks often participated in politics and the independence struggle.

Since 1948 when the country received independence from Great Britain, both civil and military governments have supported Theravada Buddhism. The 1947 Constitution states, "The State recognizes the special position of Buddhism as the faith professed by the great majority of the citizens of the Union."

The Ministry of Religious Affairs, created in 1948, was responsible for continuing Buddhism in Myanmar. In 1954, the prime minister, U Nu, convened the Sixth Buddhist Synod in Rangoon (Yangon), which was attended by 2,500 monks. It was during this time that the World Buddhist University was established. During the military rule of Ne Win (1962-1988), he attempted to reform Burma under the Burmese Way to Socialism which contained elements of Buddhism.

In the 8888 Uprising, many monks participated and were killed by Tatmadaw soldiers. The current military regime, the State Peace and Development Council (SPDC) patronises Buddhism, although persecution of persons of other religions, namely Islam and Christianity, continues.

Traditions

After the child pass 7-year age, the parents have to send him to the monastery to follow some Buddhist teachings and practice. Myanmar people are devoted to the religion and they believe in Buddhism.

According to the Buddhism, the Buddhist, when he was a prince, left his palace on the horse-back with the follower man, "*Maung San*" to practise the meditation and to dig up what the real life and how the cycle of life is rotating and how to attain Nirvana, and that life is made up of suffering and there is no self after He saw the old, the sick, the dead, the monk in the royal garden.

Myanmar people also send their children to the monastery to conduct Buddhist education.But before they are sent to the monastery, they celebrate the ceremony called "Shinbyu". In this ceremony, the male children wear the costumes like the princes. Then they ride the horse as the Buddhist did when he left for meditation.

In Burmese ceremony, they also have a follower man to this child, a monk-to-be. Then a lot of people will follow going around the city or village carrying the things, what they called, the "*Paraitkayashikba*", the things needed to be a monk including the robe. After the going around, he will be sent to the monastery. The head monk of the monastery will give some teachings.

Then he was balded and let in the robe and he also cites some Buddhist teachings and becomes a young monk. On the following day is the preaching of Buddhist teaching by the head of monastery at the parents' house with a lot of people.

The head monks, the monks from the monastery, as well as the young monks are on the traditional stage cite the teachings first. Then the head monk will give some teachings which takes at least 2 hours. All the laymen and women offer the offerings to the monk and share some traditional food with the guests, and all of them are in great interest in the teachings of Buddhist monks. Then the ceremony is closed and the young monks are sent to the monastery to study Buddhist teachings,where they have to keep the Eight Precepts. They have to study in the monastery at least 2 weeks. But all the parents in Myanmar want their children learn Buddhist teachings as long as possible during the new year festival, called Thingyan.

Politics

Buddhism made major contributions in the development of Burmese politics. Burmese nationalism first began with the the formation of the Young Men's Buddhist Associations (YMBA)-modelled after the YMCA-which started to appear all over the country. Civilian governments, after the country gained independence, patronised Buddhism donating large sums to fund the upkeeping and building of Buddhist monuments.

In addition, leaders of political parties and parliamentarians, in particular U Nu, passed Buddhist influenced legislations. He declared Buddhism the state religion which isolated minority groups, especially Kachin. This added yet another group to the growing number of ethnic insurgencies.

The present military government are such patrons of Buddhism that it has become a joke-"Burmese TV has only two colours, green and yellow"-describing the military green uniforms and monk's yellow robes or golden pagodas which cover the screen.

Shwedagon Pagoda has been a local venue for large meetings where both Aung San and his daughter Aung San Suu Kyi had made their famous speeches. The second university strike in history of 1936 was also held at that location.

Aung San Suu Kyi returned from London to lead the National League for Democracy but was placed under house arrest in 1989; since she is a devoted Buddhist and politicial, she is considered a socially engaged Buddhist.

BUDDHISM IN SINGAPORE

As of 2000, 42.5% of the Singaporeans register themselves as Buddhist by religion. Adherents of Buddhism are mostly by the Chinese majority ethnic group, although small minorities of Sinhalese and Thai Buddhists do exist as well. Chinese Mahayana Buddhism is the most prevalent form of Buddhism in Singapore. Sizeable communities following other traditions include Theravada and Tibetan Buddhism.

The best-known representative of Buddhism in Singapore is Venerable Shi Ming Yi who is the abbot of Foo Hai Ch'an Monastery and Secretary General of the Singapore Buddhist Federation. He also works as the CEO of Ren Ci Hospital.

The leading lay Buddhist organization that is the voice of contemporary Singapore Buddhism is the Buddhist Fellowship, originally called the Buddhist Graduates Fellowship.

History

The presence of Buddhism in Singapore was evident during the Srivijayan times. However, as Islam spread to the local Orang Laut population in the 14th and 15th century, the influence of Buddhism and Hinduism eventually waned and almost disappeared. Buddhism's revival in Singapore is a recent trend, although many of the Chinese inhabitants also mix in Taoism and other Chinese folk religions with worship of some Buddhist figures.

The Singapore census includes detailed data on religion and ethnicity. Figures on Buddhism in 1980 shown that 27% of Singaporeans are Buddhists, up to 31.2% in 1990 and 42.5% in 2000.

It was also noted that there is a significant increase of interest in the Buddhist teachings (Dharma) and practises (i.e Meditation).

Traditions and Ceremonies

Although many folks traditions and practises are often linked to Buddhism in Singapore, it should be noted that these practises and traditions often have nothing to do with Buddhism. As there is still much ignorance among Singaporeans, many people still consider folk traditions as linked with Buddhism, although this idea of Buddhism is gradually disappearing among the locals and local medias are giving increasing attention to the true form of Buddhism in Singapore that focuses on the dharma (teachings) of the Buddha.

Folk practises was traditionally practiced among the folk Chinese. The female form of Avalokiteœvara, Guan Yin, was introduced into Chinese traditions around the 12th century. Especially in Southern China, where Taoist traditions are strong, Buddhist beliefs gradually assimilated Chinese Taoist beliefs, and Guan Yin was frequently venerated as a Taoist deity. Furthermore, the usage of joss sticks, a Taoist practice by origin, were used for religious purposes, even in the case of worshiping a non-Taoist Guan Yin.

Such Buddhist-Taoist syncretism gave many Chinese an impressions that they were of the same religion, among many Chinese Singaporeans. Such practices continued even after the Chinese immigrants came to Singapore. Buddha and Avalokitesvara Bodhisattva (Guan Yin) were thus venerated as gods among the Chinese. However in Buddhism, gods and deities are seen as inferior to Bodhisattvas and the Buddhas, who are enlightened beings.

Especially true for the older generation, many will visit the Buddhist temples to pay homage to their ancestors on an annual basis, a tradition which is part of native Chinese practise.

The Buddhist monks recite mantras and the names of the Buddhas for the deceased and the spirits, that they may receive merit and attain more favorable rebirths in the higher realms or the Amitabha Western Pure Land. The ashes are normally sent to Buddhist temples after cremation to be stored in urns.

Traditions

The Mahayana school, Theravada school, and Tibetan Buddhism have acquired sizeable followings. Monks from Sri Lanka, Thailand and other South-eastern countries have come to teach their form of the Dharma to the Chinese in Singapore. As a result, a number of Theravada and other Buddhist temples like the Sakya Muni Buddha Gaya Temple have sprung up in recent years.

Buddhism in Modern Singapore

However, in recent years, due to the increasing publication of Buddhist books, the appearance of internet sites in English, the availability of modern Buddhist music as well as courses conducted in English, more and more English-speaking Chinese, especially the younger Singaporeans, are joining Buddhist circles. As a traditional Asian religion, Buddhism seems to be spreading back from the West to Singapore, as many of the Buddhist books are written by Western monks, sangha and writers (e.g., the Dalai Lama, Thubten Chodren, Tenzin Palmo).

Singapore's Buddhist temples and religious circles are highly organised and very often have a connection with foreign religious organisations, especially in China, Taiwan, Thailand, the USA, the UK, Sri Lanka, etc. Many foreign Buddhist associations and temples have also established branches in Singapore to propagate Buddhist teachings and activities. Buddhist temples and associations are spread all over Singapore, ranging from small to large.

The largest Buddhist temple in Singapore, Kong Meng San Phor Kark See Monastery, holds many Buddhist activities such as chanting, meditation, retreats, and dharma talks, as well as offering Buddhist courses on dharma and meditation, very often attended by thousands of adherents.

From the practice of many Singaporeans, there is the perception that Buddhism is only about burning joss sticks (which is actually a practice carried over from Taoism) and praying to Buddha. A typically fervent Chinese Buddhist will also learn the teachings of Buddhism, and practise the teaching in his daily life, such as meditation, practising mindfulness etc. He will also attend the various Buddhist activities (e.g., Om Mani Padme Hum Retreats, Insight Meditation) in the Buddhist circles and do volunteer work if necessary.

He will normally celebrate Vesak Day and place a Buddha altar at home, paying homage to him daily. If he feels he would like to be an official Buddhist, he would normally undergo a religious ceremony in the temple known as 'taking refuge in the Triple Gem'.

7

The Four Noble Truths

The first instruction of the Buddha was the teaching on the Four Noble Truths. These cannot be said to be "just Shravakayana." They are everything. Apart from the Four Noble Truths, there is nothing else in Buddhism. So they are the most important thing. The Buddha taught the Four Noble Truths in accordance with the way a person would normally solve a problem. That is, when a problem arises, first we try to find out what that problem is,we try to see its nature and depth and how much ofit is actually there. Once this is seen clearly, we can look further and find its causes. The first teaching of the Buddha isvery down to earth. No matter what kind of problem we have, first we need to see it clearly. Then we have to recognize its causes, and after recognizing these we have to find a way to eliminate them in order to achieve the result, which is freedom from the problem. This is the most important part. In this context mere understanding is not enough. We have to learn how to make use of our understanding and apply it to our lives.

When the Buddha taught the Four Noble Truths he repeated them three times, expanding them successively. First he said, "There is suffering in this world. There are causes of this suffering. There is cessation of suffering, and there are ways to reach the cessation of suffering." Then he said, "There is suffering in this world, one has to understand it. There are causes of this suffering, and one has to eliminate them. There is cessation of suffering, and one has to attain it. There are ways to reach the cessation of suffering, and one has to work upon them." The third time he said, "There is suffering in this world, one has to understand it, but actually there is nothing to understand. There are causes of this suffering, and one has to eliminate them, but actually there is nothing to eliminate. There is cessation of suffering, and one has to attain it, but actually there is nothing to attain. There are ways to reach the cessation of suffering, and one has to work upon them, but actually there is nothing to work upon." This was the first teaching of the Buddha, which he gave at Sarnath to his first five disciples: Kaundinya, Bhaddiya, Vappa, Mahanama, and Asvajit.

The Truth of Suffering

So the first subject the Buddha taught was *duhkha*a's it is called in Sanskrit, which is sometimes translated as "suffering," and also as "dissatisfaction" or "misery." I do not know which translation is best. What it means is that we have to understand whatever problem is there. We have to see it clearly and we have to accept it, not in a passive way, but by opening our eyes and looking at it. Without doing so, there is not the slightest chance to find a way to overcome any problem.

The Buddha just looked at life, at samsaric or human existence, and then talked about the problems he saw. If there were no problems, there would be no need to worry. But because there are problems, we have to talk about them and point them out in order to find a solution. It is sometimes said that Buddhism is a very pessimistic religion, since it constantly talks about suffering. But Buddhism does not aim at creating suffering or a pessimistic attitude. It talks about suffering in order to engender an optimistic outlook. It conveys the message, "Yes, there is suffering, but it can be removed." In order to do so, we have to open our eyes. If we try to pretend that everything is all right, it will not be of much avail, especially when a problem arises that is so great that it cannot be denied.

Therefore, we must understand clearly whatever problem is there, so that we can also see its causes and create the necessary conditions to be able to actually work on it. If we looked into our lives and found that there was no problem whatsoever and that everything was perfectly all right, there would be no need for Dharma. But when we look in this way, we might find that there is some problem, that we are not completely satisfied and happy. We might feel that something is not quite right, that there are things irritating us, tormenting us, and making us unhappy. This feeling will alert us to the fact that there must be something that we can do about it as well. The very recognition of the problem raises the question, "Why do I not feel completely wonderful all the time? What is it that prevents me from being happy?"

Thus the Buddha's teaching on suffering is meant to be positive and constructive. It does not mean that we cannot enjoy anything. Rather, the message is that it is possible to enjoy ourselves completely, all the time, provided we have the necessary means. As soon as we are able to remove the causes of suffering, it will cease, and there will be the possibility of continuous and uninterrupted happiness.

The teaching on *duhkha means* that we first look at our lives and try to see what kind of life we have. Is it always peaceful and happy? Is it always like walking on roses? When we look into this question, we may find that there are things which are not so nice. We may fall ill, for instance, or we may get something we do not want, or lose something we love. Then we will feel sad, dissatisfied, frustrated, and very miserable. Once these feelings arise, we will wish them away and try to ignore them. But this will not work. We have to open our eyes to what we have.

The Buddha categorized suffering into three types. The first is called "the suffering of suffering." This refers to real pain, such as being deeply hurt or having had a truly terrible experience. It is the type of suffering everybody recognizes for what it is. Nobody needs an introduction. This kind of suffering everybody knows.

Yet, apart from this, there are less apparent types of suffering that we may not even recognize. These are called "the suffering of change" and "all pervasive suffering." The first refers to a situation where we may not be experiencing the suffering of suffering. Nothing really painful is happening, we are quite happy and peaceful, and yet there is some kind of dissatisfaction. Why should this be? It is because we fear that our present fortunate situation might change. When we are asked, "How are you," we will not say," I'm happy." We will say," I'm quite all right," because we anticipate in terms of a dull understanding that something negative might happen soon. Thus the feeling of anxiety and uneasiness is ingrained even in our moments of happiness. This is the second kind of suffering.

On top of this, there is a third type of suffering, created by the fact that this changing nature is all-pervasive. Everything moves on, including ourselves, and we cannot hold on to anything. Although we long for complete security, we know that we can never get it. Our bodies are composite and impermanent, just as everything else. If! were to insure my life for a large sum of money, this would not prevent me from dying. The money would be there after my death and might be of use to other people, but it would not be useful to me. There is no real security. At the same time, every human being seeks security and longs for unchangingness. This longing proves impossible to fulfil. Everything changes all the time, and whenever change happens we experience a shock.

Once we know this, once we know the way things are and clearly see the condition of our lives, at least we will no longer be in the dark. But knowledge is not enough on its own. We have to recognize the causes and work on them. It is important to remember that the words of the Buddha are the expression of his experience. So the key is to evaluate his teachings as facts and use them in an experiential way. We cannot treat his words as if they were simply information, telling us that there are so and so many different types of suffering. We have to go beyond the words and see from our own experience whether or not there is suffering, what kind of suffering there is, what are its causes, and so forth. We have to open our eyes to our own lives. Looking directly and openly at life, we will gain an understanding of the way it functions and what it actually is. This is the true understanding we need to achieve.

Seeing life as it is will be of great benefit, even while we cannot yet see the causes of suffering. We will no longer be shocked by anything that comes to pass. We will be open to what is there and see it in perspective. It happens quite often that when people visit me, they are feeling low, and they tell me that everything in their lives is so bad. Sometimes I suggest that these people visit some Third World country. Such a comparison with other people's suffering can be helpful. Lacking a realistic perspective, we can make ourselves miserable without any need.

There is a story about a man, his wife, and their many children, all of whom were living together in a very small house, in extremely cramped conditions. This caused the man a lot of problems and increasingly he felt so oppressed that one day he went out to get some advice from a relative who was a local priest. After he had told him how he was nearly going mad with the house being so small and the children so obnoxious, his relative reflected for a while and then told him to buy a goat and take it back home. The man followed the advice, but a few days later he went back and lamented, "Oh, it is so much worse! On top of everything else, now the goat is running around in the house and making everything dirty." His relative advised him to buy a cock and take it home as well. The man did so, but it did not even take three days before he was back and said, almost choking with tears, "I cannot cope any longer. This is unbearable! Now the goat and the cock together mess up the whole house and make everything filthy." His relative thought for a moment and said, "Just go and sell the bird." After seven days, they met again and the relative asked how he felt. The reply was, "0 h, my life is much better." The relative said, "All right, sell the goat as well."

When they met a week later, incidentally, the relative inquired about the man's situation. He got the answer, "My life is just wonderful. Everything is so peaceful!"

This shows how a problem can become comparatively small or big, when seen in perspective. Thinking in this way will allow us to appreciate the full extent of all the problems that might occur and to have an eye for the various difficulties of our fellow beings, which are often much more severe than our own. Once we are able to see that, we can be more confident in dealing with whatever is at hand, it will be seen in due proportion. As long as our field of vision is narrowed down to just our own problem and our feelings about it, we get easily upset. When we look at the palm of our hand from a certain distance, it is neither too big nor too small. It is just a hand. Yet, if we hold it in front of our eyes, it blots out everything and we cannot see anything else. In addition, what we do see is completely unclear since it is far too near to our eyes. As long as we do not see clearly and in proper perspective, even the smallest thing can be completely overwhelming.

When, on the contrary, we are able to see how things are and perceive their inevitability, there will be a greater amount of clarity. We will be more broad-minded and thus gain inner strength. That is the benefit of just knowing the state of affairs. As soon as we see how things are, we know suffering, or in other words, reality. When reality is seen more precisely and in greater depth, the solution is almost at hand.

Once we know the suffering of suffering, we are able to go further: we can see that it is caused by constant change, which in its turn cannot be avoided. Change happens all the time. The reason is that nothing whatsoever has any essence of its own. Everything comes into existence due to interdependence, to different influences affecting each other. Nothing stands still. Looking into this fact more deeply, we will eventually see the interdependent nature of everything, the way everything is due to causes and effects. Then we will perceive how things really are, their actual nature. Having gained this capacity, we will see ourselves as being part of this ongoing process of change.

When we discover that we ourselves are subject to this interrelatedness, we will no longer feel separate and cut off from anything else. Usually we endeavour to be separate from everybody and anything else. We constantly try to be just ourselves, and the only measure for everything that happens is whether it is good for us. This manner of being egoistic and making ourselves the centre of our attention contradicts reality, and therefore leads to dire suffering.

Normally, we act and react in terns of 'I' and "the rest of the world." Whatever another person does is seen and evaluated in relation to ourselves. This leads to a constant need to protect ourselves, and we then become so defensive that we completely close up and experience everything as an attack or as pain. Figuratively speaking, we become like a wound filled with puss, ever so sensitive to the slightest touch. Once we change this unrealistic way of experiencing, knowing the interrelatedness of ourselves and everything else, this sensitivity and isolation is broken. We open up, and become freer and more relaxed. This will happen just by knowing the realities of life, that interdependence is the true nature of things.

The Truth of the Causes of Suffering

Once we gain this realistic view of ourselves and everything around us, as it is shown by the Buddha's teaching on the Truth of Suffering, we cannot leave it at that. We have to go deeper and see the cause. This is the most important teaching of the Buddha, his most significant discovery. It is where his whole teaching comes from, and the focal point to which it is directed.

In Buddhism, it is said that the actual and final cause of all our sufferings and problems consists of two things: karma and the mental poisons or afflictions. This constitutes, in my view, the real discovery the Buddha made. No one had said this before. In order to fully understand that karma and the mental poisons are the true causes of suffering, we have to have a genuine experience of the Truth of the Path.

To begin with, we should look into what is meant by the term "karma." Nowadays, almost everybody talks about karma. Yet, it is not that easy to understand, and there are many misconceptions about it. Karma is cause and effect. When we talk about karma, we talk about the law of cause and effect. A similar cause yields a similar result. A sweet seed will result in a sweet fruit, and a bitter seed will result in a bitter fruit. This is the philosophy of karma.

To comprehend karma, we need to understand what is meant by the term "interdependence." This does not mean that just one single thing gives rise to another. Rather it means that there are many influences on each and every thing, and each single thing in its turn affects many others. Everything comes about due to a multitude of causes of various kinds. Even not obstructing something else is a kind of cause. A flower, for example, was caused by whatever was helpful to its growth, by everything that actively furthered its development, and also by everything that did not prevent or obstruct it. When encountering a flower, I am also in a way a cause of this flower, because I do not cut it down and prevent it from growing. Furthermore, karma is not just limited to that of the individual. There is also the karma of a family, a community, a nation, the whole world, and so forth. As far as individual karma is concerned, we sometimes tend to think, "I have done something in the past, which now inevitably has to surface. Everything is predestined. Whatever my future may be, it is all written down. I cannot do anything about it." This is a misconception. Karma is not static. It is very changing and dynamic. It is true that what I am now is the result of my past actions. Whatever I did in my last life and in my lives before, whatever I have done in this life from its very beginning until the present, all of that has made what I am now. This is called the "skand has of complete ripening." I am the result of all my actions.

This result has already happened, but the way it continues into the future is not predetermined. Whatever has left a strong impression in my mind will affect my stream ofbeing and change the course of my life to a certain extent. I am like a river. If someone puts something very big into it or forcefully manipulates its banks, the course of a river will change. It can become a flood, or divide into two streams, or turn into a narrow canal. So, a certain limitation through what has already happened is there. But given this limitation, I can still go in any direction. What I do from now onward is in my own hands. Karma, therefore, does not mean that we cannot do anything. Karma is very dynamic. Every single moment a new karma is created. Thus everything changes all the time.

There are different types of karma, and thus a variety of impacts that our actions can have. Karma ripens in four ways. The strongest karma is a cause that yields an immediate result, a result experienced in this very life. The second is a cause yielding an effect experienced in the next life. The third will produce a result at an uncertain time. The fourth is indefinite in the sense that it may produce a fruit or it may not. Of these, the first is called "the karma we see and experience directly." This will take precedence over any less powerful karma such as that resulting from our last life or from the preceding ones. This means that if we make a strong decision, from now onward we can lessen or even neutralize the impact of the karma we have to deal with. Thus there is a chance to overcome it.

In short, karma means that any good and positive action will result in a corresponding fruit, in more pleasure and happiness; any negative and harmful deed will also result in its equivalent, in more suffering and pain. Neutral actions will yield an equally neutral fruit.

So how does karma function and what are its causes? In Buddhism, the mental poisons or afflictions are held to be the causes of karma; of these poisons, ignorance is the root. It is a state of mind that is extremely unclear and confused. It is delusion in the sense of not knowing how things truly are. This is considered to be the real basis of karma. Due to confusion and lack of clarity, we identify ourselves with something that is not the truth and does not correspond to the actual state of reality. Thus ignorance is basically a misconception. What does it mean when it is said that karma arises from ignorance? It is very important to understand this, but at the same time, it is quite difficult to comprehend. Thus, it is better to explain it strictly according to the tradition. In the Buddhist sense, ignorance is equivalent to the identification of a self as being separate from everything else. It consists of the belief that there is an "I" that is not part of anything else. On this basis we think, "I am one and unique. Everything else is not me. It is something different." This is what is called *atman in* Sanskrit, meaning a self or ego in terms of an existing entity. In Buddhist terminology the term "ego" means the following. When we look at ourselves, we find that we are not just a single entity. We are compounded: we consist of form, feeling, consciousness, and so forth. Nevertheless, we take all these different constituents as being just one thing. We conceive of them as an "I" and say," This is me." Thereby, we make an identification and a projection.

From this identification stems the dualistic view, since once there is an "I," there are also "others." Up to here this is "me." The rest is "they." As soon as this split is made, it creates two opposite ways of reaction: "This is nice. I want it!" and "This is not nice. I do not want it!" There may be a neutral reaction as well, but this can be neglected as it does not constitute a major problem. The first two are far more serious.

On the one hand there are those things that seem to threaten and undermine us. Maybe they will harm us or take away our identity. They are a danger to our security. Due to this way of thinking, aversion comes up, which in turn gives rise to fear and anxiety. We are afraid that the threat associated with these things might prove true. So we reject them and try to run away from them or fight them off.

Then, on the other hand, there are those things that are so nice. We think, "I want them. I want them so much. I must run after them! I have to get them! Once I have got them I cannot part with them!" Through this way of thinking, first attraction and desire occur, then clinging, and finally strong attachment arises.

In this way the mental poisons are aversion/attachment based upon ignorance, or not knowing how reality truly is. The functioning of karma is propelled by these. As long as we are subject to these three poisons, we are in samsara. Tibetans have a traditional painting called "the Wheel of Life," which depicts the samsaric cycle of existence. In the centre of this wheel there are three animals: a pig, a snake, and a bird. They represent the three poisons.

The pig stands for ignorance, although a pig is not necessarily more stupid than other animals. The comparison is based on the Indian concept of a pig being the most foolish of all animals, since it always sleeps in the dirtiest places and eats whatever comes to its mouth. Similarly, the snake is identified with anger because it will be aroused and leap up at the slightest touch. The bird represents desire and clinging. In Western publications it is frequently referred to as a cock, but this is not exactly accurate. This particular bird does not exist in Western countries, as far as I know. It is used as a symbol because it is very attached to its partner. These three animals represent the three main mental poisons, which are at the core of the Wheel of Life. Stirred by these, the whole cycle of existence evolves. Without them, there is no samsara.

Samsara, therefore, is not a place. It is a state of mind. Wherever these three mental poisons are active, samsara is present. It is a state of mind in which we are constantly running. Either we are running away from something, or we are running after something else. Being caught in this circle, there is no peace, no relaxation, and no rest. As long as our frame of mind is like that, we are in samsara and always running. Suffering is also to be understood in these terms. All our problems are rooted in either trying to get something, or in trying to avoid something else. In this constant endeavour we are never satisfied. To want something means not to have it. We are therefore in pursuit of something; we are searching and struggling for it. This is not an agreeable experience. Equally, running away from something means that we do not like it, that there is a strong apprehension and fear of it. This again is a painful experience. As long as we are in this state of mind, marked by aversion and attachment stemming from ignorance, we are in samsara and thus bound to suffering. We are in constant struggle, trying and fighting all the time.

Within this frame of mind we create karma in three different ways, through actions that are positive, negative, or neutral.

When we feel kindness and love and with this attitude do good things, which are beneficial to both ourselves and others, this is positive action. When we commit harmful deeds out of equally harmful intentions, this is negative action. Finally, when our motivation is indifferent and our deeds are neither harmful nor beneficial, this is neutral action. The results we experience will accord with the quality of our actions.

Yet, no matter how good our actions may be, as long as we are caught in a state of mind dominated by aversion and attachment based upon ignorance, we remain within the samsaric world. We can reduce our suffering and augment our happiness but cannot dispel all the causes of suffering. The true cause of all our suffering is ignorance, which gives rise to aversion and attachment. These three are called "the mental poisons," and as long as we do not succeed in uprooting these, we will continue to suffer. We can run after all kinds of things, after wealth, fame, or pleasure. We can even run after enlightenment or spiritual attainment. Yet, this kind of spiritual activity will not make any real change, it is still the same mentality, the same attitude of being constantly in pursuit of or on the run from something. Deep down inside, we all have a very basic feeling of insecurity. In a way we know that our identification with a self is not based on anything real, concrete, or substantial. There is not really anything to hold on to. For this reason, we feel insecure in a very deep-rooted way. Yet, despite our faint notion of its insubstantiality and intangibility, we try to hold on to this self. We do not want to know about or accept the truth. We want to make sure that there is something to identify with. There is the urge to define ourselves in terms of thinking, "I am here and the others are there." This is our main ignorance and it causes us to react within the pattern of aversion and attachment The Buddha has said from his experience that once we succeed in eliminating our ignorance, we will actually break the functioning of karma. There will no longer be any basis for it. Without ignorance, there will be no attachment and no aversion, and thus there will be no ground on which to create.

THE PERSPECTIVE OF THE NIKAYAS

As I indicated above, there is a sense in which both the Nikayas and the Mahayana sutras alike take it as their project to demonstrate what is required of one who wants "to follow in the footsteps of the Master." But they take up this project from these two different standpoints. I will explain first the standpoint of the Nikayas and then the standpoint of the Mahayana sutras.

The Nikayas begin with our common human condition and depict the Buddha *as starting from within this same human condition*. That is, for the Nikayas, the Buddha starts off as a human being sharing fully in our humanity. He takes birth among us as a man subject to the limitations of human life. As he grows up, he is confronted with inevitable old age, sickness, and death, which reveal to him the deep misery that perpetually lies hidden behind youth, health, and life, mocking our brightest joys. Like many other thoughtful Indians of his time, he seeks a way to liberation from life's afflictions — and as he tells it, he seeks liberation primarily *for himself*, not with some grand thought in mind of saving the world. He goes forth, becomes an ascetic, and engages in a relentless struggle for deliverance. Finally, he finds the correct path and attains the bliss of nirvana. After his attainment, he considers whether he should make the path available to others, and *his first impulse is to remain silent*. Note that he *almost* follows the route of a paccekabuddha. It is only when the deity Brahma Sahampati entreats him that he takes up the task of teaching this path to others. His major achievement is to have attained nirvana, the state free from all bondage and suffering. This is the great goal, the final end of all spiritual striving, the peace beyond all the anxiety and unrest of the ordinary human condition. By teaching the path, he makes this goal available to others, and those who follow the path reach the same goal that he himself attained.

The Buddha is the first of the arahants, while those who reach the goal by following his path also become arahants. In the verse of homage to the Buddha, it is said: "*Iti pi so Bhagava*

Araham... — The Blessed One is an arahant..." Shortly after his enlightenment, while walking to Benares to meet the five monks, a wanderer stopped the Buddha and asked who he was. The Buddha replied: "I am the arahant in the world, I am the supreme teacher" (MN 26/I 171). So the Buddha first of all declares himself to be an arahant. The defining mark of an arahant is the attainment of nirvana in this present life.

The word "arahant" was not coined by the Buddha but was current even before he appeared on the Indian religious scene. The word is derived from a verb *arahati*, meaning "to be worthy," and thus means a person who is truly worthy of veneration and offerings. Among Indian spiritual seekers in the Buddha's time, the word was used to denote a person who had attained the ultimate goal, for this is what made one worthy of veneration and offerings. From the perspective of the Nikayas, the ultimate goal — the goal in strict doctrinal terms — is nirvana, and the goal in human terms is arahantship, the state of a person who has attained nirvana in this present life. The Buddha's enlightenment is significant because it marked the first realization of nirvana within this historical epoch. We might say that the Buddha rises above the horizon of history as an arahant; in his historical manifestation he dawns upon human consciousness as an arahant.

After attaining enlightenment, the Buddha makes the path to enlightenment available to many others. Enlightenment is valued because it is the gateway to the ultimate freedom of nirvana.

In the Nikāyas, we find several descriptions of the process by which the Buddha attained enlightenment, and there are corresponding texts that describe the disciples' enlightenment in the same terms. In MN 26, the Buddha says that "being myself subject to birth, aging, sickness, and death, I attained the unborn, ageless, sickness-free, deathless, supreme security from bondage, Nibbana" (MN I 167) A few months later, when he taught the Dhamma to his first five disciples, he says of them: "When those monks were instructed and guided by me, being subject to birth, aging, sickness, and death, they attained the unborn, ageless, sickness-free, deathless, supreme security from bondage, Nibbana" (MN I 173).

Thus the attainment of these monks is described in exactly the same terms that the Buddha uses to describe his own attainment. Again, in several suttas — MN 4, MN 19, MN 36 — the Buddha describes his attainment of enlightenment as involving two main stages. First comes the attainment of the four jhanas. Second, during the three parts of the night, he realized three higher knowledges: the recollection of past lives, the knowledge of the passing away and rebirth of beings according to their karma, and the knowledge of the destruction of the *asavas*, the primordial defilements that sustain the round of rebirths. Now several suttas in the same collection, the Majjhima Nikaya, describe the enlightenment of the disciple in just this way: attainment of the four jhanas and realization of the three higher knowledges; see e.g. MN 27, MN 51, MN 53. While it is true that not all disciples attained the jhanas and most probably didn't attain the first two higher knowledges, these seemed to mark a certain ideal standard within the early Sangha — a standard that the Buddha and the great arahants shared in common.

At SN 22:58, the Buddha says that both the Tathagata and the arahant disciple are alike in being liberated from the five aggregates: form, feeling, perception, volitional formations, and consciousness. So, what is the difference between them? The answer the Buddha gives points to temporal priority as the distinction: the Tathagata is the originator of the path, the producer of the path, the one who declares the path. He is the knower of the path, the discoverer of the path, the expounder of the path. His disciples dwell following the path and become possessed of it afterwards. But they both walk the same path and attain the same final goal.

Thus the Buddha is distinguished from the arahant disciples, not by some categorical difference in their respective attainments, but by his role: he is the first one in this historical epoch to attain liberation, and he serves as the incomparable guide in making known the way to liberation. He has skills in teaching that even the most capable of his disciples cannot match, but with regard to their world-transcending attainments, both the Buddha and the arahants are '*buddho*', "enlightened," in that they have comprehended the truths that should be comprehended. They are both '*nibbuto*', in that they have extinguished the defilements and thereby attained the peace of nirvana. They are both '*suvimutto*', fully liberated. They have fully understood the truth of suffering; they have abandoned craving, the origin of suffering; they have realized nirvana, the cessation of suffering; and they have completed the practice of the noble eightfold path, the way leading to the cessation of suffering.

As the first to accomplish all these worthy achievements, the Buddha fulfills two functions. First, he serves as an example, the supreme example; almost every aspect of his life is exemplary, but above all, his very person demonstrates the possibility of attaining perfect freedom from all the fetters of the mind, complete release from suffering, release from the pitfalls of birth and death. Second, as aforesaid, he serves as the guide, the one who knows the path and can teach it in its most intricate details. As the guide, he constantly exhorts his disciples to make a dedicated effort to attain the ultimate goal, nirvana. He admonishes them to strive as diligently as a man whose turban was on fire would strive to put out the fire. The fires of the human heart are greed, hatred, and delusion; their extinction is nirvana. Those who extinguish greed, hatred, and delusion are arahants.

HOW THE BUDDHA IS DISTINGUISHED FROM OTHER ARAHANTS

Nevertheless, it would hardly be correct to say that temporal priority is *the only thing* that distinguishes the Buddha from the arahants. To bring out the difference, I want to take two stock formulas that occur many times in the texts, one for the Buddha and one for the arahants. I already quoted the opening of the Buddha formula; now let me take it in full: "The Blessed One is an arahant, a perfectly enlightened one, possessed of true knowledge and conduct, an exalted one, a knower of the world, unsurpassed trainer of persons to be tamed, teacher of devas and humans, enlightened, the Blessed One."

There are nine epithets here. Of these nine, four are also used for arahant disciples: arahant, possessed of true knowledge and conduct, an exalted one, enlightened; five are used exclusively for the Buddha: perfectly enlightened one, knower of the world, unsurpassed trainer of persons to be tamed, teacher of devas and humans, the Blessed One. Note that of these five, two (unsurpassed trainer of persons to be tamed, teacher of devas and humans) explicitly refer to the Buddha's significance for others, while, as I understand it, this aspect is also implied by the word "Bhagava." Even the epithets signifying knowledge are intended to show that he is a reliable authority; that is, by reason of his wisdom or knowledge, he is someone whom others can trust as a source of guidance. So when the Buddha is designated a *samma sambuddha*, "a perfectly enlightened one," this highlights not only the fullness of his enlightenment, but his authority and reliability as a spiritual teacher.

The formula for the arahant reads thus: "Here a monk is an arahant, one whose taints are destroyed, who has lived the spiritual life, done what had to be done, laid down the burden, reached his own goal, utterly destroyed the fetters of existence, one completely liberated through final knowledge." Now all these epithets are true for the Buddha as well, but the Buddha is not described in this way; for these terms emphasize the attainment of one's own liberation, and the Buddha is extolled, not primarily as the one who has attained his own liberation, but as the one who opens the doors of liberation for others. That is, even in the archaic suttas of the Nikayas, an "other-regarding" significance is already being subtly ascribed to the Buddha's status that is not ascribed to the arahant.

While the content of the Buddha's enlightenment, according to the Nikaya suttas, does not qualitatively differ from that of other arahants, it plays a different role in what we might call the grand cosmic scheme of salvation. The Buddha's enlightenment has an essentially "other-directed" component built into it from the start. By virtue of attaining enlightenment, the Buddha serves as the great teacher who "opens the doors to the Deathless." AN I, xiii,1 says he is the one person who arises in the world for the welfare of the world, out of compassion for the world, for the good of devas and human beings. MN 19 compares him to a kind man who leads a herd of deer (signifying sentient beings) from a place of danger to a place of safety; MN 34 compares him to a wise cowherd who leads his cows (i.e., the noble disciples) safely across the river. According to MN 35, the Buddha is honored by other arahants because he is one who, having attained enlightenment himself, teaches the Dhamma for the sake of enlightenment; having attained peace, he teaches for the sake of peace; having attained nirvana, he teaches for the sake of nirvana (MN I 235). He is perfect in all respects, and the most important of his perfections is his ability to teach the Dharma in ways that are best suited to the capacities of those who come to him for guidance. His teaching is always exactly suited to the capacities of those who seek his help, and when they follow his instructions, they receive favorable results, whether it be merely the gain of faith or the attainment of liberation.

Other arahants can certainly teach, and many do teach groups of disciples. Nevertheless, as teachers they do not compare with the Buddha. This is so in at least two respects: First, the Dhamma they teach others is one that comes from the Buddha, and thus ultimately the Buddha is the source of their wisdom; and second, their skills in teaching never match in all respects the skills of the Buddha, who is the only one who knows the path in its entirety. The Buddha can function so effectively as a teacher because his attainment of enlightenment — the knowledge of the four noble truths, which brings the destruction of the defilements — brings along the acquisition of several other types of knowledge that are considered special assets of a Buddha. Chief among these, according to the oldest sources, are the ten Tathagata powers, which include the knowledge of the diverse inclinations of beings (*sattanam nanadhimuttikatam yathabhutam nanam*) and the knowledge of the degree of maturity of the faculties of other beings (*parasattanam parapuggalanam indriyaparopariyattam yathabhutam nanam*). Such types of knowledge enable the Buddha to understand the mental proclivities and capacities of any person who comes to him for guidance, and to teach that person in the particular way that will prove most beneficial, taking full account of his or her character and personal circumstances. He is thus "the unsurpassed trainer of persons to be tamed." Whereas arahant disciples are limited in their communicative skills, the Buddha can communicate effectively with beings in many other realms of existence, as well as with people from many different walks of life. This skill singles him out as "the teacher of devas and humans."

Thus we can see the respects in which the Buddha and disciple arahants share certain qualities in common, above all their liberation from all defilements and from all bonds connecting them to the round of rebirths. And we also see how the Buddha is distinguished from his disciples, namely: (1) by the priority of his attainment, (2) by his function as teacher and guide, and (3) by his acquisition of certain qualities and modes of knowledge that enable him to function as teacher and guide. He also has a physical body endowed with thirty-two excellent characteristics and with other marks of physical beauty. These inspire confidence in those who rely on beauty of form.

THE BODHISATTVA PROBLEM

I said above that each extreme attitude — "Nikaya purism" and "Mahayana elitism" — neglects facts that are discomforting to their respective points of view. "Mahayana elitism" neglects the fact that in his historical manifestation, so far as we can ascertain through the early records of his teachings, the Buddha did not teach the bodhisattva path, which emerges only in documents that start to appear at least a century after his passing. What the Buddha consistently taught, according to the early records, is the attainment of nirvana by reaching arahantship. The problem besetting "Nikaya purism" is the figure of the Buddha himself; for in the Buddha we meet a person who, while an arahant, did not attain arahantship as the disciple of a Buddha *but as a Buddha*. In the Nikayas themselves, he is depicted not merely as the first of the arahants, but as one member of a class of beings — the Tathagatas — who possess unique characteristics that set them apart from all other beings including their arahant disciples. The Nikayas, moreover, regard the Tathagatas as supreme in the entire order of sentient beings: "To whatever extent, monks, there are beings, whether footless or with two feet, four feet, or many feet, whether having form or formless, whether percipient or nonpercipient, or neither percipient nor nonpercipient, the Tathagata, the Arahant, the Perfectly Enlightened One is declared the best among them" (AN 4:34).

Now since the Buddha is distinguished from his liberated disciples in the ways sketched above, it seems almost self-evident that in his past lives he must have followed a preparatory course sufficient to issue in such an exalted state, namely, the course of a bodhisattva. This conclusion is, in fact, a point of agreement common to all Buddhist schools, both those derived from Early Buddhism and those belonging to the Mahayana; it also seems to me to be a conclusion required by reflection. According to all Buddhist traditions, to attain the supreme enlightenment of a Buddha requires the forming of a deliberate resolution and the fulfilment of the spiritual perfections, the *paramis* or *paramitas*; and it is a bodhisattva who consummates the practice of these perfections. However, the Nikayas and Agamas, the most ancient texts, are strangely silent about this very issue. In the Nikayas, the Buddha does refer to himself as a *bodhisatta* in the period prior to his enlightenment: in his immediately preceding life, when he dwelled in the Tusita heaven, and during the period of his final life, as Gautama of the Sakyan clan, before his enlightenment. But he says nothing to suggest that he had been *consciously* following a deliberate course of conduct aimed at the attainment of Buddhahood. Moreover, soon after his enlightenment, when the Buddha considered whether or not to teach the Dhamma, he says that he first inclined to "dwell at ease" (*appossukkataya cittam namati* MN 26/I 168; Vin I 5), that is, *not* to teach, which suggests that even after his enlightenment he might not have fulfilled the function of a *samma sambuddha*, but could have become a *paccekabuddha*.

There are, however, other passages strewn across the Nikayas that prevent us from drawing the definitive conclusion that the Buddha somehow stumbled upon Buddhahood merely by chance or that his hesitation implied a genuine possibility of choice. These passages suggest, to the contrary, that his attainment of Buddhahood was already prepared for in his previous births. Though they do not say that in his past lives he was deliberately following a bodhisattva path to attain Buddhahood, the Nikayas do depict him as dwelling in the Tusita heaven in his immediately past existence (as I noted just above), destined to become a fully enlightened Buddha in his next life as Gautama of the Sakyan clan, and this implies that in his past lives he must have fulfilled the most demanding prerequisites to take on such an exalted role, to become the loftiest and most highly venerated being in all the world. When he descends into his mother's womb, a great measureless light appears in the world surpassing the light of the devas; and such a light appears again at his birth. When he is born, he is first received by deities, and streams of water pour forth from the sky to wash him and his mother. Immediately upon his birth, he takes seven steps and declares himself the best in the world (MN 123/III 120-23). The gods sing songs of delight, declaring that the bodhisattva has arisen for the welfare and happiness of the human world (Sn 686). Such passages, of course, could be seen as later additions to the Nikayas, indicative of a stage when the "Buddha legend" was already making inroads upon the most ancient texts. Nevertheless, given the law of cause and result as operating in the spiritual dimensions of the human domain, it seems virtually impossible that anyone could have attained the extraordinary stature of a Buddha without having made a deliberate effort over many lives to reach such a supreme attainment.

Despite such considerations, in the Nikayas the Buddha is never seen teaching others to enter a bodhisattva path.

Whenever he urges his monastic disciples to strive for any goal, it is to strive for arahantship, for liberation, for nirvana. Whenever monastic disciples come to the Buddha, they ask for guidance in following the path to arahantship. The monks that the Buddha praises in the midst of the Sangha are those who have attained arahantship. Lay disciples often attain the three lower stages of liberation, from stream-entry to non-returning; those who lack the potential for world-transcending attainments aim at a heavenly rebirth or for a fortunate rebirth back into the human realm. No mention is ever made, however, of a lay disciple treading the bodhisattva path, much less of a dichotomy between monastic arahants and lay bodhisattvas.

We need not, however, simply take the Nikayas at face value but can raise questions. Why is it that in the Nikayas we never find any instance of a disciple coming to the Buddha to ask for guidance in following a bodhisattva path to Buddhahood? And why is the Buddha never seen exhorting his followers to take up the bodhisattva path? The questions themselves seem perfectly legitimate, and I've tried working out several explanations, though without complete success. One explanation is that there were instances when this happened, but they were filtered out by the compilers of the texts because such teachings were not consistent with the teachings aimed at arahantship.

This hypothesis seems unlikely because, if discourses on the path to Buddhahood had the imprint of genuine teachings of the Buddha, it is improbable that the monks compiling the texts would have omitted them. Another explanation is that in the earliest phase of Buddhism, the pre-*textual* phase, the Buddha was simply the first arahant who taught the path to arahantship and did not differ significantly from those among his arahant disciples who possessed the three higher types of knowledge and the *iddhis*, the supernormal powers.

According to this account, the Nikayas are the product of several generations of monastic elaboration and thus already show traces of the apotheosis of the Buddha, his elevation to an exalted (but not yet superhuman) status. On this hypothesis, if we could take a time-machine back to the Buddha's own time, we would find that the Buddha differed from the other arahants mainly in the priority of his attainment and in certain skills he possessed as a teacher, but these differences would not be as great as even the old Nikayas make them out to be.

However, this position seems to strip away from the Buddha that which is most distinctive about him: his uncanny ability to reach deep into the hearts of those who came to him for guidance and teach them in the unique way suitable for their characters and situations. This ability betokens a depth of compassion, a spirit of selfless service, that harmonizes better with the later concept of the bodhisattva than with the canonical concept of the arahant as we see it portrayed, for example, in many of the poems of the Theragatha or the *muni* poems of the Sutta-nipata.

In the final analysis, I have to confess my inability to provide a perfectly cogent solution to this problem. In view of the fact that in later times so many Buddhists, in Theravada lands as well as in the Mahayana world, have been inspired by the bodhisattva ideal, it is perplexing that no teachings about a bodhisattva path or bodhisattva practices are included in the discourses regarded as coming down from the most archaic period of Buddhist literary history.

This remains a puzzle – for me personally, and also, I believe, a puzzle for Buddhist historiography. In any case, the texts that we inherit do not show as steep a difference between the Buddha's "other-regarding" functions and the so-called "self-enlightenment" of the arahants as later tradition makes them out to be.

The Nikayas show sufficient emphasis on altruistic activity aimed at sharing the Dhamma with others; admittedly, though, most of this emphasis comes from the Buddha himself in the form of injunctions to his disciples. Thus, several texts distinguish people into four types: those concerned only with self-good, those concerned only with others' good, those concerned with the good of neither, and those concerned with the good of both; these texts praise as best those who are devoted to the good of both. And what is meant by being devoted to the good of both is practicing the noble eightfold path and teaching others to practice it; observing the five precepts and encouraging others to observe them; working to eliminate greed, aversion, and delusion and encouraging others to eliminate them (AN 4:96-99).

In other suttas the Buddha urges all those who know the four foundations of mindfulness to teach their relatives and friends about them; and the same is said about the four factors of stream-entry and the four noble truths (SN 47:48, 55:16-17, 56:26). In the beginning of his ministry, he exhorts his disciples to go forth and preach the Dharma "out of compassion for the world, for the good, welfare, and happiness of devas and human beings" (Vin I 21).

Among the important qualities of an outstanding monk are abundant learning and skill in expounding the Dharma, two qualities that are directly relevant to the benefit of others. Also, we must remember that the Buddha established a monastic order bound by rules and regulations designed to make it function as a harmonious community, and these rules often demand the renouncing of self-interest for the sake of the larger whole.

Regarding the lay followers, the Buddha praises those who practice for their own good, for the good of others, and for the good of the whole world. Many prominent lay followers converted their colleagues and neighbours to the Dharma and guided them in right practice.

Thus, we can see that while Early Buddhism emphasizes that each person is ultimately responsible for his or her own destiny, holding that no one can purify another or rescue another from the miseries of samsara, it includes an altruistic dimension that distinguished it from most of the other religious systems that flourished alongside it in northern India. This altruistic dimension might be seen as the "seed" from which the bodhisattva doctrine developed. It might thus also be considered one of the elements in ancient Buddhism that contributed to the emergence of the Mahayana.

PRATYEKABUDDHAYANA (HINAYANA)

In Buddhism it is pointed out that our present state of mind is conditioned by previous actions. This is always true, regardless of which realm of existence one is born into. Different kinds of existence come about as a result of the infallible law of cause and effect.

The mind is the origin of all actions. The way individuals behave is based on what they think and believe. Samsara, which is a state of perpetual suffering, will continue to manifest, as long as the mind is conditioned by ignorance. This is the actual state of affairs; it is not true just because the Buddha, Shakyamuni, said so.

The Buddhist teachings are methods that remove ignorance from the mind. Since ignorance is merely a state of mind, Buddhist practice is always a mental process which attempts to bring about an enlightened state. There are two stages: to study and contemplate the way things truly are and to cultivate the resulting understanding, so that one's perception of reality becomes accurate.

The Tibetan name for Buddha, *'Sang-gye'*, illustrates this approach. 'Sang' means to awaken, that is, to awaken from the sleep of ignorance. This awakening is like the sun dispelling darkness. 'Gye' refers to the enlightened qualities that are revealed and free to manifest once ignorance is gone. This is like when a flower blossoms displaying all its beauty.

The Buddha presented three levels of teachings, which are called the Three Vehicles or the Three Yanas. The appropriate level for each individual depends upon one's understanding. These three main approaches have different goals and ways of presenting reality.

In the first approach, the Shravakayana, the two major schools of thought are the Vaibashika and the Sautrantika systems. The Vaibashika and the Sautrantika teach that the cause of conditioned existence is the ignorant belief that the individual is a permanent, lasting entity.

In order to overcome this mistaken notion, one studies the teachings which explain that the 'self' is, in fact, without essence, insubstantial, and unreal. Having arrived at a definitive understanding, one familiarizes oneself with this new way of regarding reality to the point where it becomes an integral part of one's being. This realization is called the state of an Arhat of the Shravakayana, and it is the highest point of this approach.

The second approach, the Pratyeka Buddhayana, goes further. It points out that all other phenomena also, just like the individual, are not truly existent entities, that all things are illusory like the images in a dream. As in the Shravakayana, there are two stages of development: intellectual analysis which is followed by cultivating a new way of perceiving reality, so that full realization of this approach is achieved. Practitioners contemplate the twelve phases of the process of dependent occurrence in their order of arising, that is, basic unawareness, actions and the karma they accrue, habitual patterns that colour consciousness, and so on. They also contemplate these phases in the reversed succession, starting with death, going on to aging, birth, and so on. The goal of this approach is the state of an Arhat of the Pratyeka Buddhayana. This state involves full realization of the emptiness of the individual as well as a partial realization of the emptiness of external phenomena.

The third approach, the Mahayana, speaks of compassion for all living beings and the emptiness of both the individual and all other phenomena. It teaches that the practice of the ten paramitas must be based on awareness which fully perceives the essencelessness of phenomena. The inseparability of compassion and emptiness is a main teaching in this tradition. The point is that compassion compels one to work for the welfare of others and that perception of emptiness allows one to do so in an enlightened way. Such perception of emptiness brings one to the realization of mind's true nature which, according to the Mahayana, is the union of awareness and emptiness free from the limitations of conceptual mind. In this approach, as in the two previous approaches, practice begins with a learning process, so that an accurate understanding becomes the ground for one's development. One makes effort to benefit others with the understanding that whatever occurs is empty of reality and thus illusory.

When practice is based on this understanding, the individual will not have expectations or hopes of reward. The knowledge of the Mahayana viewpoint in all its aspects is the foundation for cultivating states of mind that will gradually result in attaining Buddha, the enlightened state, which is insight into the way things truly are-the fact that any phenomenon is empty of real essence or substance. Such emptiness is not a mere nothingness; it is what allows the enlightened qualities of the three kayas to manifest.

This is a brief overview of the Three Vehicles, which include all the teachings of the Buddha. Anyone who wishes to follow the Buddhist path needs to study the teachings in detail and then put them into practice. The Buddha said that he can show the way, but it is through personal efforts alone that enlightenment is attained.

Pratyekabuddha yana — one of the nine yanas. Pratyekabuddhas, or 'self-awakened' are so-called because, having a more profound depth of wisdom than the shravakas, they manifest their own awakening through the power of their own wisdom, without needing to rely on other masters.

Entry Point

As with the entry point to the shravaka yana, the pratyekabuddhas take up any one of the seven sets of pratimoksha vows and then keep them unimpaired.

View

When it comes to the basis of their path, how they determine the view, they realize the absence of a personal self completely, but only realize half the absence of phenomenal identity, because although they realize that the partless particles of perceived objects are not real, they still believe in the true existence of indivisible moments of consciousness.

Meditation

When it comes to their path, and their practice of meditation, the uncommon approach of the pratyekabuddhas is to meditate on how the twelve links of interdependent origination arise in their progressive sequence and how they cease in the reverse order.

Conduct

Like the shravakas, they keep to the twelve rules of ascetic practice.

Results

As their fruition, those with sharper faculties attain the level of a rhinoceros-like pratyekabuddha arhat and those with duller faculties become parrot-like pratyekabuddha arhats.

Moreover, they reach their final existence as a result of three specific aspiration prayers. They pray that their last existence may be in a world without Buddhas and shravakas, that they may attain awakening by themselves, without relying on any teacher, and that they may teach the Dharma silently through physical gestures.

BODHISATTVAYANA (MAHAYANA)

The bodhisattva yana is the part of the mahayana that belongs to the vehicle of characteristics. It is called the vehicle of bodhisattvas because once it has been entered it has the power to lead someone to great enlightenment, because its domain of experience is vast, in terms of its extensive skilful methods and its profound wisdom, because it brings about benefit and happiness, in the higher realms in the short term, and ultimately at the stage of definitive good, and because it carries one to greater and greater qualities as one progresses along the paths and stages. It is called a vehicle of characteristics because it has all the characteristics of a path that is a direct cause for bringing about the ultimate fruition, the level of buddhahood.

Entry Point

The bodhisattvas practise on the basis of their wish to benefit others. They are motivated by bodhichitta, which has as its focus all sentient beings and is characterized by the wish to establish them all at the level of perfect buddhahood, free from the causes and effects of suffering and endowed with all the causes and effects of happiness. With this motivation, they take the bodhisattva vows of aspiration and application in the proper way, through the ritual of either the tradition of Profound View or Vast Conduct. They then observe the points of discipline concerning what should be adopted and abandoned, and heal and purify any impairments.

View

Concerning the basis of their path, how they determine the view, if we speak in terms of philosophical tenets, the approach of Mind Only is to assert that outer objects are not real and all phenomena are but the inner mind, and to claim that the self-aware, self-knowing consciousness devoid of dualistic perception is truly real. The approach of the Middle Way is to realize that all phenomena appear in the manner of dependent origination, but are in reality emptiness, beyond the eight extremes of conceptual elaboration. Through these approaches, on the basis of the explanation of the two levels of reality, they realize completely the absence of any personal self or phenomenal identity.

Meditation

Concerning their path and how they practise meditation, the bodhisattvas realize and train in developing their familiarity with the indivisibility of the two levels of reality, and, on the basis of the yogic meditation that unites shamatha and vipashyana, meditate sequentially on the thirty-seven factors of enlightenment while on the path of training.

Conduct

They practise the six transcendent perfections for their

own benefit and the four means of attraction for the sake of others.

Results

They attain the level of buddhahood, which is the ultimate attainment in terms of both abandonment and realization since it means abandoning all that has to be eliminated, the two obscurations including habitual traces, and realizing everything that must be realized, included within the knowledge of all that there is and the knowledge of its nature. They accomplish the two types of dharmakaya for their own benefit and the two types of rupakaya for the benefit of others.

COMPETING BUDDHIST IDEALS

The arahant ideal and the bodhisattva ideal are often considered the respective guiding ideals of Theravada Buddhism and Mahayana Buddhism. This assumption is not entirely correct, for the Theravada tradition has absorbed the bodhisattva ideal into its framework and thus recognizes the validity of both arahantship and Buddhahood as objects of aspiration. It would therefore be more accurate to say that the arahant ideal and the bodhisattva ideal are the respective guiding ideals of Early Buddhism and Mahayana Buddhism. By "Early Buddhism" I do not mean the same thing as Theravada Buddhism that exists in the countries of southern Asia. I mean the type of Buddhism embodied in the archaic Nikayas of Theravada Buddhism and in the corresponding texts of other schools of Indian Buddhism that did not survive the general destruction of Buddhism in India.

It is important to recognize that these ideals, in the forms that they have come down to us, originate from different bodies of literature stemming from different periods in the historical development of Buddhism. If we don't take this fact into account and simply compare these two ideals as described in Buddhist canonical texts, we might assume that the two were originally expounded by the historical Buddha himself, and we might then suppose that the Buddha — living and teaching in the

Ganges plain in the 5th century B.C. — offered his followers a choice between them, as if to say: "This is the arahant ideal, which has such and such features; and that is the bodhisattva ideal, which has such and such features. Choose whichever one you like." The Mahayana sutras, such as the Mahaprajna-paramita Sutra and the Saddharmapunarika Sutra (the Lotus Sutra), give the impression that the Buddha *did* teach both ideals. Such sutras, however, certainly are not archaic. To the contrary, they are relatively late attempts to schematize the different types of Buddhist practice that had evolved over a period of roughly four hundred years after the Buddha's parinirvana.

The most archaic Buddhist texts — the Pali Nikayas and their counterparts from other early schools (some of which have been preserved in the Chinese Agamas and the Tibetan Kanjur) — depict the ideal for the Buddhist disciple as the arahant. The Mahayana sutras, composed a few centuries later in a Buddhist Hybrid Sanskrit, depict the ideal for the Mahayana follower as the bodhisattva. Now some people argue that because the arahant is the ideal of Early Buddhism, while the bodhisattva is the ideal of later Mahayana Buddhism, the Mahayana must be a more advanced or highly developed type of Buddhism, a more ultimate teaching compared to the simpler, more basic teaching of the Nikayas. That is indeed an attitude common among Mahayanists, which I will call "Mahayana elitism." An opposing attitude common among conservative advocates of the Nikayas rejects all later developments in the history of Buddhist thought as deviation and distortion, a fall away from the "pristine purity" of the ancient teaching. I call this attitude "Nikaya purism." Taking the arahant ideal alone as valid, Nikaya purists reject the bodhisattva ideal, sometimes forcefully and even aggressively.

I have been seeking a point of view that can do justice to both perspectives, that of the Nikayas and the early Mahayana sutras, a point of view that can accommodate their respective strengths without falling into a soft and easy syncretism, without blotting out conceptual dissonances between them, without abandoning faithfulness to the historical records – yet one which also recognizes that these records are by no means crystal clear and are unlikely to be free of bias. This task has by no means been easy. It is much simpler to adopt either a standpoint of "Nikaya purism" or one of "Mahayana elitism" and hold to it without flinching. The problem with these two standpoints, however, is that both are obliged to neglect facts that are discomforting to their respective points of view.

Although I am ordained as a Theravada Buddhist monk, in this paper I am not going to be defending the opinions of any particular school of Buddhism or trying to uphold a sectarian point of view. For six years, I have lived in Chinese Mahayana monasteries, and my understanding of Buddhism has been particularly enriched by my contact with the teachings of the Chinese scholar-monk Master Yinshun (1906-2005) and his most senior living pupil, Master Renjun, the founder of Bodhi Monastery in New Jersey. My first purpose is to draw out from the texts what the texts say explicitly, and *also what they imply*, about these two competing ideals of the Buddhist life. At the end, when I draw my conclusions, I will clearly state them as such, and they will be entirely my own. Sometimes I will not draw conclusions but instead raise questions, pointing to problems in the history of Buddhism that I am acutely aware of but unfortunately cannot resolve. It is quite possible that what I consider a nuanced and balanced point of view will draw fire from partisan advocates on both sides of the divide. However, from the standpoint of my present understanding, I have no choice but to take this risk.

THE TRANSITION TOWARDS THE FULL-FLEDGED BODHISATTVA CONCEPT

Perhaps for a full-fledged bodhisattva doctrine to emerge in Buddhism, something more was needed than the conception of the Buddha that we find in the ancient texts of the Nikayas. Thus the common project of comparing the arahant of the Nikayas with the bodhisattva figure of the Mahayana sutras may be somewhat misguided. As I see it, one of the factors that underlies the emergence of the full-fledged bodhisattva doctrine was the transformation of the archaic Buddha concept of the Nikaya sutras into the Buddha figure of Buddhist religious faith and legend. This took place mainly in the age of Sectarian Buddhism, that is, between the phase of Early Buddhism represented by the Nikayas and the rise of early Mahayana Buddhism. During this period, two significant developments of the Buddha concept occurred. First, the number of Buddhas was multiplied; and second, the Buddhas came to be endowed with increasingly more exalted qualities. These developments occurred somewhat differently in the different Buddhist schools, but certain common features united them.

The Nikayas already mention six Buddhas preceding Gautama and one to follow him, Metteyya (Skt: Maitreya). Now, since cosmic time is without any discernible beginning or conceivable end, the inference was drawn that there must have been even earlier Buddhas, and thus the number of past Buddhas was increased; stories about some of these entered into circulation and brought them to life.

Since space was likewise unbounded, with world systems like our own spread out in "the ten directions," some schools posited the *present* existence of Buddhas in other world systems beyond our own — Buddhas still alive whom one might worship and, by means of meditative power, actually see with contemplative vision.

The texts of Sectarian Buddhism increased a Buddha's faculties of knowledge until they eventually ascribed to him nothing short of omniscience. He came to possess numerous miraculous powers. Eighteen special "Buddha-dharmas," not mentioned in the old suttas, were added. Legends and stories entered into circulation describing the wonderful ways he taught and transformed others. Some of these stories are already found in the suttas: the stories of his encounters with the serial killer Angulimala, the fierce demon Aavaka, the poor leper Suppabuddha, the angry brahmin Bharadvaja.

Bibliography

Adikaram, E. W.: *Early History of Buddhism in Ceylon,* Buddhist Cultural Centre, Dehiwala, 1994.

Beal, Samuel: *Buddhist Records of the Western World,* Paragon, London, 1885.

Birnbaum, Raoul: *The Healing Buddha,* Shambhala, Boston, 1989.

Bond, George: *The Word of the Buddha: The Tipitaka and its Interpretation in Theravada Buddhism,* Gunasena, Colombo, 1982.

Brown, R.L.: *The Dvaravati Wheels of the Law and the Indianization of South East Asia,* E.J. Brill, Leiden, 1996.

Buddhadasa, Bhikkhu: *Teaching Dhamma by Pictures,* Social Science Association Press of Thailand, Bangkok, 1968.

Coomaraswamy, Ananda K.: *Elements of Buddhist Iconography,* Harvard University Press, Cambridge, 1935.

Dallapiccola, Anna: *The Stupa: Its Religious, Historical, and Architectural Significance,* Franz Steiner Verlag, Wiesbaden, 1980.

Daniel L. : *Folk Buddhist Religion: Dissenting Sects in Late Traditional China,* Cambridge, MA: Harvard University Press, 1976.

Davidson, J. Leroy: *The Lotus Sutra in Chinese Art,* Yale University Press, New Haven, 1954.

Georges B.J. : *Recognizing Reality: Dharmakirti's Philosophy and Its Tibetan Interpretations,* Albany, NY: State University of New York Press, 1997.

Ghosh, A.: *Ajanta Murals,* Archaeological Survey of India, New Delhi, 1967.

Goldstein, Melvyn C. : *The Snow Lion and the Dragon: China, Tibet and the Dalai Lama,* Berkeley, CA: University of California Press, 1997.

Gomex, Luis O.: *The Land of Bliss: The Paradise of the Buddha of measureless Light,* University of Hawai'i Press, Honolulu, 1996.

Gray, Basil: *Buddhist Cave Paintings at Tun-huang,* University of Chicago Press, Chicago, 1959.

Holt, John Clifford: *Buddha in the Crown: Avalokitesvara in the Buddhist Traditions of Sri Lanka,* Oxford University Press, New York, 1991.

Howard, A.F.: *The Imagery of the Cosmological Buddha,* E.J. Brill, Leiden, 1986.

Ireland, John D.: *The Itivuttaka: The Buddha's Sayings,* Buddhist Publication Society, Kandy, 1991.

James E. : *Tibetan Treasury of Aphoristic Jewels,* Bloomington, IN: Indiana University Press, 1968.

Joshi, Lalmani: *Studies in the Buddhistic Culture of India,* Motilal Banarsidass, Delhi, 1977.

Kalupahana, David J.: *Causality: The Central Philosophy of Buddhism,* University Press of Hawaii, Honolulu, 1975.

Keown, Damien: *The Nature of Buddhist Ethics,* St. Martin's Press, New York, 1992.

Lamrimpa, Gen : *Calming the Mind: Tibetan Buddhist Teachings on Cultivating Meditative Quiescence,* Ithaca, NY: Snow Lion, 1995.

Lewis R. : *The Korean Buddhist Canon: A Descriptive Catalogue,* Berkeley, CA: University of California Press, 1979.

Mark D. Cummings: *Buddhism and Asian History,* MacMillan, New York, 1987.

Matthew T. : *The Tibetan Assimilation of Buddhism: Conversion, Contestation, and Memory,* New York: Oxford University Press, 2002.

Michael R. : *Buddhist Studies in the People's Republic of China, 1990-1991,* Honolulu, HI: University of Hawaii Press, 1993.

Naudou, Jean: *Buddhists of Kashmir,* Motilal Banarsidass, Delhi, 1980.

Nyanaponika Thera: *The Heart of Buddhist Meditation,* Samuel Weiser, New York, 1973.

Pal, Pratapaditya: *Light of Asia: Buddha Sakyamuni in Asian Art,* County Museum of Art, Los Angeles, 1984.

Rabten, Geshe : *The Preliminary Practices of Tibetan Buddhism,* Burton, WA: Tusum Ling Publ., 1974.

Reedy, Chandra L. : *Himalayan Bronzes: Technology, Style, and Choices,* London: Associated University Presses, 1997.

Roger Warner: *Angkor: The Hidden Glories,* Houghton Mifflin, Boston, 1990.

Shaw, Miranda: *Passionate Enlightenment: Women in Tantric Buddhism,* Princeton University Press, Princeton, 1994.

Singer, Jane Casey : *Tibetan Art: Towards a Definition of Style,* London: Laurence King/Alan Marcuson, 1997.

Sopa, Geshe Lhundub : *Cutting through Appearances: Practice and Theory of Tibetan Buddhism,* Ithaca, NY: Snow Lion, 1989.

Stcherbatsky, Theodore: *The Central Conception of Buddhism and the Meaning of the Word "Dharma",* Royal Asiatic Society, London, 1923.

Stephan V. : *The Cult of Tara: Magic and Ritual in Tibet.* Berkeley, CA: University of California Press, 1973.

Tharpar, Romila: *Ashoka and the Decline of the Mauryas,* Oxford University Press, Delhi, 1983.

Thomas J.: *The Hindu Religious Tradition,* Wadsworth, Belmont, 1982.

Thomas, E. J.: *The Life of the Buddha as Legend and History,* Routledge & Kegan Paul, London, 1927.

Weber, Andy : *Tibetan Art and Practice,* Ithaca, NY: Snow Lion, 1993.

Welbon, Guy Richard: *The Buddhist Nirvana and Its Western Interpreters,* University of Chicago Press, Chicago, 1968.

Wijayaratna, Mohan: *Buddhist Monastic Life According to the Texts of the Theravada Tradition,* Cambridge University Press, Cambridge, 1990.

Williams, Paul: *Altruism and Reality: Studies in the Philosophy of the Bodhicaryavatara,* Curzon, London, 1998.

Index

A

Abhidhamma, 42, 106, 107, 108, 109, 110, 123.
Agganna Sutta, 110.
Anagarika Dharmapala, 202, 205.
Ananda, 35, 41, 42, 79, 80, 81, 82, 94, 95, 101, 124, 125, 189, 190, 193.
Anathapindika, 95, 96, 97, 98, 99, 100, 101, 102, 123.
Angulimala, 84, 85, 86, 87, 88, 89, 90, 91, 92, 266.
Angulimala the Monk, 88.
Anguttara Nikaya, 18, 83, 99, 102.
Arahants, 32, 33, 120, 124, 246, 248, 249, 250, 251, 252, 253, 255, 256.

B

Bodhisattva, 52, 58, 66, 128, 170, 172, 181, 199, 231, 252, 253, 254, 255, 256, 257, 261, 262, 263, 264, 265, 266.
Bodhisattvayana, 261.
Brahmin Caste, 111, 202.
Brahmins, 86, 110, 111, 112, 116.
Buchasergyi Lakang Monastery, 67.
Buddha, 1, 2, 4, 5, 9, 17, 19, 21, 23, 24, 25, 32, 33, 35, 36, 37, 38, 39, 40, 41, 42, 44, 46, 47, 52, 53, 55, 58, 59, 60, 61, 63, 70, 74, 77, 79, 80, 81, 82, 83, 84, 85, 87, 88, 89, 90, 91, 92, 93, 94, 95, 96, 97, 98, 99, 100, 101, 102, 107, 108, 110, 111, 112, 113, 115, 116, 117, 118, 119, 120, 121, 122, 123, 124, 125, 126, 133, 134, 135, 136, 138, 141, 144, 145, 146, 148, 153, 160, 166, 167, 171, 176, 177, 178, 179, 180, 181, 182, 183, 184, 185, 186, 190, 191, 193, 204, 206, 210, 212, 213, 216, 221, 232, 233, 234, 235, 236, 238, 239, 241, 242, 247, 248, 249, 250, 251, 252, 253, 254, 255, 256, 257, 258, 259, 260, 261, 262, 265, 266.
Buddhism in India, 26, 75, 185, 187, 200, 201, 202, 203, 204, 205, 211, 212, 263.
Buddhist Cosmology, 37.

Buddhist Doctrine, 2, 21, 118, 214.
Buddhist Monasteries, 45, 57, 63, 180, 181, 191, 210.
Buddhist Philosophy, 1, 2, 5, 60, 109, 182, 184, 210.
Buddhist Teachings, 21, 23, 38, 63, 92, 106, 126, 157, 228, 229, 231, 232, 258.

C

Chandra Dynasty, 185.
Changzhu Temple, 67.
Chionin Temple, 156.
Chudamani Vihara, 59, 213.

D

Dalit Buddhist Movement, 203.
Deer Park Monastery, 60.
Development of Buddhism, 173, 220, 263.
Dharma, 4, 8, 23, 41, 51, 60, 61, 62, 63, 70, 71, 79, 107, 158, 186, 201, 212, 231, 232, 236, 251, 257, 261.
Digha Nikaya, 79, 110.
Drepung Monastery, 67, 69.
Drigung Monastery, 68.
Dzogchen Monastery, 69.

E

Eastern Philosophy, 1, 3, 14, 15.

G

Ganden Monastery, 69, 70.
Gautama Buddha, 1, 58, 83, 141, 143, 144, 189, 205.
Ghoom Monastery, 61.

I

Islamic Philosophy, 8.
Ivolginsky Datsan, 65, 66.

J

Jewish Philosophy, 10.

K

Kudara Kannon, 164.
Kurjey Lhakhang, 49.

L

Labrang Monastery, 54, 55.
Longxing MonTharpa Choling Monastery, 45.

M

Mag-Dhog Yolmowa Monastery, 46.
Magnolia Village, 46.
Mahamevnawa Buddhist Monastery, 47.
Mahamoggallana, 118, 120.
Mahapajapati Gotami, 92.
Mahayana, 5, 19, 21, 23, 27, 41, 48, 91, 102, 104, 108, 126, 173, 180, 181, 182, 185, 186, 192, 201, 208, 213, 225, 230, 232, 246, 252, 253, 256, 257, 259, 260, 261, 263, 264, 265, 266.
Mahayana Buddhism, 5, 19, 23, 48, 185, 201, 208, 225, 230, 263, 264, 266.
Majjhima Nikaya, 84, 85, 248.
Maoism, 10, 11.
Maudgalyayana, 118, 119, 126.
Menri Monastery, 70.

N

Namgyal Monastery, 71.
Noble Truths, 1, 5, 22, 23, 24, 29, 32, 33, 47, 121, 234.

P

Phenomenology, 1, 16, 18, 19.
Pratyekabuddhayana, 258.
Provincial Temple, 127, 134.

R

Ralung Monastery, 72, 73.
Religious Traditions, 4.
Rumtek Monastery, 56.

S

Sakya Monastery, 74.
Samsara, 20, 32, 37, 243, 244, 257, 258.
Samyutta Nikaya, 18, 20, 21.
Sarvastivada Abhidharma, 109.
Schools of Buddhism, 102, 135, 173, 191, 213.
Shalu Monastery, 71, 72, 75, 76.
Shechen Monastery, 57.
Sutta Pitaka, 42, 80.

T

Tamshing Lhakhang, 49.
Tantric Schools, 105, 213.
Tashilhunpo Monastery, 52, 53, 77, 78.
Tathagatagarbha Sutras, 19.
Teaching of Theravada, 22.
Textual Sources, 84.
Theravada, 18, 22, 23, 25, 26, 27, 28, 30, 32, 35, 36, 37, 38, 41, 42, 43, 44, 85, 105, 108, 109, 120, 122, 123, 124, 188, 191, 205, 211, 212, 217, 220, 230, 239, 240, 241, 242, 243, 244, 245, 248, 250, 266.
Tibetan Buddhism, 5, 45, 53, 54, 57, 61, 70, 72, 105, 188, 192, 193, 201, 212, 213, 215, 230, 232.
Tibetan Buddhist, 54, 55, 56, 57, 58, 66, 71, 72, 184, 188, 192, 194.
Tsurphu Monastery, 54.

V

Vajrayana, 102, 105, 188, 191, 192, 196, 197, 198, 201.
Vedas, 8, 17, 182.

W

Wat Florida Dhammaram, 45.

Y

Yonghe Temple, 57, 58.
Yumedono, 162, 164.

Z

Zang Dhok Palri Phodang, 46.

❑❑❑